The Only Job Hunting Guide You'll Ever Need

The Most Comprehensive Guide for Job Hunters and Career Switchers

Kathryn and Ross Petras

Poseidon Press

New York   London   Toronto   Sydney   Tokyo   Singapore

Poseidon Press

Simon & Schuster Building
Rockefeller Center
1230 Avenue of the Americas
New York, New York 10020

Published by the Simon & Schuster Trade Division

POSEIDON PRESS is a registered trademark
of Simon & Schuster Inc.

POSEIDON PRESS colophon is a trademark
of Simon & Schuster Inc.

Manufactured in the United States of America

10 9 8 7 6 5 4 3 2 1
10 9 8 7   *(pbk)*

Library of Congress Cataloging in Publication Data
Petras, Kathryn.
  The only job hunting guide you'll ever need.
  Includes index.
  1. Job hunting—Handbooks, manuals, etc.
2. United States—Occupations—Directories.
I. Petras, Ross. II. Title.
HF5382.7.P48 1989 650.1'4   88-31638
ISBN 0-671-67842-6
ISBN 0-671-63648-0 (pbk)

Contents

Preface

The idea behind this book is simple. You can get almost any job you want—provided you know what you're doing.

Of course, a great deal depends on luck, educational background, and circumstances beyond your control. But a great deal depends on you. On how well you write your resumes and cover letters. On how effectively you sell yourself in an interview. On how well you research job opportunities. These are the things you can control.

This book takes all of these factors in your control, each and every aspect of your job hunt from start to finish, and tells how you can do them effectively, quickly, and better than before.

It is based on years of job hunting experience, thousands of interviews, and hours of listening. This book is very comprehensive—it not only lays out the basics, it is crammed with tips and techniques that make a difference.

To some degree, each and every job hunt is the same. It is a series of steps, starting from the first step of setting a job objective, and ending with the last step of saying yes to a job offer. In between are such steps as researching, writing resumes and cover letters, answering ads, conducting mail campaigns, and going on interviews.

We've set out all this information chronologically, step by step, so that the book accompanies you on every step of your job hunt. But we've also arranged the book so that you can use it as an encyclopedia and look up what you need when you need it.

We've also included a comprehensive research section and an

even more comprehensive reference guide—the best and most comprehensive career reference section we've ever seen. We think this is maybe the single most valuable aspect of this book: the information on how and where to research your way into a job. As Americans, we've all been deluged by the information revolution. But all too few of us know how—and where—to find vital information. We show you how to use the information deluge to your advantage.

The job search is really about being noticed—for the right reasons. The average Fortune 500 company receives over 250,000 unsolicited resumes every year. A daunting fact. But remember, *someone* always gets an offer, no matter how many applicants there are for a given position. And the person who does is the person with the most organized, most effective, job hunting technique.

Which is what this book is all about.

1 Setting a Job Objective

INTRODUCTION

Before you begin your job hunt ask yourself a few questions—and answer them. What do you want to do? What are you trying to do? What kind of job do you want?

By answering these questions at the outset, you create a job hunting *goal*, a clear, targeted objective you use to focus your resumes, cover letters and interviews.

Most problems that surface during the job hunt itself have their beginnings in decisions you avoided—or didn't make—before you started. Poor early planning or a lack of career focus leads to lackluster interviewing, a badly managed job hunt, and a bad track record later in your career. It's hard to be dynamic during an interview when you have only a vague idea of why you're there in the first place. For the same reason, it's even harder to get a job offer.

> **EXAMPLE: A man in a stable state government job quit to enter an MBA program at a local university. Talks with friends and extensive reading had led him to conclude that private sector or nongovernment jobs were more rewarding financially and personally. After graduating, he interviewed at over thirty corporations with no success. Problem: His job hunt was scattered across industry and functional lines: he knew he wanted *a* private sector job, but had no idea of what *kind*. Result: He returned to state government after losing two full years and tuition costs.**

The best way to avoid the problems and decide on a career is through a step-by-step approach. By tackling all of your job uncertainties and career dilemmas in a methodical and deliberate manner, you can progress from indecision to a plan of action. And you avoid the second most common problem of job or career changers—hopping from idea to idea, with no real plan or direction in mind.

The five basic steps to take are:

1. *Self-assessment*—deciding who you are, what you like, and what you want.

2. *Job assessment*—researching the job/career areas that fit your interests and needs.

3. *Informational interviewing*—talking with people in the career areas that interest you.

4. *Weighing career alternatives*—determining whether to quit your job, whether to look for a job in a new area, or whether to stay right where you are in the same job or career.

5. *Career counseling*—meeting with career counselors, who can take you through the entire process from administering assessment tests to helping you assemble a job hunting or career changing program. This step can be taken at *any* time . . . or not at all.

In general, deciding what to do is usually harder than doing it, but decisions made early in your job search pay dividends later. As always, the goal is to become an informed, targeted job hunter—the type of person who gets job offers.

GENERAL TIPS ON A STEP-BY-STEP APPROACH

■ **The key idea is to *organize* yourself so you can arrive at some decisions about your job or career quickly and with the least amount of ambivalence.**

A step-by-step approach breaks things down into parts or tasks and helps you avoid the major problem facing anyone looking for a job or thinking about a career change—a scattergun approach in which the person looks at almost anything that pays a salary. Although it may seem practical, it's not. Particularly in today's competitive job environment, employers can pick and choose. Applicants who are unfocused and untargeted don't present themselves as winners. They just sound like they don't know what they're doing.

The time you spend on each step depends on how sure or unsure you are about your career objectives. Someone who *knows* she is a born stockbroker may take only a few minutes with the self-assessment and job-assessment steps. On the other hand, someone who is deeply dissatisfied with his current career may take much more time.

■ **Don't worry if you're caught deciding between two careers—you can manage a job search in two or even more avenues, as long as you're focused on a definite plan.**

A common mistake is to be overly vague about your goals: "I want to remain in the health field, as a hospital administrator or a social worker supervisor, or in the public health service or maybe overseas with an aid agency. . . ." It's better to have one clear goal, or two, or even three, and *concentrate* on them.

> **EXAMPLE: A person with a degree in international relations and no real idea of what he wants out of life can start by picking several *defined* careers in which to research and interview. For example, he can choose diplomacy (the State Department), international banking, and import-export firms.**

■ **Don't be afraid to change: the idea is to move into a job or career where you will flourish.**

As more information about possibilities and opportunities becomes evident, you may realize that your original plan needs changing. Fine. Change your plan. The best way to manage a job search is to be flexible, and to keep narrowing your goals until you form realistic job targets. Jumping from interview to interview with no real purpose but a hope of getting hired will get you nowhere. The bottom line is always to keep yourself organized and your job planning under control.

STEP ONE: SELF-ASSESSMENT

■ **Chart your interests, values, skills and abilities, and personality type.**

Many people have been so busy working that they have very little idea of what genuinely interests them or motivates them beyond getting a paycheck. If you are unsure about what you want, be prepared to take some time and let your mind wander through various possibilities. Stop and think of what jobs or school courses you most enjoyed, what hobbies you have had, what kind of friends you prefer. In the beginning, try not to limit yourself; let yourself go and think of what you actually *like,* not what you *should* like.

> **TIP:** A quick way of getting a feel for your interests is to fan through a college catalogue, particularly a night-school catalogue that includes job-related courses. Note which course descriptions you stop to read, which interest you enough to actually consider taking the course. If you have the time and money—*take* the course.

> **TIP:** What makes you *angry?* Many people get angry with things that concern them the most: an idea might be to find a job in that area. For example, someone who is upset and concerned over acid rain or other forms of pollution might consider looking for a job with an environmental agency; someone who feels passionately about apartheid might consider a job with Amnesty International, the United Nations, or international human rights groups.

■ **Be honest with yourself.**

What kind of lifestyle do you want? What kind of people would you like to work with? What really motivates you: competition, a job well done, helping others, analyzing trends? Or making money first and foremost?

> **TIP:** Be careful not to overdo this phase of the job hunt. Many people spend half their lives trying to figure out exactly what motivates them with career counselors, career authors, and psychologists, but never get anywhere. Don't mistake self-analysis for action.

■ **List key factors of your personality and job needs.**

Think back to where and when you have felt most satisfied. What job elements made you the happiest and most productive? What do you want to get out of a career and out of life? What do you want to be remembered for?

Self-assessment is difficult, and the major questions can't be sketched out in a few pages. Many people need professional help and outside perspectives. If so, consider:

1. Career counseling. See pages 24–29 for a full discussion.

2. Personality and vocational testing. See pages 24–27.

3. Books. Many books offer detailed methods of self-examination and ideas for discussion. A few of the better known are:

> *Wishcraft*
> Barbara Sher with Ann Gottlieb
> Ballantine Books (New York, 1983)

> *Where Do I Go From Here With My Life?*
> John C. Crystal and Richard Nelson Bolles
> Ten Speed Press (Berkeley, CA, 1974)

> *What Color Is Your Parachute?*
> Richard Nelson Bolles
> Ten Speed Press (Berkeley, CA, 1987)

STEP TWO: JOB-ASSESSMENT

What Kind of Job Do I Want?

Knowing yourself is only the beginning; your ultimate goal should be to answer two questions: *What do I want to do? Can I reasonably expect to do it?*

Surprisingly, very few people can answer either question. You should start by facing up to them and trying to establish some answers. Given what you know about yourself or what you've learned during self-assessment, pick one or more job areas that seem to suit your personality and interests. Don't worry about practicality yet, just try to determine the areas you are drawn to.

■ **Research the jobs and careers that interest you.**

Go to the career section of your local library. This is the best place to find specialized magazines or trade journals that will give you an inside view of employment and hiring trends. (See Chapter 3, "Research," for details on researching job and career areas.)

■ Stop to reassess your position.

Ask yourself: *Do I still* really *want to do this? Would a new field or job provide me with advancement opportunities? Would I be happy? Would I be challenged and interested?* Again, don't be afraid to change your mind.

Even in the early exploratory stages, you'll find yourself narrowing down the list of possible jobs or careers. For example, a highly ambitious person might read in a management magazine that advancement in a certain career is too slow or too predictable; he or she might then be better off reading about other areas before committing to this career. This commonly occurs with very idealistic and imaginative people. They may get all caught up in the *romance* of being an art historian at a major museum and ignore the problems of low pay and low advancement potential until it is too late. Look before you leap into a new job.

> TIP: Given the bad climate for middle managers, be careful when assessing advancement potential. Ask yourself: *Regardless of what the company says, where does this job or career* really *lead?*

> EXAMPLE: *Forbes* magazine of April 6, 1987, listed the following executive areas as potential dead-ends in large firms: purchasing, data-processing, human resources, public relations, internal auditing, and international work. *Note:* This is not a problem if you *want* this career. Just accept that the odds of making CEO are probably small, unless you plan on transferring out.

> TIP: If unemployed, be particularly careful when assessing new jobs or careers. Low self-esteem may cause you to look at less challenging or competitive careers more readily than you normally would. A common mistake is to make a decision based on *only* one criterion: will they hire me?

By the end of your research, you should have several major career areas or job choices that you want to pursue in depth—preferably by informational interviewing.

STEP THREE: INFORMATIONAL INTERVIEWING

■ **Informational interviewing—interviewing experts in the fields that interest you—is the best way of assessing other careers.**

By asking the right people about their jobs and companies, you avoid having the common complaint *after* the job hunt is over: "If only I had known. . . ." During this phase of your research, concentrate on getting a *feel* for the industry or the job itself. Sometimes the information you uncover can save you a great deal of time by giving you a true picture of your dream job.

> **EXAMPLE:** **A man had long dreamed of leaving his present field and entering the medical profession. Helping others, earning a stable and high income, and keeping away from the fractious worlds of law and business were goals that he thought would be met by a career in medicine. In fact, when he spoke with doctors and health-care workers in person, he discovered that high stress, lawsuits and insurance problems, overwork, and variable incomes were also common aspects of many medical careers. In this case, he chose to stay in his field and satisfy his desire to help others through volunteer work.**

How to Interview

■ **Start the interviewing process by gathering personal contacts through friends and co-workers.**

Most people know someone you should talk to, or at least have a friend who does. Ask for that person's name, phone number, and position. Call and make an appointment to come in and talk about jobs. Stress that all you seek is information: you're not looking for a position now. This is important because it is necessary to put your interview targets at ease if you want the truth, and not some nervous response to keep you from asking them for a job.

■ **Cold-calling—contacting people you haven't met or been referred to—is another tactic to consider. Cold-call the companies where you don't have a personal contact.**

From the library, you can get the names of companies or organizations that interest you; now is the time to call them and ask to speak to the people who can give you specific information about the jobs and careers they provide. You can get the names of managers from friends, magazine articles, and annual reports.

> **EXAMPLE:** "Mrs. Jones, my name is Paul Jobseeker and I'm interested in eventually pursuing a career in your field. Your name was given to me as an example of one of the company's most successful managers. I'd appreciate it if you could give me a few minutes of your time to describe the pros and cons of the field. Would coffee next week be okay?"

> **TIP:** If you don't have names, call the company and say you're updating a mailing list or telephone directory, and need the name and number of the marketing director, or whomever. It's usually best not to ask for names directly because many companies will not give out the names of individuals over the phone. You can check association listings or directories (see pages 265–305) for names and titles. Or you can attempt to track down the authors of magazine articles in professional journals. Usually, addresses and titles are listed. Then look up the name in the phone book and call.

Even though hundreds of people are doing it, cold-calling works: the trick is not to be discouraged by rejection, and to keep on trying until you get someone to meet with you. Cold-calling can be intimidating and awkward—but it is still one of the quickest ways to get through to the right people. If you rely only on friends to give you names, it may take weeks; one day of cold-calling can yield two or three contacts.

> **TIP:** If cold-calling seems too intimidating, start with an informational letter campaign. Write to knowledgeable people in the field, and give a date and a time when you will call.

■ **Take night-school courses in the area you've targeted.**

These courses are usually taught by professionals, one of whom might give you a referral, or you might make contacts through people in the class, who often work in the industry or know people who do.

What to Ask

■ **During your informational interview, ask your contact about the best and worst parts of the job or career.**

Try to get them to tell you the truth and not a puffed-up version of how great things are. People inside the company have a tendency to tell outsiders only the positive aspects of a job. What a person says to the public and what he or she really feels can be two entirely different things, so tell him or her that the conversation is personal and completely off the record.

These are some of the questions you should ask:

1. Are there job opportunities available?

2. What kind of person fits in well?

3. What are the best and worst points of the job or career?

4. Does the company give you advancement opportunities?

5. Would you work in this profession if you could do it all over again?

6. What advice can you give me about getting into this business?

7. What training, education, skills do I need?

8. Considering my background, what problems or advantages would I have that might affect my chances or performance?

9. Could you give me the names of other people to talk to, either in this company or the field in general?

■ **Be sure to get the names of other people to talk to.**

You need information from at least three or four people in the field in order to get a more balanced view and to build up a network of contacts. Also, if you're getting along well with the person, you should ask more specific and personal questions: What would you recommend *I* do to get a job? Do you think *I* have the right qualifications, background, experience?

STEP FOUR: WEIGHING CAREER ALTERNATIVES

■ **The hardest part of job hunting comes after you have finished the research and informational interviewing:** *Now what do I do?*

You may only need a few hours or days or weeks to reflect on what you've researched or heard, but the average job changer takes six months to come to a firm career decision. Mid-level managers in depressed industries may take upward of eighteen months before moving successfully into a new job. Quite naturally, it's hard to be positive at this stage: you're usually weighing alternatives, and wondering if you'll ever get hired or rehired. Over and over and over.

■ **Now is the time to assess how much experience or extra education may be needed to make a job or career switch, and to decide if it's worth it.**

Thoughts of what you want to do may change when you realize the entry requirements—that you may need extra schooling or training; that you may have to work for a long period in a low-level position—or when you discover that there is a lack of jobs in the area.

TIP: If you *really* want to have a particular career and are barred by a lack of education or experience, consider sneaking in through the back door. Try working at a lower level in the field while you go back to school or start working in a similar area to gain experience. You might be able to apply your current skills to a different kind of job in the same field.

■ **One thing you shouldn't do is decide at the outset that the dollar cost of changing your job or career is too high.**

Many unhappy employees stay stuck in bad jobs because they're convinced that they can't afford a major career or job change, so they refrain from making any change whatsoever.

■ **As much as possible, avoid thinking of depressing scenarios.**

Concentrate on alternative methods of getting what you want. If you want something strongly enough, there is often a way of overcoming the odds against accomplishing your goal. By being negative or depressed, you lose sight of possible opportunities. Psychologists agree: positive thinking works!

> **EXAMPLE:** A man in his mid-thirties, with a wife and two children, realized that law, rather than a job in the housing industry, was his genuine interest. Instead of giving up the idea as wildly impractical, he began taking night courses at a local law school. After many grueling years he finally graduated, and was offered a legal position in the same housing company.

■ **If you want to enter a competitive field or position, but feel discouraged by the potential obstacles in your path such as the lack of money or time, face these problems directly.**

Go back and call the people you've interviewed and ask them for advice. Your contacts may know of shortcuts, means of funding, or other jobs in the field. Continue to expand your network until you have exhausted every possibility. Then, and only then, can you reasonably decide that you can't do something for "practical reasons."

Ultimately, a career decision boils down to two variables: (1) Would I like another job or career better? *Or:* Do I *have* to leave my current job? (2) If so, can I find a way of improving my situation without putting myself or my family at too much risk? There are no set rules on how to answer these questions—but these are some things you should ask yourself.

Should I Quit My Current Job Before Getting Another One?

■ **The first question most people start with is: "Should I quit my current job?" In general, the answer is no.**

It's easier to find new employment when you are presently employed. Statistics show that it takes longer for unemployed people to find jobs. Like bank loans, jobs go to people who don't seem to need them.

■ **The real question to ask yourself is:** *Should I start looking for a new job?*

Before making *any* kind of job or career change, look once again at the new position or career you've targeted. Compare it to what you are already doing. Many people find that their dissatisfaction with their current job or career is less of a problem than they had thought;

their research has told them that alternative careers would be worse. Or at least not better.

Think long and hard about leaving your current job or career. *Remember:* You originally chose to do what you're doing now for good reasons. Are you sure those reasons are no longer valid?

Before deciding to move, ask yourself several questions, particularly if you feel burned-out or overly tired in your current job:

1. *Would a vacation change my attitude?* Sometimes, temporary burnout makes you feel negatively toward your employment in ways that are unjustified. This frequently occurs in high-stress positions. A vacation may recharge you and allow you to see things in a different light.

2. *Do I have a personal problem with my boss?* Tough or unfair employers can be dealt with directly or through grievance procedures *before* you quit a job in protest or disgust.

3. *Would more (or less) of a workload make me happier?* Sometimes the main problem with a particular job is boredom or overwork. Assess how a change in work responsibilities (e.g., hiring temporary help or taking on extra projects) might affect you.

4. *Would a lateral move be better?* Before jumping ship, consider the advantages of transferring within your current company. Especially in today's tough employment market, it's easier to stay in a place where your past record has more value. However, do not mistake longevity with tenure. Don't make a decision to stay on merely because upper management will reward your loyalty.

5. *Do I really want to change my situation?* A common problem you might face is having well-meaning friends and relatives convince you to leave a job for something better. Don't try something new unless you are *certain* that's what you want. Be careful of fads. Many dissatisfied managers switched into the faster-moving computer industry in search of quick promotions and big money, then the industry suffered a recession. Many of the same managers would have been better off remaining in their original fields.

6. *Am I glamorizing other jobs or industries?* Good research and contacts should answer this question. It's not unusual to convince yourself that things are much better at another firm or in another career. Make sure you know what the realities are before you consider leaving your current situation.

Good Reasons for Leaving a Job or Career

There are many *good* reasons for leaving a job or career.

You should strongly consider leaving if:

1. *You've tried everything, but still are not excited by what you're doing.* A gold watch aside, the rewards for staying in a job or career you really don't like are few. *Remember:* In today's competitive environment, you must be at your best. If you are unhappy, you won't work up to potential, and you may find that your loyalty to a company or career is rewarded with a termination letter. It's better to start thinking of alternatives *now*.

2. *Advancement is blocked, or you know you are in a dead-end job.* Coldly and rationally assess your advancement potential. If you are ambitious and know you are blocked by relatives in a family-owned business, or by a new management team coming in to replace the old, start thinking of moving. *Remember:* If you stay in a dead-end job too long, interviewers and recruiters won't necessarily think you're loyal, they may think you're unambitious and a slow mover.

3. *The company or organization is badly managed, losing market share drastically, or not responding to business or professional challenges.* Birds of a feather flock together. Don't remain a member of a management team that doesn't work, if you're convinced that nothing will be done to improve things. You will remain frustrated, and the longer you stay, the more closely you will be associated with failure. *Note:* This is also the case with lower-level jobs. One administrative assistant who had worked for ten years at a badly run firm was told during her interview: "How could you have stayed at that place? There must have been something you *liked* about its sloppy procedures." She wasn't hired.

4. *You're not adequately rewarded for your work.* This doesn't just mean salary. It might mean recognition, benefits, fair commissions, proper respect. First try to obtain satisfaction *within* the company. If things don't work out, consider leaving, particularly if you're convinced other firms will recognize your achievements. Also, it is sometimes difficult to "grow up" in a company and get substantial salary increases. You can be taken for granted and not be seen as the true professional you really are.

5. *You feel you* have *to try to fulfill your lifelong dreams.* Don't underestimate the power or importance of your own dreams. Even if you're

relatively happy in your work, an unfulfilled entrepreneurial or creative dream can hurt you in your *current* job by making you feel bitter toward the company and yourself. If you're determined to do something special and know how and why you must do it, then make the break and take the risk of trying to accomplish it.

> **EXAMPLE: A young coffee-shop owner in Georgia dreamed of an acting career. After years of being told to forget his impractical dream, he hired a manager for his shop and went to New York. He failed miserably for five years, but was finally hired as a casting director's assistant. From there he began a slow move up the ladder, happy to have finally entered a field he truly loves. Today he is a successful Hollywood producer.**

■ **In general, *you* usually know if you should leave a job or a career and go somewhere else.**

The considerations listed here are designed to objectify a decision that probably has been lingering inside of you all along. The problem is getting it out. The best rule of thumb throughout a job hunt is: be honest with yourself.

STEP FIVE: CAREER COUNSELING

■ **Go to a career counselor if you can't work out your career decisions or problems on your own, if you need help in planning your job hunt, or if you just want an independent opinion about you and your career.**

Because jobs and careers are changing so rapidly, many people now go to a counselor for a "career check-up" whenever they are contemplating a major job or career move.

Career counseling is normally a three-step process. A good career counselor will help you assess yourself, help you decide on a career area, and then advise you on job hunting techniques.

Career Testing: Interests and Aptitudes

■ **As part of the counseling process, many career counselors administer psychological tests designed to measure interests and abili-**

ties, and with your participation they will analyze and interpret the results.

Many people only go to career counselors to take aptitude or personality tests, wrongly expecting to find some sort of easy "scientific" answer to a career or job dilemma. Of course, this is a mistaken assumption. Any test should be viewed *only* as a component of a total counseling session, and you should expect to work and analyze your situation independently, as well as with a counselor. All the same, there's something very compelling about career testing. Many experts and job or career changers find them helpful as a starting point.

Most common are the personality preference tests, which are designed to help you arrive at some answers you may have difficulty answering honestly on your own: *What do I like to do? Are there other fields or careers that I've overlooked where I might be happier or more productive? What kind of employee am I? What do I value in my work?*

■ **Two of the most commonly used tests, the Myers-Briggs Type Indicator and the Strong-Campbell Interest Inventory, are multiple-choice tests that are designed to give you an idea of your personality, your interests, and suggest possible career areas.**

Testing should be administered under the auspices of a career counselor or psychologist, who can offer professional counseling and guidance based on the results. The Strong-Campbell test is the 325 question test that focuses on specific types of work and general interests as well as the individual characteristics that make up one's personality. Essentially, the test is a series of lists: lists of professions, school subjects, activities and so on. As a test-taker, you are supposed to rapidly fill in your likes or dislikes in each category, or decide on preferences between categories; for example, whether you would prefer being a stockbroker or a warehouse manager, or are indifferent to both, or just can't decide. Your scores are then analyzed and matched against the scores of other people who are successfully involved in various professions and who have taken the test. Certain conclusions are drawn. For instance, even though you are currently a data-processor, your responses may be found to strongly match those of veterinarians. This may prompt you to look more closely at this or related careers. This test is widely respected and is the principal vocational interest test given by counselors.

Whereas the Strong-Campbell test is primarily concerned with career, the Myers-Briggs test concentrates on personality. The test is a three-section series of 126 questions that deal with choices between activities and attitudes, and between opposite or different words. It deals with how you behave, how you want to be perceived, and how you view yourself. For example, one question might ask if you would rather be considered a gentle person or a tough person; another might ask you to decide which of two words appeals to you more: "innovative" or "traditional."

When the test is scored, you will be designated as one of sixteen personality types, based on four scales of opposites: extroversion–introversion, sensing–intuition, judgment–perception, thinking–feeling.

The Myers-Briggs test has many satisfied customers, including top executives. The premise behind the test is that certain personality types do better in certain types of careers than others. Many people have found that it has accurately predicted or assessed their "unscientific" gut-level preferences in careers, or specific jobs within careers. In conjunction with the Strong-Campbell test it is particularly valuable in helping you decide among career choices. Again, a good counselor will view the results of these tests *only* as a guide, not the final word.

■ **An implicit danger with career testing lies in taking them too literally—some people feel compelled to explore careers in which they have very little interest, just because of the test results.**

This is where a good career counselor comes in: he or she can interpret your test results more abstractly and help you make a better career move that takes into account your particular situation. For instance, an unhappy stockbroker whose tests show a strong correlation with those of a research scientist might find some aspects of the results valuable without deciding to jump into molecular biology. A counselor can help him find other similarities in the same profession. In this case, the unhappy stockbroker ended up as a stock analyst, a career that contains certain elements of scientific research. It was far closer to his own interests in business and economics.

To locate a career counselor who offers one or both of these tests, call career counselors in your area or write:

Consulting Psychologists Press
577 College Avenue
Palo Alto, CA 94306

■ *Aptitude* tests are not as commonly offered by professional counselors for a very good reason: just because you perform well at some activity doesn't mean you should be doing it as a career.

Many counselors prefer to assess known interests, and feel that aptitude stems more from conscious motivation and less from natural talent. In other words, if you know what you like, you can usually find a way of doing it successfully, while an aptitude test may discourage you from even attempting to work in those areas that are not highlighted by the test results. There is some truth to this. One undergraduate student reported testing high on law and very low on science and mathematics. After majoring in pre-law programs, he finally decided to take a chance and study geology; today he is a successful environmental specialist who ended up marrying a lawyer instead of becoming one.

Choosing a Career Counselor

■ **Choose a career counselor with the same care you would use in choosing a doctor or psychiatrist.**

Be careful of charlatans, people with quick, sure-fire techniques, and counselors who are linked with recruiters, headhunters, job-placement firms. With the latter, if they're promising a job, the advice you get will depend on the openings they have on hand. You won't get the *independent* advice you need. Moreover, some job placement/counseling firms are fraudulent. These companies typically demand a large up-front fee for their services, which are often little more than a few brief sessions and a promise to circulate your resume.

Before committing yourself or your money to anyone, check the counselor's credentials, background, experience, and price per session. Most important, be certain that the two of you are compatible.

■ *Interview* the counselor first.

Make an appointment to have an exploratory session so you can get a feel for his or her techniques. Make certain you are being listened to as well as spoken to; a counselor shouldn't launch into a three-minute monologue ("This is what we can do for you") without first listening to your problems and questions. One common complaint and tip-off to disreputable or ineffective counselors is that they give a great high-powered sales pitch but then don't stop and pay attention to your needs. You need a dialogue, not a egotist's monologue.

There are six questions to ask and rules of thumb to think about when interviewing a counselor:

1. *Ask about his or her general approach.* You should feel comfortable with your counselor's approach and feel it is something you need. Some people prefer a trained psychologist or social worker, others prefer a personnel or out-placement specialist who has contacts in the Fortune 500. If you think you need career testing, be sure the counselor offers them as a normal function—you want someone trained and experienced in analyzing the results.

2. *What does he or she view as a success?* Your definition and the counselor's definition should match, but don't be swayed by someone who makes grandiose promises or guarantees you a job.

3. *What is the price per session?* The price of such consultations can vary enormously. The normal range is $30 to $75 per session. Most counselors usually require a minimum of five sessions to investigate your problem. Some nonprofit organizations have counselors who charge on a sliding scale that is relative to your income. Be wary of exorbitantly priced counselors—usually you can get the same or better counseling services at lower prices.

4. *What other resources are available?* Good counselors are aware of what's out there in terms of jobs, careers, and career literature. Many are affiliated with groups that have career libraries, databases, and networks.

5. *What are the counselor's references?* Ask if the counselor is affiliated with any particular group, such as a university or corporation. Ask to see references, such as a list of previous clients, and see if it is possible to call any of these people.

6. *What are the career counselor's credentials and endorsements?* Credentials and endorsements aren't everything, but they do certify that certain standards have been met and maintained, especially for those who are members of the National Board of Certified Counselors.

The major agencies or groups that certify career counselors are:

The National Board of Certified Counselors (NBCC) and *The National Career Development Association* (NCDA)

(Both are divisions of the American Association for Counseling and Development.)
5999 Stevenson Avenue, Alexandria, VA 22304
—The major certifying agency for career counselors. Certified counselors all have degrees in the field or a related field from accredited schools and a minimum of three years experience.
—Accredited counselors have the initials "N.C.C." after their names.

Catalyst National Network of Career Resource Centers
Catalyst
250 Park Avenue South, New York, NY 10003
212/777-8900
—Lists reputable member counselors in its nationwide listing of career centers for women. Call or write for a pamphlet listing members.

Directory of Outplacement Firms
Kennedy & Kennedy, Inc.
Templeton Road, Fitzwilliam, NH 03447
603/585-2200
—Lists names and addresses of outplacement firms.

Executive Employment Guide
American Management Association
135 West 50th Street
New York, NY 10020
212/586-8100
—Lists career counselors, including name, address, number and specializations.
—Has extensive listings of executive search firms, employment agencies and job registers.

Other state and national licensing associations:
—Most states do not regulate career counseling, although many regulate counseling and psychological services. In these cases, psychologists and social workers will have degrees and licenses that show state certification for counseling services. Some churches, universities, and civic groups maintain listings of reputable counselors; these listings are usually reliable.

Other Types of Job/Career Counseling

The *John C. Crystal Centers* offer an interpersonal approach to counseling based on the best-seller *Where Do I Go From Here With My Life?* by John Crystal and Richard Bolles. In groups or as individuals, people are led through a unique series of in-depth exercises and counseling sessions designed to help them discover who they are, what they want to do, and then how to go about accomplishing it. The founder, John Crystal, was an ex-OSS officer and businessman whose practical and theoretical approach to self-analysis and job hunting parallels his successful espionage and business experience during and after World War II. A network listing of successful job and career changers is maintained, and the centers offer lectures and talks by businessmen, entrepreneurs, and experts in career changing and self-motivation.

For a complete listing of centers and courses, call or write:

The Crystal-Barkley Corporation
111 East 31st Street, New York, NY 10016
212/889-8500

Dale Carnegie Institute offers specialized courses in public speaking and general topics that may be usefully applied to a job hunt; many Fortune 500 companies offer these courses to employees.

For a complete listing of centers and courses, call or write:

Dale Carnegie Associates
1475 Franklin Ave.
Garden City, NY 11530
516/248-5100

2 *Resumes*

INTRODUCTION

You can write an effective resume just as easily as you can write an ineffective one. In both cases, you are outlining your work experience, education, and skills on paper. The difference is that an effective resume sells you; an ineffective one merely recites the bare facts about you.

Telling prospective employers the facts is never enough. You have to market yourself as a product, position yourself, and target your campaign until you land a job. One of the strongest marketing tools you can use is a good resume.

WHAT A RESUME SHOULD AND CAN DO

Remember two crucial facts as you begin to put together your resume:

> Fact #1: You have only one chance to sell yourself with a resume—the first time someone reads it.

It takes less than a minute for a potential employer to scan a resume and decide yes, no, or maybe. In those few seconds, your resume must come across.

When you sell yourself on paper, you don't have a second chance to make a first impression. It isn't like an interview, in which you can correct yourself or amend responses according to the interviewer's reaction. With a resume, you put yourself on the line immediately. If it doesn't grab the person's attention, it can't sell you. Your resume must stand on its own.

Fact #2: A successful resume gets you an *interview.* Not a job.

This is an important distinction to realize—a good resume makes someone want to meet you in person.

A resume is just one tool in your job hunt, a means to begin the process of selling yourself. An effective resume should make you sound like someone you would want to hire, someone you would want to find out *more* from.

A *targeted* resume takes both facts into consideration and helps you to overcome the odds. It sells you more efficiently because it deliberately positions you for a specific job. The work experience, achievements, and skills you include to emphasize the abilities you need for that job. Relate your background to meet the needs of a prospective employer. You give him or her a *reason* to interview you because you have already answered a key question: Does this person have the qualifications and experience we need?

HOW TO PLAN A TARGETED RESUME

■ **The first step toward developing an effective targeted resume is to zero in on your objective.**

Your objective can range from the very specific (a position as a junior sportswear buyer in a specialty store based in the Southwest) to the general (a middle-management position in marketing that would involve travel). Whatever the case, it is essential that you keep that objective in mind at all times. If you're vague about your job objective, your resume will wind up just as unfocused. In other words the more clearly you define your objective, the more effectively you can focus your resume.

TIP: If you have more than one objective, it is wise to write different resumes for each. That way you can tailor them to the specific needs of each job.

■ **Approach your resume like a basic marketing plan.**

Your goal is to construct an effective means of selling your way into an interview. To meet this goal, you must take into account your intended audience—prospective employers. Everything about your resume should be designed to satisfy those people. Continually ask yourself what they would want to see, what qualities they are looking for in a prospective employee, what kind of experience is relevant to their needs.

Engineer your resume in three main areas:

- Style: choosing how to package yourself

- Contents: the essential parts of a resume

- Presentation: the actual writing, length, and appearance

STYLE: THE DIFFERENT RESUME TYPES AND WHEN TO USE THEM

■ **There are three basic resume styles to choose from: chronological, functional, and a chronological/functional combination.**

Each resume style contains the same information—employment history, education, skills, accomplishments, and objectives—but the presentation of that data differs. The different styles work best in different situations. Following is a description of the three basic resume styles, a sample resume in each style based upon the same work history, and an explanation of when to use and when to avoid the different styles.

Some general hints about selecting a resume style:

- Don't choose a style purely on the basis of taste or appearance. Instead choose a resume style according to your situation (recent graduate with no employment experience, career switcher, etc.) and what aspects of your background you plan to stress.

- Because they serve different needs, one style is not necessarily worse or better than another. In general, however, we recommend avoiding the functional resume unless absolutely necessary. Use the chronological or combination style instead—on the whole, they have fewer drawbacks and come across more positively.

THE CHRONOLOGICAL RESUME

A chronological resume is the type most commonly used. The focus is on time and job continuity. Employment experience is presented in reverse chronological order, starting with the present (or most recent) job and going back in time.

In a chronological resume, you list job title, company name, the dates you held each job, and a brief description of your duties and accomplishments.

Strengths

Because it is arranged by time, a chronological resume is the easiest to organize and write. It is also easy to read—a plus in selling yourself. It's difficult to go wrong with this choice since the chronological style is the standard, tried-and-true resume format.

Drawbacks

Any gaps in your employment history, and short tenures, are immediately noticeable. Short of lying, you can't hide job hopping or periods of unemployment. Limited work experience can stand out harshly. And if your experience isn't logically related to your objective, you may have trouble demonstrating on paper why you're suited for the job.

Who Should Use It

Almost anyone. It's best for people looking for a job in the same or a closely related field and people who want to stress their solid work record in one area.

Who Should Avoid It

Job hoppers; people with long gaps of unemployment. Depending upon the specifics, career switchers and people with part-time or limited work experience might do better with the combination resume.

SAMPLE CHRONOLOGICAL RESUME

Karen Charles
227 East 27th St.
New York, NY 10017
(212) 222-1111

WORK EXPERIENCE:

Manager of Public Relations   12/86–present
    ABC Publications, Inc., New York, NY
—Coordinate public relations and media relations for 15 top trade publications
—Designed and supervised promotion activities for successful trade workshop—resulting in
  heavier media coverage and a 28% increase in attendance
—Improved market share 23% through introduction of innovative publicity campaign, based
  upon editorial roundtable forums and tie-ins with major industry events

Public Relations Writer/Project Associate   4/85–12/86
    ABC Publications, Inc., New York, NY
—Wrote brochures, direct mail letters, press releases
—Created new media kit format for different trade magazines
—Devised and implemented marketing plans for trade publication products

Producer of News Inserts   9/83–4/85
    WYYY-TV, New York, NY
—Produced news and feature stories requiring special production techniques
—Supervised control room staff and floor crew
—Acted as editorial director for taped commentaries of prominent New York individuals

Research Manager   7/82–9/83
    WYYY-TV, New York, NY
—Coordinated all research for nightly news show, documentaries and special news series
—Established guidelines and procedures for newly created information services department
—Designed and implemented computerized videotape library system

Associate Producer   3/81–7/82
    WYYY-TV, New York, NY
—Field-produced show segments; produced special features
—Wrote news and events copy; coordinated talent for on-set interviews

Production Assistant   2/80–3/81
    WYYY-TV, New York, NY
—Supervised editing of two-inch videotape and oversaw taping of international feeds
—Trained new personnel, operated character generator and acted as graphics assistant

EDUCATION:
  Bachelor of Arts, New York University, January 1980
  Major: English Literature
  Dean's List/Creative Writing Award

ACTIVITIES:
  Member, American Women in Radio & Television
  Member, Public Relations Society of America

THE FUNCTIONAL RESUME

A functional resume focuses on functions, skills, and responsibilities. Instead of having job titles as headings, the resume is organized by functional titles that explain a general area of expertise.

Under each function heading, write a brief paragraph explaining your accomplishments in that area. The accomplishments don't have to be purely work-related; you can use examples from school and outside activities. Including company names and exact job titles in the descriptions is optional.

In a typical functional resume, dates are omitted. The emphasis is squarely on what you did, not when you did it. You can brush over gaps of time between jobs, length of time you have held jobs, and periods of unemployment.

Strengths

You can tailor functional resumes to highlight the skills a particular job requires. Even if your job history doesn't strictly lend itself to the position you are applying for, a functional resume can help you bypass the problems of little or no formal work experience by concentrating on the knowledge you have acquired.

Drawbacks

Because career counselors and books recommend functional resumes to cover up a spotty or unqualified job record, many employers red-flag them and immediately believe you are trying to hide something or cover up a weak employment background.

Who Should Use It

Anyone who feels that showing dates would hurt their chances; frequent job switchers; people reentering the work force after many years; people who have been unemployed for a long period of time; people with little or no formal work experience.

Who Should Avoid It

Almost anyone who can avoid using this style should do so, especially people who want to emphasize their employment stability to capitalize on the companies with which they have been affiliated.

SAMPLE FUNCTIONAL RESUME

Karen Charles
227 East 27th St.
New York, NY 10017
(212) 222-1111

OBJECTIVE: PUBLIC RELATIONS DIRECTOR for a television station, using my public relations experience, knowledge of television production and managerial and administrative skills.

EXPERIENCE:

PUBLIC RELATIONS: Manager of public relations for a top trade magazine publisher. Oversee all aspects of public and press relations for 15 publications and industry-wide trade workshop. Designed and supervised promotion activities for successful trade workshop—resulting in heavier media coverage and a 28% increase in attendance. Improved market share 23% through introduction of innovative publicity campaign, based upon editorial roundtable forums and tie-ins with major industry events.

As public relations writer for the same publisher, wrote press releases, direct-mail brochures, and other promotional pieces.

Member of the Public Relations Society of America.

TELEVISION: Producer of special inserts session for leading New York independent television station. Oversaw implementation of special effects and production techniques. Working knowledge of three-quarter-inch editing machines, character generator and other television equipment. Field production and special segment production, including in-studio work.

Member of American Women in Radio & Television

ADMINISTRATION: As public relations manager, supervise staff of fifteen. Coordinate and schedule all activities. $250,000 budget responsibility.

As research manager for the television station, oversaw research staff of three and directed them in all phases of newsroom research. Established all procedures for newly created information-services department. With news director, researched and purchased computer system for computerization of archives system.

EDUCATION

Bachelor of Arts, New York University, January 1980
Major: English Literature
Dean's List
Creative Writing Award

THE COMBINATION RESUME

A combination resume uses elements of both the chronological and functional styles.

The bulk of a combination resume is functional, organizing your background by skills and function rather than by job title. A list of job titles and companies is given in reverse chronological order at the end.

This is the current hot resume style, recommended in articles and by career counselors, because it uses elements from both styles and crosses over well.

Strengths

As with the functional resume, you can tailor an explanation of your job history to fit the job you're applying for. At the same time, you can show continuity in your job record.

Drawbacks

Because descriptions of accomplishments are under functional headings, specific positions and titles are downplayed and specific job duties aren't spelled out. This can be confusing to the reader and can also look unwieldly—you have to take special care in layout.

Who Should Use It

Career switchers who want to fit their past jobs to a different area; recent graduates with little formal work experience.

Who Should Avoid It

People with strong, consistent experience in the same area as their objective; people who want to emphasize particular jobs and companies.

BASIC COMBINATION RESUME

Karen Charles
227 East 27th St.
New York, NY 10017
(212) 222-1111

OBJECTIVE: PUBLIC RELATIONS DIRECTOR for a television station, using my public relations experience, knowledge of television production, managerial and administrative skills.

SKILLS:

PUBLIC RELATIONS:

—As manager of public relations for a top trade magazine publisher, oversee all aspects of public and press relations for 15 publications and industry-wide trade workshop.
—Designed and supervised promotion activities for successful trade workshop—resulting in heavier media coverage and a 28% increase in attendance.
—Improved market share 23% through introduction of innovative publicity campaign, based upon editorial roundtable forums and tie-ins with major industry events.
—As public relations writer for the same publisher, wrote press releases, direct mail brochures, and other promotional pieces.

TELEVISION:

—As producer of special inserts session for leading New York independent television station, produced news and feature pieces requiring special effects and production techniques.
—Extensive field production and special segment production experience, including in-studio debates and audience participation talk shows.
—Working knowledge of three-quarter-inch editing machines, character generator, and other television equipment.

ADMINISTRATION:

—As public relations manager, supervise staff of fifteen. Coordinate and schedule all activities. Profit and loss responsibility for $250,000 budget.
—As research manager for the television station, oversaw research staff of three and directed them in all phases of newsroom research.
—Established all procedures for newly created information-services department. With news director, researched and purchased computer system for computerization of archives system.

EXPERIENCE:

4/85–present ABC Publications, Inc., New York, NY
          Manager of Public Relations
          Public Relations Writer/Project Associate

2/80–4/85 WYYY-TV, New York, NY
          Producer of News Inserts
          Research Manager
          Associate Producer
          Production Assistant

EDUCATION

    Bachelor of Arts, New York University, January 1980
    Major: English Literature
    Dean's List
    Creative Writing Award

ACTIVITIES

    Member: American Women in Radio & Television
             Public Relations Society of America

CONTENTS: THE CHIEF PARTS OF A RESUME

Regardless of format, a resume must cover certain areas of information. Those areas constitute the five key parts of a resume.

The length of each section, the information you include, and how you present it, all depend on your background and objective.

1. Personal Data:

Name, address, and telephone number.

These three basic facts are all your personal data section should contain; anything else is a waste of space. Don't bother with height, weight, marital status, or health. There is absolutely no reason to include any of those.

> TIP: Put your name, address, and phone number in the upper *right hand corner* instead of the middle of the page. When people flip through a stack of resumes, your name is immediately noticeable.

2. Career Objective (optional, but recommended):

A brief statement of your immediate goals that targets your resume; six lines are the absolute maximum, less if possible.

A career objective isn't essential, but it does tell your target audience exactly what you're after. Many prospective employers flip through a stack of resumes, reading only the objectives. If there isn't an objective that grabs them, or there isn't an objective at all, they may scrap the resume.

In light of this: *make it specific.* A general objective doesn't sell you; if anything, it weakens your resume. You should state succinctly *exactly* what you are looking for.

> EXAMPLE: *Objective:* A position in human resources with a retailing company that will enable me to apply my 12 years of experience developing and overseeing training programs for retail management.
> *Not:* A position in human resources that will utilize my communications and business skills.

Avoid mushy nonstatements like the second example. General phrases such as "utilize my business skills" mean nothing to a prospective employer. It comes across as if all you're doing is filling in the blanks. If the only objective you can come up with is this kind of bland statement, you're better off omitting the objective entirely.

You can skip the objective if you don't want to target your resume for a specific job. Also, if you have a well-grounded background that fits your job target and shows continuity and logical progression, you can omit a career objective without really worrying.

3. Work Experience:

Your past jobs and accomplishments arranged either by date or by function, depending on the format.

This is the real heart of a resume. The information you include and how you present it can make or break you. Take your time planning and writing your work history, always keeping your target audience and objective in mind. Tie your experience to your general objective.

If you've included a job objective on your resume, you *must* be able to back it up with the information in this section. Stress the achievements and jobs you've had that most underscore your ability to meet your objective. Take advantage of past experience that isn't directly linked to your objective by writing it up so that it relates *indirectly.*

EXAMPLE: A Houston morning talk-show producer wanted to make a move into the record industry. *Problem:* All of her work experience was exclusively in TV production. *Solution:* She played up the shows she had done about music, recording stars, and radio, emphasizing her interest in and knowledge of the field and supporting her objective.

EXAMPLE: A recent college graduate used his part-time job as a salesperson in a gourmet food shop to back up his ability to become an effective management trainee at a large industrial company. He explained that at the shop, he trained new personnel, managed it on weekday nights, oversaw the other part-time workers, and devised a new inventory system. Those specific examples demonstrated his ability to take on responsibility and stressed his innovative managerial skills—qualities that most management-training programs are looking for in new recruits.

Where you place certain facts about your work history can make a huge difference in how you are perceived. Use placement to emphasize the strongest aspects of your experience. Highlight the information that directly relates to your objective by positioning it prominently in your resume: at the top of lists or at the beginning of paragraphs.

In a chronological resume, emphasize your most recent job. List your accomplishments, your achievements, and your duties—four examples is a good number to aim for. A prospective employer will pay most attention to your recent achievements. The further you go into the past, the less information you should include—usually two or three key points are enough.

> **TIP: To make the work experience section of a chronological resume even more hard-hitting, write a brief paragraph that summarizes your responsibilities under each job title, *then* list three to four examples of specific achievements.**

You should apply the same general principle to a functional or combination resume. The function that is the most crucial to your objective should get the most detailed information; write less in the lesser function areas.

> **TIP: Don't stress the key areas of your experience (most recent job or strongest function area) at the expense of the rest of your work experience. If any part of your background looks sketchy, prospective employers become wary.**

4. Education:

School, degree(s), year in which you earned your degree, major, any honors.

Generally speaking, the longer you have been out of school, the less space it should take on your resume. However, *if you're a recent college graduate or a student,* expand the education section by adding such information as dean's list, college activities, and awards. You can also include courses you think might stand in your favor. This works especially well if your major isn't directly applicable to your career objective, or if you have specific knowledge in another field that can enhance your candidacy.

> **EXAMPLE:** A young woman who was applying for an executive trainee position in retailing listed a few computer courses she had taken in college. *Reason:* She knew that buyer trainees had to use computers. *Result:* She was snapped up quickly.

In addition, list education *before* work experience on your resume if you're a student or recent graduate seeking an entry-level position. Usually your work experience is limited, so prospective employers will place more weight on your educational background.

> **TIP:** If you were involved in a work/study program or co-op program, mention it briefly under "Education," but also include a description of the job itself under "Work Experience."

> **TIP:** A phrase to include under education that impresses prospective employers is: "Earned XX% of college expenses." If you had a part-time, free-lance, or full-time job, you should add this phrase to your resume. It never fails to get a good reaction.

5. Activities (Optional, but recommended):

A brief list of outside activities, memberships, civic involvement, etc.

Don't write this category off as fluff. Extracurricular activities can play a big role in getting you an interview or a job. Not only do they differentiate your resume from others, making you come across as an individual, they can also strengthen your career objective.

Work-related activities underscore your expertise and professionalism. If you are a member of a trade or professional association, list it prominently. Also include any professional awards or honors you've received. If you've written any articles, you can list them here as well.

Be sure to list activities that reflect positive personal characteristics, such as volunteer work.

> **TIP:** Shy away from mentioning groups that are overtly political or controversial. The person reading your resume may have strong views—the opposite way.

> **TIP:** List hobbies *only* if you have limited or no formal work experience and need to flesh out your skills and capabilities. If you

have a few years of solid work experience to show, *don't* list hobbies, unless they mesh extremely well with the position you seek.

Note: There should be *no* reference section in which you list the names of references; i.e., people who would speak in your favor. Except for very rare exceptions, there is absolutely no need to write out your references.

As for the common compromise, "References Available Upon Request," don't bother. The person who reads your resume will assume you can provide the names of references if you're asked for them. There's no point in wasting space on the page saying so.

WRITING A RESUME THAT SELLS

■ **The simplest way to begin drafting a resume is by making a resume worksheet, following the format you have chosen, and then filling it in.**

Start by listing your job duties. Flesh out your experience with summaries and examples of your accomplishments, skills, and abilities. This will give you a foundation upon which to build the substance of your resume and help you to organize your thoughts along the right lines. Always keep your job objective in mind, focusing on the qualities that a prospective employer would want for that job and how you can prove on paper that you have them.

At the same time, remember to play up the *general* qualities that employers like to see.

Be sure to include:

- examples of productivity/profit-mindedness
- patterns of accomplishment and upward movement
- examples that present you as a team player
- evidence of stability and direction

■ **Expect to write at least two drafts.**

The first draft will be your worksheet. Write more than you need, and don't worry much about phrasing and style. Cite as many examples and descriptions as you can. You can use the first draft as raw material and boil down the information to come up with the strongest facts to put in the final version. Edit with an eye to the reader and your job objective.

■ **Have friends and colleagues read and critique your resume.**

Make sure you have supported your objective, given enough specific information, and written clearly and interestingly.

> TIP: **Give your resume to someone in the same position as your career objective. That person will know what should be stressed and probably can give you some helpful advice.**

■ **One last point as you write, edit, and rewrite your resume: Don't forget that how you say something is as important as what you're saying.**

Someone with a weaker background can win an interview over someone more qualified, if that person is a better communicator. The key to writing a strong, effective resume is *presentation.*

Little things make a difference—length of sentences, the words you use to describe your experience, layout, and general appearance. Don't overlook anything. You want your resume to sell you, so make it as solid as possible in every way, from contents to presentation to appearance.

FIVE BASIC GUIDELINES WHEN WRITING A RESUME

1. Be Brief

A resume should demonstrate your ability to communicate by summarizing and consolidating information clearly.

Some guidelines:

- Use short words. A resume isn't the place to demonstrate your impressive vocabulary. Avoid bureaucratese and jargon.

- If you have little experience or little to say, fine. Don't resort to puffery. When you puff up a resume, it shows.

- Use fragments instead of complete sentences. They read more quickly, take up less space, and force you to omit unnecessary words.

TIP: Use bullets in the body of your resume to set off each piece of information under a heading.

- Plunge right into your statements and avoid using "I." Say "Produced award-winning television commercials," not "I produced . . ." Everybody already knows you are the subject of the resume.

2. Be Specific

Try to come up with concrete *examples* of achievements rather than writing in terms of straight job duties or skills. Vague descriptions about your past jobs won't sell your experience effectively. Outlining specific results will. The more specific you are, the better you demonstrate your skills and accomplishments.

You want to underscore your ability to step into a job and begin producing results immediately. Listing the results you've already produced is the most convincing way to do this.

TIP: Aim for ten specific accomplishments on your resume. This amount makes your background look solid.

Some guidelines:

- Never include phrases such as "worked in a department that dealt with . . ." or "worked for a company that . . ." You should be specific about what *you* did, not what the company or department did.

- Avoid general comments such as "knowledge of," "helped with," "aided in." They make you sound like a nonachiever, someone who stood around and watched or lent an occasional hand.

- Whenever possible, use numbers or percents. Statistics stand out and make a resume look even more precise. Also, people are more inclined to believe numbers.

EXAMPLE: Managed $2,000,000 procurement and supply budget and saved the company $250,000.
Supervised staff of 45.
Increased productivity 23%.
Note: Don't write out figures, especially when you are talking about money. Two hundred fifty thousand dollars doesn't jump off the page like $250,000 does.

TIP: If you are unsure about a number but still want to use one, avoid common numbers such as 50, 100, etc. Odd numbers sound less manufactured.

3. Be Active

Always use strong words that show action; avoid passive descriptions. Action words bring a resume to life. Most important, they make you seem like an achiever, a person who is a doer.

When you use action words in a resume, you underscore your skills and abilities subtly and succinctly. Certain words have the power to create a positive image, one that is implied as much as stated.

Especially strong words . . .

. . . to emphasize your innovative and creative abilities:

conceived	developed	launched	produced
created	established	originated	set up
devised	initiated	planned	structured

. . . to emphasize leadership skills:

coordinated

administered	delegated	headed	oversaw
authorized	directed	led	spearheaded
controlled	guided	managed	supervised

. . . to emphasize your contribution to productivity and growth:

expanded	generated
increased	strengthened

. . . to emphasize efficiency and problem-solving skills:

expedited	revamped	streamlined
improved	revised	
reorganized	simplified	

. . . and some good all-purpose words:
completed   implemented
conducted   maintained
demonstrated

To further strengthen your resume, use strong adverbs and adjectives as modifiers. But use them sparingly. Too much descriptive language becomes annoying and looks slightly suspicious. If you overdo the glowing words, it looks as though you're trying too hard—and probably exaggerating.

Some good modifiers to use are:
actively   comprehensive   cost-effectively
dramatically efficient   effectively
far-reaching innovative   solid
significantly strong   substantially
successfully

> **TIP:** When you use a phrase such as "dramatically increased," be sure you include the figures or facts to back it up. Otherwise it may sound like an inflated claim.

4. Be Selective

Don't think that the more examples you list and the more information you pack into a resume, the more qualified you appear.

Think before you list job duties, skills, and accomplishments. Decide what aspects of your previous jobs apply to the position you want. By being selective, you target yourself and your resume more precisely.

Prospective employers want to determine your qualifications for a specific job. They don't want to wade through useless material to get to the pertinent information.

> **EXAMPLE:** "Able to build, motivate, and cultivate brilliance." This phrase, taken from an actual resume, is the type of comment you should cut to make room for concrete statements. The major problem—it isn't backed up with any specific examples. It also smacks of overstatement, something that adds nothing to the salability of the candidate.

If you clutter your resume with unimportant facts, examples, and claims of ability, you distract the reader from the information that sells you.

Focus only on the positive aspects of your background. Although you should be honest on your resume, you don't have to confess all.

5. Be Honest

Don't lie.

False statements and claims on your resume hurt more than they can help. At some point, your background may be checked or you may be asked to elaborate. Stick with the truth and you will have much less to worry about.

PRESENTATION: THE RIGHT APPEARANCE

■ **A clear, readable typeface, cream, white, or off-white bond paper, and black print always look good.**

Stick with the basics and you can't go wrong. If possible, prepare your resume on a computer with a letter-quality printer. It is less expensive than having it professionally printed because you don't need to order hundreds of copies. Instead you can print out as many as you need, when you need them. You can also update your resume whenever you want without doing as much retyping. If you don't have access to a computer, many word-processing services type, print, and store resumes for you.

> **TIP: If you do use a computer, be aware of the justification. Most word-processing programs automatically justify the text, which makes the right margin even instead of ragged. While a smooth block of text normally looks sharp, it can pose problems in resume-writing—especially if you write short sentences or fragments. The letters wind up being oddly spaced, with large gaps in between.**

Having your resume professionally printed is another option. It used to be the rule of thumb. This option has changed somewhat. It is still a good idea if you're planning to do a massive mailing—you don't have to print or run off hundreds of resumes yourself and you're assured of having resumes that are neat and professional looking. But there are drawbacks to having your resume typeset—it's costly to make changes; you usually have to order a large quantity; and people may think you're mounting a resume blitz. If you do decide to have your resume typeset, steer clear of anything but the standards in terms of paper color, typeface, and layout.

Photocopying a typewritten resume is a strong option, in spite of what many people think. It's easy and inexpensive, and you can control the number of copies according to need. Just be sure to use bond paper (25% rag content) instead of copier paper; it prevents the print from smearing and also makes it less obvious that you used a copier. Also be sure that the original is aligned perfectly. Nothing gives away the fact that you've photocopied your resume more quickly than having it come out slanted.

Flashy layouts, colored paper, and ornate fonts are recommended *only* for creative positions. If you are applying to be an art director, an artist, or a photographer, and you feel the urge to show how clever you are with your resume, go ahead. But proceed at your own risk. Even in the creative fields, sometimes it is wiser to err on the side of conservatism. Your work should demonstrate how creative you are; your resume doesn't have to do that for you.

■ **Don't crowd information onto the page.**

Appearance is more than paper and type. It is also layout, an aspect of resume preparation that too many people downplay. Don't make that mistake—layout matters. If your resume is laid out poorly, people won't read it as carefully. Any artist will tell you that negative space is as important as positive space. *Translation:* Don't fill up the page with print. Leave space in between the major parts of the resume and between the paragraphs in those sections as well. There is nothing more difficult to read than a large unbroken block of text. It looks dull and threatening. Let your resume breathe.

Length

■ **There are no hard-and-fast rules governing the length of a resume; make your resume as long as it has to be, no more and no less.**

Forget all the articles that say your resume *must* be two pages long or you *must* summarize twelve years work experience in one page.

A couple of qualifiers:

- A resume should fill one page minimum. If you have little information to include, lay it out with a lot of spacing and wide margins.

- The trend is toward resumes over one page long. Some career counselors say employers want to see more information than they need from prospective employees. But select your information judiciously and be sure it is relevant. Don't take this trend as an excuse to pad out a meager resume with extraneous details and data just so you can fill up space.

SIX SPECIAL PROBLEMS AND HOW TO OVERCOME THEM

It can be difficult, but you can hide or disguise job-related problems on your resume. Following are six of the most common problems and what you can do about them.

Problem #1: Being Labeled Overqualified

Two things on your resume can immediately flag you as being over-qualified: too many jobs and too many *higher-level* positions.

To get around this problem, omit information on your resume and minimize the importance of certain jobs. The trick is to do both without undermining your qualifications.

Some tips on how to do this:

- Assess your background and determine what information is not crucial to support your career objective. Sometimes you can completely omit a few jobs—positions you held furthest in the past, lateral moves are safe cuts. *Remember:* You are trying to make your experience look like less than you actually have. The fewer positions you list, the less weighty your resume will seem.

- If you worked at the same company and received several promotions, combine two or more jobs into one. Don't bother listing each step.

- Picking up on job titles is a quick and easy way for a prospective employer to determine if you're overqualified. Don't give him or her the ammunition. Recognize which titles are triggers and replace them with equally descriptive but less imposing titles. For example, instead of referring to yourself as a vice president, call yourself a department head.

- To avoid drawing attention to dates and job titles, use a combination or functional format. Focus on experience.

Problem #2: Being Considered Too Old

Age discrimination is illegal in most cases—but it happens all the time. Sometimes otherwise ideal candidates are told they are "overqualified"; other times they are just not called back. To avoid the problem before it arises, consider *age-proofing* your resume.

Try the following:

- Adjust your resume accordingly by omitting or downplaying dates. Make certain to notice all the references to age in your resume: dates you attended school, dates you held jobs, military service, even the types of activities you list.

- Use a functional or combination format instead of chronological. If you prefer the chronological format, don't display dates prominently by setting them off. Bury dates in parentheses right after the job title. They'll attract less immediate attention.

- Eliminate mention of your earliest jobs. There is no point in advertising the number of jobs you have held, nor the number of years you have been working.

> **TIP:** While we don't advocate lying, some people do knock a few years off their age. Warning: If you do that, be sure to be consistent. Take into account your spouse's age, your children's ages, how old you were when you graduated, and other important dates in your life. One man was convinced he had completely snowed his interviewer—he had dyed his hair, he knew his new (and more recent) year of birth, the revised date of his college graduation. But the interviewer looked a bit askance at him when he confidently blurted out the actual year of his wedding anniversary. Given his new age, he had apparently gotten married at the tender age of fourteen.

Problem #3: Spotty Work Experience: Job Hopping/Jobs in Different Areas

Prospective employers often view spotty work experience as a negative signal: the person isn't a stable worker, can't hold a job, has no career direction.

You can fight against this perception. The key point in your favor is that despite your job hopping you do keep getting hired, so you must be doing something right. You want prospective employers to see the situation that way. Your resume should make them want to hear the reasons you changed jobs or career direction.

Some ways of doing this:

- If you held numerous jobs in a short amount of time, use the combination or functional style resume to make the number of jobs and the duration of those jobs less obvious.

- Consolidate jobs under similar function headings or omit mention of certain jobs entirely. If you held a job for only a few months, feel free to drop it. Gaps of a few months don't look that questionable.

- Focus on achievements, but don't get carried away. If you held a job for only a short while, no prospective employer is going to believe you dramatically increased profits or turned around a failing division.

- Arrange your resume so that the reader can see a constant upward movement. You may have switched jobs, but you kept advancing.

- If you took a demotion, don't make it appear as such. Stress the different duties and different areas the job comprised.

- If you shifted career directions, emphasize the common bonds between the jobs you held in different fields. For example, if you went from retailing to computers, stress the computer literacy you needed to function as an assistant buyer. Downplay the non-computer functions.

Problem #4: Odd Match between Background and Objective

An employer has two chief concerns about a person attempting a career shift: Can this person's qualifications be applied to a different career, and is he or she committed to acquiring enough new knowledge to make it work?

When your experience is seemingly unrelated to your objective, you must figure out ways to convince a prospective employer that you have the qualifications and the background to fill the job.

By concentrating on the elements of your background that relate in any way to your job objective, you can skew your resume and present yourself as a strong candidate.

Try the following:

- Start by examining your past experience and recognizing any patterns in it that connect to your current job objective. Regardless of your primary duties, have all your jobs involved similar aspects—such as intense personal contact, communication skills, analytical ability? Did you volunteer to take on responsibilities outside of your job description, responsibilities that you can tie to your new objective? Play up anything that shows you have been interested in your objective for some time.

- Pay special attention to minor aspects of previous jobs that relate in any way to your new objective. Be creative in finding connections where it looks like there are none.

  EXAMPLE: You're trying to move into a sales position after having had experience as an audit accountant. Mention the extensive contact you have had with different kinds of people and how you have had to sell them on your presence in the company that was being audited.

- In the descriptions of your jobs or functions, minimize or omit any specialized experience you can't tie to your objective.

- Stress leisure activities, even hobbies, that demonstrate your interest, abilities, or experience in your objective.

- Take continuing education or professional courses. Depending on the course, list under education or activities.

- Join professional associations and list them prominently. Even if you are a new member and have attended few, if any, meetings, it signals your interest in and commitment to this new field.

Problem #5: Unemployed/Fired/Laid Off

Being unemployed when you're job hunting is a situation that is becoming more and more common and there is not the same stigma attached to it as there used to be. Still, problems exist. People often prefer to hire people who have jobs. It's not fair, but it's human nature: when a job candidate is holding a responsible position, prospective employers assume he or she is a solid, responsible person.

A well-designed resume can help you bypass some of the problems of being unemployed. It can hide your unemployed status or de-emphasize it by focusing on your abilities and contributions to companies in the past.

A few tips:

- *Don't* explain on your resume why you were or are unemployed. Some people want to make sure prospective employers realize that they were laid off, not fired. They add a comment such as "position was eliminated due to corporate cutbacks" at the end of a job description. This is a strategic error. Explanatory comments don't make you sound more qualified. If you feel the need to explain your present unemployment or any other gap in your record, do so in the interview or cautiously in a cover letter.

- In general, it's best to go with the combination or functional resumes. Either of these formats is more helpful when you're trying to concentrate on skills rather than dates and trying to make it less apparent that you're currently out of work.

- If you have a solid work record and you're looking for a job in the same general area, you *can* use the chronological format. Capitalize on your stability and consistency. These will outweigh your recent unemployment.

- Do free-lance or part-time work. Even if you only do a little, you can have a present job to put on your resume. For example, an unemployed attorney began taking on charity cases for no pay on a limited basis. That way, she could honestly state on her resume that she maintained a private practice.

- Ways to hide unemployment on your resume: 1) If you have a friend who owns his or her own business, ask if you can arrange a trade: you get a job title, he or she gets free assistance from you. This way you can legitimately list a job on your resume for the period in which you're unemployed. 2) If you left your last job on good terms, check with your employer to see if you can list the job as "current" on your resume.

Problem #6: Reentering the Work Force

When you are reentering the work force after a short or long absence, your chief concern is to prove on paper that you have the right qualities and experience to fill a particular job—despite your time away.

Your resume must convince prospective employers that your employment gap hasn't affected your skills and ability to contribute and that you have maintained a level of professionalism.

One of the best ways to prepare a strong resume is to plan ahead. Lay the groundwork for reentering the work force by becoming active *before* you start a formal job hunt. Keep abreast of developments in your field, join professional groups, recontact colleagues, take short courses.

Some tips:

- Begin by *honestly* assessing your background, paying special attention to the years you have been out of the job market. Think about everything in terms of marketability. Don't think that because you haven't held a formal job, you haven't had salable experience. Civic activities, leisure activities, hobbies, childcare— you can use any or all of them on your resume to show your abilities and experience.

- Use a functional or combination resume, so you can emphasize your abilities and nonwork experience as opposed to the time between your last formal job and the present.

- List on your resume any volunteer work you've done as if it were regular work. Be specific about duties and accomplishments.

- Include any brush-up courses or refresher courses you've taken.

- Be sure that you carefully target everything. Don't list activities just to prove that you've been active. If you can link only a few of them to your objective, fine. It's best to have a small amount of strong information, well presented and targeted, than lists of unrelated activities.

RESUME EXAMPLES: BEFORE AND AFTER

To give you a clear sense of how to critique and evaluate your resume, what follows are some actual examples. We have commented on their strengths and weaknesses, then reworked them to make them as strong as possible.

RESUME #1—BEFORE

<u>RESUME</u>

[Comment: Titling the resume "RESUME" is absolutely unnecessary. The reader *knows* what this is. Omit.]

Mark Wilson

129 Washington Street

Atlanta, GA

(404) 555-2222

<u>Summary of Achievements</u>

- designed the procedures for inventory control of components and finished products; implemented the system to reduce inventory costs.

[Needs expansion—was the system successful? How much money was saved?]

- coordinated and oversaw the regional implementation of a corporate obsolescence policy that resulted in a cost savings of over $250,000.

[Good example—the dollar figure stands out.]

- participated in "Administration Resources Seminars" and served on four integrated quality management teams.

[All right, but would be better if it were explained what these programs/teams are.]

[Comment: The above section is a good place to emphasize the job hunter's top accomplishments, but it would be stronger if he began with a career objective statement, then used this summary to outline his strongest qualifications.]

<u>EXPERIENCE</u>

May 1985 to Present   Tri-Lab Products, Inc., Duluth, GA

<u>Current Position</u>: Production Scheduling Supervisor, Production Control Department

Responsible for the supervision and coordination of scheduling the production of over 235 million pieces of consumer health products. Forecasting according to a "Just in Time" concept.

[The information in this section is good, but it isn't presented as well as it could be. "Responsible for" deadens the section. Final statement needs clarification.]

<u>June 1983 to April 1985</u>—Components Analyst/Scheduler, Production Control Department

[Above date is buried, not consistent with the rest of the resume.]

Responsible for the scheduling of all lines for a three-week sales cycle; planning and supervising a production group on a daily basis; expediting ingredients and components; organizing the obsolescence program.

[Again, "responsible for" should go. Choice of verbs is good, but it would be better if they were in the active voice.]

July 1982   Factors Walk Trading Co., Savannah, GA
to May 1983
             Position: Export Assistant

             Responsible for market research, product information, freight forwarding, and
             feasibility reports.

[Because this job was not a recent one, the description can be this brief. But this needs work—action verbs, explanation of accomplishments.]

August 1980 InfoNetwork, Inc., Atlanta, GA
to June 1982
             Position: Researcher

             Responsible for coordinating research study on consumer buying habits.

[This should be put into the active voice.]

[Comment: Layout in this section needs work—job titles are buried, dates stand out more than company names or positions held. Job descriptions could be stronger.]

EDUCATION
    Masters in Business Administration
        Emory University, Atlanta, Georgia
        Graduation: June 1984
        Major: Industrial Management
        Thesis: "Just in Time" Inventory Management: Inventory and cost reduction through
                short-term integral planning

    Bachelor of Science
        Duke University, Durham, North Carolina
        Majors: Political Science and Economics
        Graduation: May 1980

[Comment: Too much space given to above section. Layout could be consolidated.]

REFERENCES
    Available upon request

[Comment: Unnecessary section.]

General Comments About Resume #1

This isn't a bad resume—there are many strong things about it. But it could be much better.

On the plus side: The writer has chosen good, specific examples of his achievements and has used numbers to underscore those examples. The "summary of achievements" section immediately points out his top accomplishments.

The problems are chiefly layout and writing style. The layout is confusing and doesn't draw the reader to the most important information. The writing style could be punched up. The writer has taken several excellent examples and strong verbs and watered them down.

RESUME #1—REVISED

MARK WILSON
129 Washington Street
Atlanta, GA
(404) 555-2222

OBJECTIVE: PRODUCTION/INVENTORY CONTROL MANAGER for a health & beauty aid
manufacturer

SUMMARY OF ACHIEVEMENTS
- designed and implemented inventory control system for health & beauty aid components and finished products, reducing inventory costs 21%
- coordinated and oversaw the regional implementation of a corporate obsolescence policy that resulted in a cost savings of over $250,000
- chosen by upper management to participate in "Administration Resources Seminars," and served on four integrated quality-management teams

EXPERIENCE
Production Scheduling Supervisor, Production Control Department
Tri-Lab Products, Inc., Duluth, GA   (May 1985–present)
- supervise and coordinate production scheduling of over 235,000,000 pieces of consumer health products
- saved company over $110,000 in inventory costs by introducing "Just in Time" short-term planning method
- plan and forecast according to that method, maintaining minimum inventory and maximizing cost efficiency

Components Analyst/Scheduler, Production Control Department
Tri-Lab Products, Inc., Duluth, GA   (June 1983–April 1985)
- scheduled all company product lines for a three-week sales cycle
- planned and managed production group on daily basis
- expedited ingredients and components
- organized cost-saving obsolescence program

Export Assistant
Factors Walk Trading Co., Savannah, GA   (July 1982–May 1983)
- conducted market and product research surveys
- handled freight forwarding
- researched and prepared export feasibility reports

Researcher
InfoNetwork, Inc., Atlanta, GA   (August 1980–June 1982)
- coordinated research study on consumer buying habits
- gathered and analyzed data

EDUCATION

Masters in Business Administration

Emory University; Atlanta, GA—June 1984

Major: Industrial Management

Thesis: "Just in Time" Inventory Management: Inventory and cost reduction through short-term integral planning

Bachelor of Science

Duke University; Durham, NC—May 1980

Majors: Political Science and Economics

RESUME #2—BEFORE

Veronica Carlin

Permanent Address:	Temporary Address:
208 Maple Avenue	55 East 10th Street
Ridgewood, NJ 07450	New York, NY 10003
(201) 555-5555	(212) 555-1234

OBJECTIVE   Application programming position with the opportunity for growth and advancement

[Comment: A bit too general. Be more explicit about the kind of company; add a qualification statement.]

EDUCATION
9/83–Present   New York University
                      B.S. in Computer Science **[No abbreviation]**
                      Graduation Anticipated June 1987 **[Reword]**
                      Grade Point Average: In Major: 3.7/4.0
                                            Overall: 3.5/4.0

[Comment: Since this job hunter is still a student, this section belongs up top, but layout is poor.]

WORK EXPERIENCE

<u>Well-Known Computer Company</u>   Burbank, CA
   Programmer
   Summer Supplemental—1986
   —Using PL/I and IMS wrote software that generates and maintains a
     telecommunications network.
   —Tested software in test environment in which I had to modify and
     update a database.
   —The software I wrote and tested is now being produced.

<u>Telecommunications Company</u>   Morristown, NJ
   Programmer
   Computer Science Internship—Fall 1986
   —Using SAS and RPF, wrote interactive software that simulates
     communication noise levels along power lines, and generates a table
     and graph for interpretation.

<u>Electronics Co., Inc.</u>   New York, NY
   Summer 1985, Summer 1984
   —Office Clerical—Handled various office tasks including word
     processing and switchboard.

[As phrased, this adds little to the resume. This should either be written to tie in with the objective and be presented as an example of the job seeker's work ethic, or should be dumped.]

[Comment: As this work history is set up, companies are highlighted and skills downplayed—a mistake. While the information given is specific and should be effective, this doesn't emphasize the job hunter's qualifications enough.]

COMPUTER SKILLS

Hardware used:

IBM 308X	IBM 370	INTEL 8080	VAX 785

Software used:

ADA	ADF2	APL	COBOL
FORTRAN	IMS	JCL	LISP
MVS	PASCAL	PL/I	RPF
360/370 ASSEMBLER		8080 ASSEMBLER	

[An excellent addition to a technical resume and one that clearly shows the writer's expertise. Could be laid out to be more readable, but that is the only improvement this would need.]

EXTRACURRICULAR
ACTIVITIES

—member IEEE/ACM

[Comment: Mentioning trade association membership is a good idea, but this is buried under the long section heading. Writing out the association title would make it more prominent]

REFERENCES

Available upon request

[Comment: Again, a useless addition that does nothing for the resume.]

General Comments About Resume #2

This is similar to many student resumes we've seen. The writer has made the mistake many people make: she follows a strict chronological format.

Because the job hunter is still a student her experience is limited to summer work, but her qualifications are quite strong. The resume would be much more effective arranged functionally, playing up her skills rather than the jobs she has held. Opening with a summary, followed by results-oriented highlights, then closing with a brief synopsis of the companies and dates, would sell this job hunter more successfully.

RESUME #2—REVISED

Veronica Carlin

Permanent Address:
208 Maple Avenue
Ridgewood, NJ 07450
(201) 555-5555

Temporary Address:
55 East 10th Street
New York, NY 10003
(212) 555-1234

OBJECTIVE

Application programming position in a computer or telecommunications company, giving me an opportunity for growth and advancement

EDUCATION

New York University
Bachelors of Science expected in June 1987
Major: Computer Science
Major Grade Point Average: 3.7
Overall Grade Point Average: 3.5
Earned 43% of tuition costs

EXPERIENCE

- Using PL/I and IMS, wrote software generating and maintaining a telecommunications network. Software is currently in production.
- Tested software in BTS test environment—requiring accessing, modification, and updating of database.
- Wrote interactive software using SAS and RPF, simulating communication noise levels along power line and generating a table and graph, used by technical staff.
- Operated word-processing equipment and switchboard, and assisted office manager of an electronics company, to pay for college expenses.

1986
(summer)

Programmer
Well-Known Computer Company, Burbank, CA

1985
(fall)

Programmer
Telecommunications Company, Morristown, NJ

1985, 1985
(summers)

Office Assistant
Electronics Co., Inc., New York, NY

COMPUTER SKILLS

- write and test software; working knowledge and experience in:

ADA	ADF2	APL	COBOL
FORTRAN	IMS	JCL	LISP
MVS	PASCAL	PL/I	RPF
360/370 ASSEMBLER		8080 ASSEMBLER	

- hardware used:

  | IBM 308X | IBM 370 | INTEL 8080 | VAX 785 |

ACTIVITIES

Member, campus chapter of International Electrical and Electronic Engineering (IEEE).

RESUME #3—ORIGINAL

CARL McMANUS   205 Wilshire Blvd.   Business: (213) 555-1234
                Los Angeles, CA 11111   Home: (213) 555-6789

[Comment: Bad layout. Name doesn't stand out.]

BUSINESS EXPERIENCE
L&B ADVERTISING—LOS ANGELES, CA 8/78–Present
    Account Supervisor 9/83–present: Super Wine Coolers
    —Manage strategic planning and execution for the multimillion-dollar, national introductory
    campaign of a new product line. This includes numerous duties, including market research
    and sales promotion activity.

[This is his current position, yet he says next to nothing about it. Needs more description, more results.]

    Account Executive 8/79–9/83: A&A, Tip-Top, Suncool
    —11/82–9/83: Managed A&A Inc. account, including successful introduction of A&A Aspirin
    and relaunch of A&A Cough Syrup. A&A's market share grew from 0.3% to 3.7% during this
    period.
    —8/79–11/82: Responsible for both the Tip-Top hair-care and Suncool sun-care product line.
    Accomplishments included the Suncool's tan accelerator new product introduction, the
    Tip-Top sweepstakes program, as well as development of direct response and gift-with-
    purchase promotions.

[Could be punched up, made more active and results-oriented.]

    Assistant Account Executive 5/78–8/79
    —Assisted on top national accounts including Tip-Top, Valkyrie Wine, Taylor's Toothpaste,
    SilkSense Hosiery.

[Because this was in the past, this description should be brief.]

KNIGHT & DAY ADVERTISING—LOS ANGELES, CA 8/76–5/78
Media Planner: Planned national broadcast and print advertising for Roast Beef Ranch,
Sophisticated Lady Cosmetics, Vintage Wines, Amalgamated Chain Stores.

[Format isn't consistent with above.]

EDUCATION
1976   University of California at Berkeley
    Master of Science in Communications.
    Graduated 3.5 cume.
1974   University of California at Berkeley
    Bachelor of Arts in English/Sociology with honors.
    Graduated 3.6 cume.

1981–85   Selected to participate in advanced Agency Management Seminars
1980–83   Additional Graduate Courses: Public Relations, Sales Promotion, Business Writing

[Could be tightened up. Grade-point average is unnecessary, because writer has been out of school for over a decade.]

AWARDS AND HONORS
1976   Who's Who in American Universities and Colleges

[Since there is only one "award and honor" and it isn't a professional award, this section should be omitted entirely.]

General Comments About Resume #3

This job hunter is right in choosing a chronological format: it effectively shows off his stable work history and consistently upward movement.

The overriding problem with this resume is that his current job description is *much* too brief. In general, the writer has relied too much on listing account names and too little on outlining results-oriented accomplishments.

The layout is confusing, cluttered, and inconsistent, making it difficult for the reader to get through and digest the information.

RESUME #3—REVISED

CARL McMANUS
205 Wilshire Blvd.
Los Angeles, CA 11111
(213) 555-6789

EXPERIENCE:

<u>L&B Advertising</u>, Los Angeles, CA

1983–present ACCOUNT SUPERVISOR: Super Wine Coolers
- Managed strategic planning and execution of successful $18-million, national introductory campaign of new product line.
- Designed and coordinated multi-media consumer and trade promotions, market research, and extensive sales promotion—winning 3.4% share of market for product.
- Extensive client interaction, resulting in agency retaining the account despite outside agency competition.

1979–1983 ACCOUNT EXECUTIVE: A&A, Tip-Top, Suncool
- Oversaw successful relaunch of A&A cough syrup and introduction of A&A aspirin—during which A&A's market share grew from 0.3% to 3.7%.
- Directed Suncool tan accelerator national roll-out, planned and implemented the Tip-Top sweepstakes program, and developed Tip-Top direct response and gift-with-purchase promotions.

1978–1979 ASSISTANT ACCOUNT EXECUTIVE
- Assisted on top national accounts including Tip-Top, Valkyrie Wine, Taylor's Toothpaste, SilkSense Hosiery.

<u>Knight & Day Advertising</u>, Los Angeles, CA

1976–1978 MEDIA PLANNER
- Planned national broadcast and print advertising for Roast Beef Ranch, Sophisticated Lady Cosmetics, Vintage Wines, Amalgamated Chain Stores.

EDUCATION:

<u>University of California at Berkeley</u>
1976	Master of Science in Communications
1974	Bachelor of Arts in English/Sociology, with honors
1980–83	Additional graduate courses in: Public Relations, Sales Promotion, Business Writing
1981–85	Selected by supervisors to participate in advanced Agency Management Seminars

RESUME #4—BEFORE

Leonard Paulsen
79 West 84th Street
New York, NY 10000
(212) 555-9999

OBJECTIVE: <u>General Manager</u>
Extensive background—improving cash flow and ROI, strengthening product lines, cutting costs, reducing inventory, building organizations . . . and profits.
   · General Manager—P&L responsibility
   · Entrepreneur—organized $3 million company
   · Marketing Vice President—$55 million company

[A good idea—combining objective with statement of qualifications in this way—but the objective is too general (general manager of what type of company?).]

<u>GENERAL MANAGER</u>
   U.S. subsidiary of major European multi-products company (1979 to date)
   P&L responsibility of $21 million division, reporting to President. Direct 40 people thru controller, sales warehouse, and service managers.
   <u>Products</u>: Mopeds, bicycles, accessories

[Good, brief summary of job responsibilities. But slang spelling "thru" is jarring.]

   • Established new U.S. market for mopeds thru comprehensive marketing and service program for the now-leading (and highest priced) moped. Increased sales from 18,000 to 32,000 units, for 34% market share and 36% rise in profit contribution.
   • Positioned company as significant new factor in bicycle business; changed supply sources, developed new product line and created dealer sales programs. Sales jumped from 21,000 low-price units to 33,000 high units, with 31% increase in profitability.
   • Cut number of warehouses from 5 to 2, without decrease in customer service and with $256,000 expense savings.
   • Saved $110,000 in telecommunication costs and reduced waiting time on dealer calls from 9 to less than 1½ minutes at season peak.

[This example doesn't come off well. It sounds like the writer is trying too hard.]

[Comment: In general, a strong section. Good use of action verbs, numbers, and specific examples.]

<u>VICE PRESIDENT, MARKETING</u>
   American Container Corporation, New York, NY (1973–1978)
   Responsible for marketing strategies and sales programs of $55 million multi-products company, reporting to President. <u>Products</u>: Garden products, sporting goods, apparel, specialty chemicals:

- As acting General Manager, improved market share of sporting goods company during poor market period. Reduced excess inventories. Set up new distribution system; prepared new catalogs; secured product publicity and set up successful consumer sweepstakes.
- Increased high-profit garden products company sales 18%, at lower selling expense. Repositioned product line, developed new products, redesigned packaging, and revised price structure. Established new sales organization.
- Turned around earnings of apparel company $1.3 million, despite poor market. Prepared business plan, trained sales manager, and developed two-tier sales organization and key-account sales program.
- Created innovative corporate-wide business planning system to enable divisions to prepare objectives-oriented action programs that could be monitored. Introduced inventory management program that cut inventory $900,000.

[Comment: Again, generally well-written, but it gets a bit verbose. A few examples could be cut without weakening the effect.]

GENERAL MANAGER

Bright Lights, Inc., New York, NY (1971–1973)

P&L responsibilty of $5 million company, reporting to Group Vice-President. Directed 90 people thru two factory managers, controller, and two sales managers. Products: Lighting fixtures, home furnishings.

- Reversed long-term profit decline and loss, to profit. Slashed inventory 19%, cut product line 44%, with 5% sales increase from better balanced inventory. Negotiated union agreement and achieved cooperation during wage-control period.
- Repackaged profitable but slow-moving product line for first-year 77% sales increase, to $800,000. Established separate organization to capitalize on this opportunity. Product is an accepted leader.

VICE PRESIDENT, OPERATIONS/MARKETING

Innovation Corporation, New York, NY (1968–1971)

As co-founder of $3 million multi-products company, responsible for selected operations and all sales, reporting to President. Directed 30 people thru operations manager and 12 sales representatives thru two sales managers. Products: Furniture, boats, and marine accessories.

- Stemmed losses of $1.8 million boat company, as acting General Manager. Renegotiated financing; operated company on cash flow. Improved margins 9% with smaller factory force and sales organization.
- Improved furniture company margins by redirecting shift in product mix.
- Negotiated acquisition of two companies, as principal, and secured $715,000 working capital financing.

PRINCIPAL MANAGEMENT CONSULTANT

Avaco Services Inc., New York, NY (1960–1968)

Responsible for management consulting projects in North America, Europe, and Middle East for leading management consulting organization. Directed four consultants. Products: Paints, plastics, packaged foods, construction materials, electronic components, real estate.

- Identified $10 million market for packaged food company and developed market-entry plans; secured 8% share in first year at targeted profit.
- Initiated plan to establish sales effort in $400 million market for construction company; firm is a leader in this market.
- Revised paint marketing and plant expansion program, for $1.2 million savings.

EDUCATION   M.B.A., New York University
              B.A., New York University

[Comment: Job hunter omitted dates purposefully—to avoid drawing attention to his age. But since preceding information is so dense, this section leaps out as sparse. It needs to be laid out differently to avoid drawing attention.]

PERSONAL   Married, 2 children
             Excellent health

[Comment: Personal section is unnecessary. Adds nothing to resume.]

General Comments About Resume #4

A very strong resume and one that works well to sell the job hunter. It is a good example of a longer-style resume, one that leaves little information to the reader's imagination.

Note: **Although this is technically a chronological resume, the writer has buried the dates in parentheses, drawing more attention to his experience and achievements and downplaying actual time. This works especially well for job switchers, career changers, and older job hunters who wish to avoid a functional resume but brush over time as much as possible.**

To make this resume stronger, all it needs is fine-tuning and polishing. A clearer objective, the deletion of a few excessive descriptions, and the addition of one or two words—and the resume would be highly effective.

RESUME #4—REVISED

Leonard Paulsen
79 West 84th Street
New York, NY 10000
(212) 555-9999

OBJECTIVE: GENERAL MANAGER for a multi-products company
Extensive background—improving cash flow and ROI, strengthening product lines, cutting costs, reducing inventory, building organizations . . . and profits.
- · General Manager—P&L responsibility
- · Entrepreneur—organized $3 million company
- · Marketing Vice President—$55 million company

EXPERIENCE:

GENERAL MANAGER
U.S. subsidiary of major European multi-products company (1979 to date)
- P&L responsibility of $21 million division, reporting to President. Direct 40 people through controller, sales warehouse, and service managers. Products: Mopeds, bicycles, accessories.
- Established new U.S. market for mopeds through comprehensive marketing and service program for the now-leading (and highest priced) moped. Increased sales from 18,000 to 32,000 units—a 34% market share and 36% rise in profit contribution.
- Positioned company as significant new factor in bicycle business; changed supply sources, developed new product line and created dealer sales programs. Sales jumped from 21,000 low-price units to 33,000 high units, with 31% increase in profitability.
- Decreased expenses $256,000 by cutting warehouses from 5 to 2 with no decrease in customer service; saved $110,000 in telecommunications costs.

VICE PRESIDENT, MARKETING
American Container Corporation, New York, NY (1973–1978)
Developed and managed marketing strategies and sales programs of $55 million multi-products company, reporting to President. Products: Garden products, sporting goods, apparel, specialty chemicals.
- As acting General Manager, improved market share of sporting goods company during poor market period. Reduced excess inventories. Set up new distribution system; prepared new catalogs; secured product publicity and set up successful consumer sweepstakes.
- Increased high-profit garden products company sales 18%, at lower selling expense. Repositioned product line, developed new products, redesigned packaging and revised price structure. Established new sales organization.
- Turned around earnings of apparel company $1.3 million, despite poor market. Prepared business plan, trained sales manager and developed two-tier sales organization and key account sales program.

- Created innovative corporate-wide business planning system to enable divisions to prepare objectives-oriented action programs that could be monitored. Introduced inventory management program that cut inventory $900,000.

GENERAL MANAGER
Bright Lights, Inc., New York, NY (1971–1973)

P&L responsibility of $5 million company, reporting to Group Vice President. Directed 90 people through two factory managers, controller, and two sales managers. Products: Lighting fixtures, home furnishings.

- Reversed long-term profit decline and loss, to profit. Slashed inventory 19%, cut product line 44%, with 5% sales increase from better balanced inventory. Negotiated union agreement and achieved cooperation during wage-control period.
- Repackaged profitable but slow-moving product line for first year 77% sales increase, to $800,000. Established separate organization to capitalize on this opportunity. Product is an acepted leader.

VICE PRESIDENT, OPERATIONS/MARKETING
Innovation Corporation, New York, NY (1968–1971)

As co-founder of $3 million multi-products company, managed selected operations and all sales, reporting to President. Directed 30 people through operations manager, and 12 sales representatives through 2 sales managers. Products: Furniture, boats, and marine accessories.

- Stemmed losses of $1.8 million boat company, as acting General Manager. Renegotiated financing; operated company on cash flow. Improved margins 9% with smaller factory force and sales organization.
- Improved furniture company margins by redirecting shift in product mix.
- Negotiated acquisition of two companies, as principal, and secured $715,000 working capital financing.

PRINCIPAL MANAGEMENT CONSULTANT
Avaco Services, Inc., New York, NY (1960–1968)

Handled management consulting projects in North America, Europe, and Middle East for leading management consulting organization. Directed four consultants. Products: Paints, plastics, packaged foods, construction materials, electronic components, real estate.

- Identified $10 million market for packaged food company and developed market entry plans; secured 8% share in first year at targeted profit.
- Initiated plan to establish sales effort in $400 million market for construction company; firm is a leader in this market.
- Revised paint marketing and plant expansion program, for $1.2 million savings.

EDUCATION: Master of Business Administration, New York University
Bachelor of Science, Business Administration, New York University

3   *Research*

INTRODUCTION

Research is one aspect of job hunting that everyone knows about, but most people could do it better. The typical problem is that too many people don't realize how many ways they can use research to help them find a job. It's much more than just compiling a list of business names and addresses or reading articles about a company before an interview.

Done correctly, research can assist you in every step of your job hunt: from writing a more targeted cover letter, to knowing key information that you can bring up during an interview, to laying the groundwork for effective networking. You can even find out about the existence of jobs where you thought there were none. In short, research is a way of making yourself more successful. It gives you the information you need to sell yourself effectively.

USING RESEARCH TO STRENGTHEN YOUR JOB HUNT

You can strengthen your job hunt in seven vital areas through research.

Too many people walk into a library, collect a few company names and addresses, and walk out, convinced they've done enough research. They're making a mistake. Research can broaden your job hunt and increase your potential for landing a job.

You should use research to:

1. *Determine in advance which companies are good prospects and which aren't.* Although this is an obvious use for research, it's not often approached correctly. By reading articles in trade publications, talking with people at the company, reading corporate public relations literature, even by checking Who's Who directories and reading about the managers, you can get a good picture of the people and the company you might want to work for.

   The questions to answer: *Does this company have job openings in my area? Does it plan to have any in the future? Can I create a job?* In short: *Is this company a viable target?*

2. *Position yourself more precisely toward a company/industry/objective.* From day one in your job hunt, you will need to target yourself. The only way of doing that accurately is by knowing the particulars of a company's or an industry's goals, and then applying them to your own.

   The questions to answer: *What are recent trends or developments in the industry or company, and how can I use them to sell myself? Who is the ideal candidate, and how do I match up? Is my objective a realistic one?*

3. *Help sell yourself in an interview or letter.* This is one of the biggest pay-offs of thorough research. It will help you take the general targeting information a step further and apply it directly to your letters, resumes, and interviews. By finding out about a company's management style, recent events and developments, and its policies and outlook *before* you contact them, you can increase your chances of fitting their criteria. You can refer to up-to-date information in your cover letter, skew yourself to match a company's style, anticipate their needs, and ask questions of an interviewer that will show off your knowledge.

   The questions to answer: *What in my background should I emphasize and what should I play down? How should I present myself, either in person or on paper?*

4. *Expand your list of potential employers.* A simple proposition, but one that's ignored by many job hunters. All it requires is an open mind. When you assemble a mailing list, take a few extra moments to check out related industries or companies. When you are reading

about a specific company or industry, make note of other companies, competitors, or ones in related fields. Through research, you might find job openings that fit your objective in companies or industries you hadn't considered.

The questions to answer: *What other industries hire people with my background? Have I overlooked any potential employers? How can I apply my work experience and/or educational background to different fields or companies?*

5. *Discover opportunities in the hidden job market.* This is one of the most rewarding outcomes of effective research: finding out about jobs before they are announced and, in effect, getting a jump on any other candidates. By following industry and company news, and reading between the lines, you can pick up clues that can mean a job in the offing. Be on the lookout for information on impending mergers, proposed expansions, relocations. Take notice of items on a smaller scale: personnel moves, promotions, and the like. When someone is promoted, his or her old job may still be available. Also, a newly hired manager may want to hire new staff members to create his or her own "team."

The questions to answer: *Will jobs be opening up? Can I meet a specific need that will come up as a result of the company's move/merger/reorganization/expansion?*

6. *Create a job opening or position.* This requires more insight and more thought, but the rewards can be far-reaching. Relying mainly on trade publications, newspapers, and general business magazines, you can follow the news of a particular company or industry, read about its trends and developments, and put yourself in a position to *create* a job. A company that is relocating may need someone to scout out real estate; a company that is cutting back staff may hire an outplacement counselor; an expanding company may need someone to design training programs.

The questions to answer: *In what ways could my background fill a need of theirs? What evidence is there that the company needs a new position? How can I sell the company on both the position and myself.*

7. *Lay a foundation for networking.* Research can make it easier to set up a network of contacts. By checking directories, you can find out the names and locations of trade organizations; reading current trade journals can give you the names of the reporters that cover the industry, the people in your field who contribute articles or are interviewed, and the industry movers and shakers; reading regional newspapers can give you the names of influential people in

the immediate area. The possibilities are numerous and the effort required is minimal.

The questions to answer: *What trade associations are in my field, and how can I contact them? What trade events, conventions, or conferences are upcoming? How can I meet employees from the company that interests me? Who are the most prominent people in my objective position, and how can I reach them? Who can introduce me to people in hiring positions?*

You can accomplish all of the above by relying on only three general sources: the *library,* the *public relations departments of individual companies,* and your *friends and colleagues.* Between these three, you can research your job hunt sufficiently.

The trick is knowing how to use these sources to meet your needs. This chapter will identify specific techniques and sources, explain what kind of information they can give you and how to apply it to your job hunt.

USING THE LIBRARY EFFECTIVELY

■ **The simplest and most logical place to start researching is also the most common: the library.**

Beginning your research at the library is a time-saving first step because of the wide variety of information you can find there to fit every aspect of your job hunt. Start with the most basic—the addresses, phone numbers, and names of the top officers of the companies you want to contact—and then expand to the less basic but equally useful—facts about jobs and companies you can use to target yourself in a letter. It is even possible to find out information as esoteric as the hobbies, birthplace, and club memberships of the vice-president of sales who is going to interview you tomorrow.

This range of information is what makes the library such a valuable tool. But that very variety may lead you to one chief problem—accumulating too *much* information. To research successfully, you have to ignore most of the data clutter. If you try to take advantage of *all* the resources in the library, you will only make your research too confusing. You should be able to locate what you need by consulting just three library sources: *reference directories, trade publications,* and *magazine and newspaper indexes.*

REFERENCE DIRECTORIES

Reference directories—books of lists on a variety of subjects— provide an excellent quick-and-easy way of finding basic information that you'll need for different phases of your job hunt. They help you:

- *contact companies*—by providing the company names, addresses, phone numbers, and names of key executives that you can use to compile a mailing list;

- *build a network of contacts*—by providing the names, addresses, and phone numbers of trade associations, plus information on conventions, trade events and more;

- *add to your salability*—through directories, you can find financial statistics about companies, biographical information about executives, and other information about specific companies and industries that you will use in cover letters or interviews.

■ **The following four directories are all you'll need for obtaining the most basic information: the trade associations to contact for networking; company names and addresses for a resume mailing list; the names of trade publications you'll need to read for want ads and the information that can target you; and more.**

1. *Encyclopedia of Business Information Sources* (Gale Research Company)

- An all-purpose directory listing magazines, newsletters, handbooks, and other sources in over 1,100 business-related topics.

- Use this for one-stop researching: to put together an immediate "career database." It isn't as comprehensive as the other directories, but it's a good place to start, especially if you're in a hurry and need information quickly. But don't stop here.

2. *Directories in Print* (Gale Research Company)

- Lists about 8,000 directories, both general business and industry-specific.

- Use this to find industry-specific directories, which will be the basis for a resume mailing list.

3. *The Encyclopedia of Associations* (Gale Research Company)

- Lists over 20,000 trade and professional associations.

- Use this to find information on trade associations that you can contact for further information and networking. Pay special attention to the entries—many associations also offer career counseling, seminars, job-referral services, and other helpful programs.

4. *Standard Rate & Data Service—Business Publications Rates & Data* (Standard Rate & Data Service)

- Over 3,000 business, trade, and technical publications listed by industry groupings.

- Use this to put together a list of trade journals. Pay attention to circulation figures—in general, those publications with the wider circulation have more extensive classified ads.

A strong point of the above directories is their wide scope. It's unlikely you'll miss anything that could be of help to you. You should also look under more than one subject heading. Don't stay within one narrow field or industry category. Be sure to check related topics and fields as well. Something that only seems marginally related might actually trigger job alternatives.

> **TIP:** *One word of warning:* **Many of the directories use illogical definitions and group subjects under headings that don't immediately come to mind. For example, in** *The Encyclopedia of Associations,* **under the "computers" category you'll find mainly associations of retail dealers in computers. If you're interested in associations of computer professionals such as systems analysts or programmers, you have to check under "data processing" and "information processing." There, among the word-processing groups, you'll find the associations you want. It's a bit of a headache trying to figure out the editors' classifications, but stick with it. The information you can pull out of these directories is definitely worth the time.**

Corporate Directories

- **If your job search centers around manufacturers and other industrial companies, banks, finance companies, and other Fortune-500**

corporations, focus on *corporate directories* **(such as** *Dun & Bradstreet, Moody's, Standard & Poor's***).**

They provide the most general corporate information: addresses, phone numbers, names of key executives, financial statistics,
number of employees, and the like—which you can use for mailing
lists, company selection, and general background preparation.

Their biggest asset is the number of corporations they cover,
which makes them great timesavers and streamlines your work. By
looking through only one directory, you should be able to locate
information on as many companies as you need.

The four most helpful corporate directories are:

1. *Dun's Million Dollar Directory* (Dun & Bradstreet)

- Lists 160,000 U.S. businesses in a variety of industries, including
  utilities, industrial, transportation, banking, finance.

- Listings include name, address, phone number, top executives'
  names and titles, financial statistics.

- Alphabetical, geographic, and industry classification.

2. *Standard & Poor's Register of Corporations, Directors and Executives*
   (Standard & Poor's Corporation)

- Lists over 45,000 U.S. corporations; includes names and titles of
  over 400,000 corporate officials, corporation's principal bank
  and law firm.

3. *Moody's Industrial Manual* (Moody's Investor Service, Inc.)

- Lists 3,000 companies listed on the New York or American Stock
  Exchanges as well as international companies. (Moody's also publishes directories for Bank & Finance, Public Utilities, Transportation, Municipals.)

4. *Thomas Register* (Thomas Publishing Company)

- 12-volume directory of U.S. manufacturers. Volumes 1–6: alphabetical listing of products/services; Volume 7: brand names.

- Volume 8 is an alphabetical listing of U.S. manufacturers, including name, address, phone number, product lines, executives, branches, representatives, and distributors.

Industry-Specific Directories

■ **For information about a *specific* industry, avoid the corporate directories and go straight to the industry-specific directory for your field.**

For example, if you're looking for a public relations job, read *O'Dwyers Guide to Public Relations Firms;* for retailing, read *Fairchild's Financial Manual of Retail Stores*. Most industries have at least one directory listing companies alphabetically. *Note:* See the Appendix, "Sources," for list of industry-specific directories.

As with corporate directories, use the industry-specific directories to compile a list of companies that interest you, to put together a resume mailing list, to get the names of contacts, and to find out basic information (finances, sales/revenues/earnings, number of employees, branch offices, forecasts, and the like).

Another good use for industry-specific directories is to find fields and businesses related to your target industry—suppliers, service industries, etc. Often these allied fields contain potential employers you hadn't considered.

Biographical Directories

■ **Biographical directories contain brief biographies of corporate executives, usually upper management, and include information such as place and date of birth, education, and club and association memberships—all of which makes them ideal for pre-interview prepping.**

Knowing the person's background can help you sell yourself more effectively. Pay special attention to any similarities you may share—same hometown, same associations, same school, etc.

Use biographical directories even if you aren't being interviewed by someone listed in them. They work well to give you a picture of management style and corporate culture. Read about top officers in a particular company and look for similarities in their backgrounds. Did they all go to Ivy League colleges? Are many of them members of the same associations? Read between the lines. Use this information to position yourself in cover letters and interviews.

The two most helpful biographical directories are:

1. *Dun & Bradstreet Reference Book of Corporate Managements* (Dun & Bradstreet)

   - Profiles include address, phone number, education and employment history, place of birth, memberships, clubs, civic and political activities.

   - The biggest plus is that, in addition to listing top corporate managers such as presidents, CEOs, and directors, it also includes biographies of vice presidents—who often are the people interviewing you.

2. *Standard & Poor's Register of Corporations, Directors & Executives (Volume 2)* (Standard & Poor's)

   - Contains biographies of 75,000 executives and directors, covering information such as business and home addresses, date and place of birth, and organization/association memberships.

   - Often more readily available in libraries than the Dun & Bradstreet.

Other Reference Sources

Ward's Directory of 51,000 Largest U.S. Corporations
(Ward Publishing Company)
—Lists name, address, phone number, president's name, sales and financial data.
—Not as easy to read as either Dun's or S&P's directories. Use this as a fallback if the others are unavailable.

Ward's Directory of 49,000 Private U.S. Companies
(Ward Publishing Company)
—Companion directory of the above. Lists the same information on the most successful privately held companies.

Standard Directory of Advertisers
(Standard Rate & Data Service)
—Commonly called "the Red Book," this lists about 17,000 companies that place national and/or regional advertising.
—For each company, lists management, financial, advertising, and marketing executives—names and titles.
—Because of its diversity and lists of executive names, this is a great one-stop reference for a mailing list.

Dun's Top 50,000 Companies
(Dun & Bradstreet)
—The top 50,000 companies of the 160,000 listed in the Million Dollar Directory.

Career Employment Opportunities Directory
(Ready Reference Press)
—Four volumes: 1 for Liberal Arts, and Social Sciences graduates; 2 Business Administration, 3 Engineering, 4 Sciences.
—Lists companies that are currently hiring. Describes employment opportunities, locations, special programs.
—Especially worthwhile for recent graduates seeking entry-level employment.

Business Information Sources
by Lorna M. Daniels
(University of California Press)
—Although this isn't technically a directory, it is one of the most comprehensive general business reference books. Includes information on general business, as well as specific sections on management, accounting, computers, corporate finance and banking, insurance, and marketing.
—Lists handbooks, books, magazines, newspapers, and associations on different industries.
—Excellent lead to other sources of information about a particular industry, but doublecheck addresses and phone numbers of publications and associations.

The Career Choices Encyclopedia
by Career Associates
(Walker & Company)
—Aimed at recent college graduates, this covers 31 industries/fields.
—Explains jobs, salaries, lists books and magazines to read.
—Good for entry-level people, but too basic for most others—even career changers.

Directory of Career Training & Development Programs
(Ready Reference Press)
—Lists management and executive training programs, professional development programs, etc.
—Listings include name, program title and purpose, how people are selected, type of training, qualifications, selection process, name and address of contact.
—Good basis for entry-level mailing list.

AMBA's MBA Employment Guide
(Association of MBA Executives)
—Lists over 1,000 companies that employ MBAs.

—100 companies that conduct heavy on-campus recruitment activity are profiled in depth.

—Good basis for entry-level/MBA mailing list.

Who's Who in America
(Marquis Who's Who, Inc.)

—Brief biographies of prominent people, including top business executives.

—Since only the biggest names are profiled, this is only useful for very general background information.
(See also the regional *Who's Who in the East, Who's Who in the Midwest, Who's Who in the South and Southwest, Who's Who in the West.*)

Who's Who in Finance and Industry
(Marquis Who's Who, Inc.)

—Profiles business executives in finance, insurance, international, commercial and investment banking, international trade, and other areas of finance/industry.

—Each listing includes career history, memberships, special awards and achievements, civic and political activities, home and business addresses.

Note: For other directories, including industry-specific directories, see the Appendix, "Sources."

TRADE PUBLICATIONS

■ **Nothing works better for you in a job hunt than trade publications —the magazines, journals, and newspapers that cover specific industries in depth.**

Every industry—from the largest and most prominent to the smallest and most obscure—has some sort of newspaper, magazine, or newsletter covering it; most have dozens. For example, the retail industry depends on *Women's Wear Daily;* jewelers read *Modern Jeweler;* the tire industry is mesmerized by *Rubber and Plastic News.* The list, variety, and scope are endless.

If you're not reading the appropriate trade journals already, start to do so as soon as you decide to look for a job and never stop. They're the easiest and fastest way to get an insider's view of the industry and they can help you in every aspect of your search—from writing cover letters to networking to finding job openings.

By regularly reading trade publications, you can:

- tap the hidden job market by anticipating job openings
- learn specific information about a company to use in your cover letter or interview
- gain salary information about your job objective
- get the names of people in your field who can serve as contacts
- fine-tune your job campaign by knowing industry trends

Locating Trade Journals

■ **Start with the *Standard Rate & Data Service Business Publications* directory to see which publications are put out in the industries you're pursuing.**

The directory lists publications by specific business or industry, so you can quickly see what is available in your field. Short editorial profiles give you an immediate idea of the contents and how helpful each publication can be to you. Listings include name and number of publisher as well as subscription information.

There is another easily used and readily available directory: the *Standard Periodical Directory,* which lists over 60,000 titles on 250 different subjects: magazines, newsletters, and directories.

■ **Don't choose only one publication; choose a few to read regularly.**

The depth of coverage can differ and you want to be sure you're getting the news that's on the cutting edge of the industry.

TIP: Try to find out which publication is the "industry bible" and pay special attention to it. (For example, in the auto industry, the weekly *Automotive News* sets the standards.) The stories it prints are the ones you'll want to remember to talk about in an interview and write about in targeted cover letters. If the publication issues industry awards, take special note of the winners. The companies that receive coveted industry awards like hearing about them.

TIP: Get the publication of the major *trade organization* in your field. The information it contains is often invaluable—especially in

terms of networking potential. Take special note of the people who write articles in the journal. They are usually well connected and make excellent contacts.

Getting the Most out of Trade Publications

■ **Read trade publications** *creatively.*

The trade papers can give you a solid foundation in what's happening and who's who in the industry and can put you into a better job hunting position because you're keeping abreast of current events in the field. But you can take it a step further by asking: *How can what I'm reading help me get a job?*

A few guidelines:

• *Look at the stories for hidden hints on employment opportunities.* In trade publications, you can read about employment trends in the industry: which companies are hiring and which are laying people off. If you read between the lines, you can find first-rate, first-hand information that can give you an edge over other job candidates.

> **EXAMPLE:** In **Women's Wear Daily,** a woman read about the unprecedented success of a retail chain. Because of its success, the company was planning to expand into new locations across the country. The woman realized that expansion meant the creation of new jobs. She sent the company a letter, congratulating its success and outlining her interest in being part of the expansion efforts in her region. She got an interview and a job *before* the company began any official recruiting.

• *Always be aware of how you can make practical use of the information you find in the trade publications.* Unlike the more general business magazines such as *Forbes, Fortune,* and *Business Week,* almost everything you read in the trade publications can be exploited to help you in some area of your job search. Pay special attention to the columns that briefly list new businesses, accounts, and clients. "Business Digest" or "New Business" columns can give you hot job leads.

TIP: The "Executive Changes and Promotions" or "People in the News" columns can be helpful. Take note of the people who are with the companies you're interested in. See if you notice any trends: Are all the promotions occurring in one office or in one department? Is there a new department head?

In some cases, you should drop a congratulatory note to whoever was promoted, even if he or she isn't in a hiring position. It's especially effective if you have something in common with that person: the same college, hometown, or associations. Mention your common ground, congratulate him or her, and briefly mention that you're applying for a job in the same company. Drop it there. Your aim is to have someone on staff who knows you and thinks well of you.

TIP: Most trade publications have an "Upcoming Events" or "Conventions and Trade Shows" column. It's wise to keep track of what's coming up in your area. It might be worth it to attend some seminars or meetings to make contacts.

- *Don't ignore any segment of the trade publications.* Sometimes the most helpful information seems minor. For example, always read the want ads even if you don't plan to answer any of them. They're a great source of information that's difficult to get anywhere else—like current salary ranges. By reading the Help Wanted section, you can get an idea of what salaries are being offered in different parts of the country, for various positions. It's handy information to know when you're being interviewed or when you're offered a job.

- *Find out about special issues.* There are two types of special issues that you should keep an eye out for: the "scoreboard," or "top 100 companies," issues and the issues that focus on a specific aspect of an industry or include special sections.

Use the scoreboard issues for quick reference: to compare different companies in terms of financial standing. Since the information in them is brief, they're good to have on hand for thumbnail sketches.

The special-focus issues are ideal for in-depth looks at particular segments of an industry. For example, *Advertising Age* puts out issues that focus on such topics as direct marketing and telemarketing, advertising to minorities, and liquor advertising. By reading these special issues, you can get a real feel for those areas that are brushed over in regular issues.

TIP: Look at the ads in special-interest issues to get the names of companies that service this aspect of the industry. The advertising is often as focused as the articles are. Pay close attention to the classifieds in special issues as well. Recruitment advertising is often more plentiful in this type of issue.

To find out about special issues, check:

Guide to Special Issues & Indexes of Periodicals
(by Miriam Uhlan/Special Library Association/New York)

- Lists the types of special issues—features, statistical surveys, directories—that each magazine puts out. Also lists indexes of periodicals.

- Because it's so thorough, you can get information on virtually any "scoreboard" or special-interest issue that's published. It even includes trade association magazines, and lists when they put out their "member's directory" issues. One drawback is that the magazines are listed alphabetically. To avoid spending time checking through the subject index at the back, it's best if you already know the names of the magazines you're interested in.

Note: For a list of trade publications, broken down by industry, and special issues of the top business magazines, see the Appendix, "Sources."

PERIODICAL INDEXES

■ Besides directories, periodical indexes—which categorize and list magazine and newspaper stories by subject and date—are a quick and easy source of library information.

Since they handle articles from a wide range of newspapers, consumer and business magazines, and technical journals, periodical indexes are useful for a wide variety of subjects. Use them to find more general information on industry trends and forecasts that can help you define your career objective and focus your job hunt, to find articles about related industries, and to get information on your career objective.

The four indexes you will use most often are:

1. *Business Periodicals Index*

- Indexes about 300 magazines, including *Forbes, Fortune,* and *Business Week,* as well as the top trade publications.

- This is ideal for a quick overview of an industry. Because of its focus and depth, you won't miss much if you only use this index. It's also useful for general employment trends and career outlook articles.

2. *Predicasts F&S Index United States*

- Indexes and abstracts from over 1,000 trade journals, business and financial publications, newspapers, government reports, and more.

- Don't be intimidated by how complicated this looks; it's actually not difficult to use and can save you a great deal of time. Often the abstracts give you so much detailed information that you can bypass reading the actual article.

3. *Wall Street Journal Index*

- Monthly index of the *Journal;* has both corporate news and general news sections.

4. *The New York Times Index*

- Comprehensive index of *The Times;* extensive business coverage in general index.

■ **Also take a look at the indexes of other major papers, such as *The Washington Post,* the *Los Angeles Times, USA Today* or the *Chicago Tribune.***

Geographics play a large role in choosing the most appropriate newspaper index. For example, to find articles on the film industry or on specific film companies, look at the *Los Angeles Times* index first; for articles on money center banks, go first to the index for *The New York Times.*

> **TIP: Don't limit your reading to articles about the company that you are interviewing with. Read about competing companies as well, so you can have a general idea about the climate of the market-**

place. You can sell yourself on the basis of this kind of knowledge.

> TIP: When you use newspaper indexes, look only at entries for the past six months to a year. Otherwise you will wind up spending too much time on stories that, by now, are old news. There is an exception to this rule: If the company was involved in a major news story (a takeover battle, massive cost-cutting, a merger, a new product introduction) within the last two years, take the time to review that story.

■ **Always check the major newspaper of the area in which the company's headquarters are located and in which the company does the most business.**

For example, if the company you are interested in has headquarters in Louisville, you can bet that the local Louisville paper will cover that company more extensively than any other paper—including *The Wall Street Journal.*

To find local and regional newspapers, use:

Gale Directory of Publications (formerly Ayer's)

- Lists newspapers, magazines, and trade publications.

- Is indexed geographically, which makes it easy to find newspapers and magazines that cover a particular area of the United States.

If you have the time—check the *Reader's Guide to Periodical Literature (not* "Business Periodicals"). This directory indexes general-interest magazines by subject and author. Although it isn't a business index, it often leads to useful articles in nonbusiness magazines that you might otherwise overlook.

A Final Good Library Source: Value Line

■ **If your job hunt is centered on major companies in the U.S. that are traded on the major stock exchanges, be sure to look at:**

Value Line Investment Surveys
(A. Bernhard/New York)

- A stock investors' guide that reports on 1,700 companies in over 95 industries.

Value Line is a best bet for one-stop research of major companies and industries. Updates come out weekly, rotating through different industries so that each company is updated quarterly.

Industry sections examine trends and discuss the general climate in the industry, giving you insight into employment possibilities.

Company reports are easy to read and packed with information beyond the usual financial statistics and forecasts. The brief text beneath the stats and charts gives you an immediate feel for the company. It includes a look at the recent past, developments that have shaped the company, and its outlook for the future.

Use *Value Line* to get a grasp of a company's management style, where it has been, and where it is headed. It's a great source to glance through before an interview.

COMPUTERIZED RESEARCH: INFORMATION SOURCES ONLINE

■ **Everything from the top reference directories to national newspapers to consumer magazines to the more obscure trade publications is available through computer databases.**

The major asset of researching online instead of in the library is *speed.* A computerized information search is much faster than any other method. You can search through hundreds of sources in a matter of minutes without having to do the physical and tedious work of looking up every item.

The major drawback is *cost.* Searching through databases isn't inexpensive. For example, using Predicasts online can cost you $90 to $150 per hour depending on the vendor.

Typically, you access databases by going through a database vendor, a system that offers a wide selection of databases. Costs, necessary expertise, and services vary from vendor to vendor.

The top database vendors that cover business and careers are:

BRS
1200 Route 7
Latham, NY 12110
518/783-1161
800/345-4277

- Three database systems: BRS/SEARCH, the main system that offers over 100 databases; BRS/BRK-THRU, that offers discounts; and BRS/After Dark.

- Among the databases: *Harvard Business Review;* ABI/Inform —covering over 680 business publications; *Predicasts.*

DIALOG
3460 Information Services, Inc.
3460 Hillview Avenue
Palo Alto, CA 94304
800/528-6050

- Offers over 250 databases, 62 specifically about business.

- Databases include: *Predicasts, Standard & Poor's, Harvard Business Review, Encyclopedia of Associations.*

NEXIS
Mead Data Central
9393 Springboro Pike
P.O. Box 933
Dayton, OH 45401
800/227-4908

- Over 125 databases, including full text of *The New York Times.*

ORBIT
SDC Information Systems
2500 Colorado Avenue
Santa Monica, CA 90406
213/453-6194
800/421-7229

- Over 70 databases.

THE SOURCE
1616 Anderson Road
McLean, VA 22102
703/821-6666
800/336-3366

- One of the best-known online systems.

- Its Management Contents, Ltd. database includes over 100 business-oriented publications such as *Barron's, Business Week, Forbes, Fortune,* etc.

VU/TEXT
1211 Chestnut Street
Philadelphia, PA 19107
215/665-3300

- Includes major metropolitan, local, and regional newspapers as well as over 60 other databases, such as *Facts on File.*

Note: For extensive information on database searches, see:

How to Look It Up Online
by Alfred Glossbrenner (St. Martin's Press, New York: 1987)

USING COMPANIES AS A RESEARCH TOOL: WHAT THEY CAN TELL YOU

■ **Once you know which companies you're interested in, you can turn to a primary source of information outside the library—the companies themselves.**

Generally, you should call the company switchboard and ask for the public relations, public affairs, corporate communications, or personnel offices. It usually doesn't matter to whom you speak: you're only after general information, not contacts.

Contacting the companies where you'll eventually be applying for a job saves you time and effort. They can give you answers to questions about their operation that you need to know. Approaching them instead of searching out answers from secondary sources makes sense. Two of the best reasons for contacting companies are to doublecheck a mailing list and to get background information.

To Doublecheck a Mailing List:

Always call the companies directly to find out the exact name and title of executives. Don't depend on articles, directories, even company literature. Typos are common, executives leave positions, titles change.

Before you send a letter, call the company first and doublecheck the names, titles, spelling. Whenever possible, also find out what floor the executive's office is on. That speeds things up and makes it more certain that your letter won't be delayed or wind up sitting in the mailroom.

Never call and ask to whom you should address your resume. General inquiries usually get you the name and title of a personnel manager. Instead be specific. Don't make it apparent that you're intending to send in a resume. Sound authoritative and ask for the name of the manager of a specific department or whoever is responsible for a certain division.

Be straightforward rather than elaborate. Some people recommend clever tricks such as asking for a false person and waiting to be corrected, pretending to be a supplier, or calling a different department and asking for information. These ploys often work—but they're usually not necessary.

> **TIP: Try telling the truth when you're asked why you need an executive's name and title. For example, a woman putting the final touches on her resume mailing list called each company to make sure that she had the correct information. Whenever someone asked her why she needed the executive's name or title, she said, "I'm updating a mailing list." It was the truth—and it satisfied everybody.**

To Get Background Information:

Calling or writing for printed information is one of the best and most efficient ways to gain insights into the company's corporate culture: how it perceives itself and how it *wants* to be perceived.

It's simple to get information directly from a company. Forget all the articles that tell you to lie and concoct a story about the article you're writing or the informational interview you want to do. More often than not, all you have to do is contact the public relations or corporate communications department and ask them to mail you current literature about the company.

Ask for a copy of the annual report, a media or press kit, and, if you're interested in an entry-level job or training program, recruitment brochures.

Annual Reports

■ **Be suspicious of annual reports.**

Because of federal disclosure requirements, corporate annual reports are honest, but very often the "real truth" is hidden behind a mass of healthy-looking figures and healthier-looking balance sheets. Unless you're an accountant and know how to factor the numbers in the footnotes—contingent liabilities and the like—look at the numbers only for trends. Are sales healthy and increasing yearly? Are provisions for discounts and returns stable? Are the basic relationships between revenues and profits stable or increasing? Has there been a major sale of assets that makes the overall picture better than it really is?

Even with trends, don't get a false sense of confidence if everything looks rosy. Many high-tech firms had great trends. The numbers kept going up, until the high-tech crash in the late 1980s when many companies fell into bankruptcy.

■ **It's best to read the annual report to get a *feel* for the company's direction.**

Inevitably, company divisions or plans are emphasized, certain attributes are talked about, and you will pick up clues on how to behave during interviews. For example, the 1984 General Electric annual report has all the normal fluff about paring down bureaucracy and creating a good environment, but concluded that its main goal was to expand. A year and a half later G.E. bought RCA.

■ **Read the management statements for corporate style as well as for facts.**

As always, be aware of buzzwords that signal trouble. For example, "We look forward to facing exciting challenges ahead" usually means that the company is in trouble and just wishes those challenges would go away.

> **TIP: Read the annual report along with a photocopy of *Dun's* or *Value Line*'s report on the company. In this way, you can read between the lines and make a realistic assessment.**

In addition, you can get tips about the company's corporate culture by looking at the photographs used to illustrate the text, by reading the quotes, and by seeing who figures prominently and why. Some corporations are top-heavy with financial types, others with marketing, and some with the original founding entrepreneurs. Each one has a different make-up that will affect *your* interview and *your* job.

> **TIP: By checking the list of corporate directors and officers for women's names, you can tell how far women have advanced in the company.**

Media/Press Kits

■ **Media kits contain the information that companies want people to know, which makes them ideal ammunition for a job hunter.**

Because they're designed for reporters or potential clients, media kits typically include an annual report, reprints of favorable articles about the company, pamphlets about the company's business, products, or services, and recent press releases.

See what achievements they stress in their literature and mention them in your cover letter or interview. Cite specific examples of your own experience that mesh with theirs.

> **EXAMPLE: In its media kit, an ad agency constantly referred to the extensive training programs they offered to every level of management. A man applying for an account executive position mentioned in his cover letter that he was impressed by their emphasis on education. He added that he had been responsible for setting up training programs for new employees at his current agency. Although the programs he had set up were far less extensive, he had made his point. The account executive who read his letter thought the man would fit in perfectly.**

■ **Media kits can show you how to package *yourself* when you go for an interview.**

A lot of company literature is commercial puffery. But if you're savvy enough to know how to interpret them, media kits can give you a good idea on how well you'd fit into the company. For example, you should notice their appearance and layout. Is a particular media kit pushing a modern, sleek image or one that's more staid? Is the writing dry and technical or more like an advertisement? Do the pamphlets stress tradition and emphasize the company's long history? Or do they talk about groundbreaking, new ideas? Knowing the company's slant helps you to see if that's where you belong and how to present yourself to them.

> **TIP: Compare media kits from different companies in the same industry. You will notice the subtle differences between them and how to better target yourself.**

> **TIP: Sometimes what *isn't* included is as informative as what is. Pay attention to omissions.**

Take special note of any press releases that are included in the kit. They tell you what recent developments the company wants to publicize. If those developments are important enough to prompt the company to write a press release, they're definitely important enough for you to mention in interviews or letters, if only to show how much you know.

Piece together information and draw conclusions. Press releases and articles about new lines of business can mean the company is planning an expansion; new products or marketing ploys can signal a shift in management style.

> **EXAMPLE: In the media kit of one of the auto giants, a woman read a press release about the innovative aerodynamic styling that was being introduced. Since the company previously had been very traditional, she took that to mean that it was moving away from its old-fashioned image to a more aggressive stance in the marketplace. She applied for a job in purchasing, mentioning that she chose this company because it appeared to be more on the cutting edge of the industry than the others. By stressing the new corporate image that management had just started pushing, the woman got a job.**

Recruitment Brochures

■ **Recruitment brochures give you the facts on training programs or entry-level positions, and usually explain company divisions, recruiting methods, and employment policies.**

Beyond the very basic nuts-and-bolts information, recruitment brochures are just another sales tool for the company. Take them with a grain of salt. Approach them like the public relations material they are. As with media kits, read between the lines to get an idea of corporate style. See if the same words keep cropping up. Also take a look at the type of training programs offered: are they highly structured, or do they keep talking about personal initiative and "intrapreneuring"?

Take note of the photographs in recruitment manuals, as well. Even though they are usually posed, pseudo-candid shots, they give you a general idea of what the company likes in its workers. Are all the employees wearing corporate suits, ties, and button-down shirts, or are they dressed less traditionally? Are there many photographs of employees at "play"—playing sports, or at home?

■ **Realize that recruitment brochures are trying to present the ideal corporate image—and that you can play the same game when you present *yourself* to them.**

USING FRIENDS AND COLLEAGUES TO GIVE YOU THE INSIDE STORY

■ **For the most accurate information on companies, industries, and jobs, speak with people you know.**

Friends and colleagues can give you the real lowdown. Tell them to give you the unvarnished truth. This isn't the time to mince words. Ask them pointed questions that will offer you a definite picture of the company: *How long does it take to get promoted? What about raises? Is there a distinct management style? Does there seem to be a model for the ideal employee?*

With the detailed information that you get from reliable sources, you can figure out how to best sell yourself to the company. Knowing about the company's atmosphere makes you better prepared.

■ **Don't shy away from subjects that might seem unimportant.**

Sometimes it's the little things that actually get you hired. Find out what sports teams they have at the company, if people go out together after work or if they go straight home. Every piece of information contributes to a clearer sense of the corporation and its environment.

4 Networking

INTRODUCTION

Networking is another way of using friends and colleagues in your job hunt. It is more than just a casual conversation between people about jobs. It's a *focused* method of developing and building a pool of contacts: people who can provide career information that can lead you to a new and better job. It can range from career advice to being recommended for a job to being hired. Each person you speak with brings you one step closer to getting hired.

The idea behind networking is simple: talking to people gets you jobs. Most job openings—estimates range up to 90%—are filled by word of mouth, before job advertisements and recruiters get into the picture.

The aim of networking is to move you into the center of a hidden job market even if you're starting well out of bounds. Beginning with a few people, you can work to develop and expand your list of contacts until you reach the ones who can hire you for the job you want.

> **EXAMPLE: A man with no experience in property management started talking with friends about his eventual goal of working in the field. One of them advised him to take a real estate course at a local community college. There, he met a city employee who introduced him to a real estate developer, who introduced him to several other**

property owners. One told him how to get the right experience, and hired him part-time. Two years later, he was fully employed in the field.

There are four basic steps to setting up a strong job-finding network:

1. Building a base of contacts

2. Expanding your contact base

3. Getting and using referrals

4. Following up

Don't expect immediate results, although it can happen. Instead, spend time developing a circle of people who are aware of the kind of job you want and the kind of job you can do. Concentrate on getting your name and skills talked about, and almost inevitably you'll get the right lead and a job. A good networking set-up is like a chain letter. The only difference is that networks work.

STEP ONE: BUILDING A BASE OF CONTACTS

■ **Start by talking with friends or close business associates—people with whom you feel comfortable.**

Don't worry if they're not employed in the field you're interested in. They may know someone who is, or at least someone who can get you closer to the right people.

Remember: You're trying to get *information* from these people, not a job. Asking friends or close business associates for a job outright can put them off and make you sound over-anxious or desperate. It also distracts them from their main function: to get you the names of *their* friends and career information about your field.

■ **Base your approach on how well you know and trust each person.**

Let him or her know that you're looking for a job and that you'd welcome advice, suggestions, and ideas. Bring up the subject of your job hunt generally; then ask if you could sit down and discuss it later. You want to make certain your friend has time to spend with you and is given the chance to give your job search some advance thought.

Don't be afraid to call on people whom you haven't talked with for a while; most people are flattered when they are asked for advice.

During the discussion be as open as possible. Go into detail about the industries and companies that interest you, the plans you've made, and the status of your job.

> TIP: **With friends, be honest about your shortcomings. You may cause problems by neglecting to admit your personal limitations. One man couldn't handle the stress of his high-pressure sales job. He really wanted to find a job that was lower-key and based locally. He avoided discussing this aspect of himself with a close friend, who talked to his boss, who then hired the man based on his friend's recommendation. The man was flattered by the high base salary but was too embarrassed to turn down a job he wasn't up to doing, so he accepted it. He was fired ten months later—and lost a friend.**

STEP TWO: EXPANDING YOUR CONTACT BASE

> ■ **You should now be getting more confident and better prepared, and thus ready to contact people you know less well, such as those you've met at associations and professional organizations, people in different departments at your present company, and people in other companies or organizations.**

You never know *who* can help you. Talk to as many people as you can. Quantity matters as well as quality when you're setting up a network. The more people you're in touch with, the better your chances of winding up with a job lead.

> TIP: **Alumni groups and trade associations are good places to get contacts. (See the Appendix, "Sources," for a list of associations broken down by industry.) Alumni groups are particularly good sources if you went to a small, out-of-the-way, or unprestigious college. Inevitably, someone made it big and that person is usually happy to help someone else from the same background.**

> TIP: **Don't stop with job-related groups. Hobbyist clubs, night-school classes, etc. may be *better* networking sources, because you share a strong common interest with potential contacts. One applicant got a job through someone in his stamp-collecting club—he spe-**

cialized in British stamps and so did the CEO of a local firm who needed an assistant.

■ **Regardless of who your contact is,** *focus* **your aims and your requests.**

Don't throw your job hunt into someone else's lap and expect that person to know how to help you. Be specific—even to the extent of making appointments with people to talk about your job search.

> EXAMPLE: **"I've decided to make a move from public relations to marketing. I'm particularly interested in working for a smaller company in packaged goods. Since you've been in marketing for so long, I'd appreciate your thoughts on the subject. Would Tuesday at twelve be a good time to meet for lunch or drinks?"**
>
> *Not:* **"I'm leaving my job in public relations and I'm looking for a job in marketing. Do you think that you could help out?"**

■ **Strive for a** *concrete* **result from each conversation.**

Don't make the all-too-common error of letting the conversation drift into vague advice: "To get a job in this industry you've got to be tough . . ." Get specific help, such as the name of another person to talk to, a meeting time when you can go over your resume, the names of companies that might be hiring.

In this sense, it's important for you to direct the conversation and let the person know exactly what he or she can do for you. The more explicit you are, the more help you'll be given.

> EXAMPLE: **"As you know, I speak French fluently, and I'm interested in combining that skill with my commercial banking background. Do you have any contacts in international banking?"**
>
> *Not:* **"I speak French. Do you know of any jobs around that might need that?"**

> EXAMPLE: **"Yes, I know filmmaking is a tough field to break into. But I read that many people start out by working on location shoots as unpaid assistants. Do you know how I could find that sort of opening?"**

STEP THREE: GETTING AND USING REFERRALS

■ **The most important information you can get from people is the names of *other* people you can contact.**

Very often the second circle of contacts—or referrals—is the most useful to you in your job hunt. Make it clear to your contacts that you're not asking only for the names of people who can hire you, you're also looking for people who can help you in general. Ask them for the name of *anyone* who can be of some use, such as people who work at the companies that interest you, or who work in a position similar to the one you want, or who work in the general industry. Someone who isn't in a hiring position can often lead you to someone who is.

> TIP: Keep a networking file of 3 × 5 index cards with each contact's name and number, the date that you met or spoke, and the information that he or she has given you. Each time you're given the name of another possible contact, make a new card and write down the name of the person who referred him or her. You should continue to update this file of contacts throughout your job hunt and after you've been hired.

■ **Go through your card file or list of names and determine which referrals look as though they could help you the most.**

Although you should still be concerned with adding to your network, at this point it pays to be discriminating. Since these referrals may be people you haven't met personally, networking with them can be a little more time-consuming and often more stressful. Get the best pay-out by starting with the best names.

How to Cold-Call Referrals

The hardest part of networking for most people is cold-calling referrals. You don't know them, they don't know you, and it can be difficult to ask strangers for advice. But sooner or later it pays off. Even if you're out of work and feeling down and out about it, resist the temptation to avoid calling. Surveys of the unemployed consistently show one thing: those who keep calling, get jobs.

▪ **Start by trying to make it easier for yourself. Ask your personal contacts to write a letter of introduction; arrange an introductory meeting; or place a call, mention your name, and say you'll be in touch.**

An introductory call or letter can pave the way for your call and ensure that you'll get through to the person with no difficulties.

If your contact phones ahead and tells the referral to be expecting your call, make certain that you do so *promptly*. Don't delay or decide at the last minute that you don't want to speak with the referral after all. Your contact is helping you; don't let him or her down. You could damage your chances for any further help and destroy a potentially valuable relationship.

> **EXAMPLE: An editor at *Vogue* magazine complained that networkers rarely follow up on her referrals. Once she had called editors at other magazines and told them to expect a call from a certain woman who had asked her for contacts. The woman never called any of them. Instead, months later, she sent in a resume to *Vogue*. The editor threw it away.**
>
> *Note:* **This type of situation is surprisingly common. Once you've started getting referrals, you *must* follow through.**

More often than not, you'll end up calling a referral without a formal introduction, so be sure to ask your contact if you can use his or her name.

For those with a nonsales personality, cold-calling can be intimidating. You just have to jump in and do it: the first call is the hardest. Most people find it easier after calling five or more people. Ask your contact for the best time to call the referrals that he or she has given you.

> **TIP: Early in the morning, in the middle of the week, is usually the best time to call. For extremely important or very busy people try to call *very* early in the morning (before regular work hours). *Rule of thumb:* Don't call on Monday, Friday, lunch hour, or late afternoon if you can help it. People are either busy, tired, eating, or cranky. Think of how you would feel at those times.**

▪ **On the telephone, be swift and get quickly to the point of your call, which is *only* to introduce yourself, to briefly explain why you're calling, and to arrange for a meeting.**

Always mention your mutual friend as soon as possible to legitimize your call and your request for time. If the referral sounds busy, acknowledge it and say you won't take much time.

> **EXAMPLE:** "This is Mary Carter speaking. Sally Jones from XYZ Corporation tells me that you're the person I should speak to about _____ [a field of interest, an industry, a company]. She suggested that I call to see if we could get together. Would coffee on Thursday morning be convenient?"

There are two things you shouldn't do on the phone:

1. *Don't ask about possible job openings—even if your source has told you there are some.* While the referral may be in a hiring position, this initial phone call is not the time to mention it. Putting people on the spot rarely works to your advantage. They get defensive; you get the cold shoulder.

2. *Don't ask for specific advice.* During your introductory phone call, be brief and courteous. You don't want to waste the referral's time, and you don't want to give the referral the clever idea that it might be easier to advise you over the phone. You want a *personal* meeting, not a five minute pep-talk.

> **TIP:** If the referral suggests that you come to his or her office, choose a time outside of regular working hours when possible. Avoid the probability of interruptions so that the person can devote more time and attention to you. Almost always, the earlier in the morning, the better.

Meeting with Referrals: How to Get the Most Out of Them

■ **Get the referral interested in you *without* directly asking him or her for a job.**

In the back of your mind, you want a job from the people you are meeting. You know it and it's very likely that the referrals know it, too. Just don't ask for one. Instead, mention your job hunt generally, and your need for names, information, and advice specifically. Get the referrals *interested* in you.

> **TIP:** Before meeting with referrals, call back your initial contacts. Thank them and explain that you're about to meet their friend.

Ask them for ideas and suggestions on how to deal with them: their likes and dislikes, etc. Then tailor your style to fit their personalities.

■ **Summarize your objective.**

Even though on the phone you've already sketched out the information you're seeking, repeat it at the beginning of your conversation. Be specific and straightforward. Explain why you're there and what you hope to get out of the meeting.

> **EXAMPLE:** "As I mentioned to you over the phone, I want to move into direct mail copywriting. Jack Bryant said you're the best person to speak with to get an idea of the ins and outs of the industry. I'm especially interested in hearing about the new trends you see in direct marketing. . . ."
> *Note:* Not only have you explained once more the general information you need, you have also reestablished your common acquaintance.

■ **Be an active participant.**

Keep up your end of the conversation. Well-thought-out questions, a concise summary of your job hunt, and clearly defined goals show that you've prepared for the meeting and are in charge of yourself.

For example, explain where your job hunt stands. Let the person know what you've already done, where you hope to be headed, and in what areas you need guidance. Ask directed questions that invite an active response.

> **EXAMPLE:** "Because I've been staging conventions for ten years now, I've gotten to know hotel management people and problems pretty well. How would you suggest I start a job search in hotel management with my background?"

■ *Personalize* **your questions when you can.**

Even if you are asking the same questions of a few referrals, shape them to fit each person's area of expertise. Make the referral understand that he or she can make a real difference to your job hunt. Give your referral a good reason for wanting to help you.

> **EXAMPLE:** "I've followed your company's innovative advertising for years now—both inside the industry and out. And I

know the importance of your role in beginning the trend. Now that I'm unemployed, I've decided to target the best and most innovative companies I can find. Which companies do you feel share your approach?"

■ **Don't underestimate the importance of your initial meeting with your sources.**

On the surface, this is only an informational interview, but it's still an interview. Treat it like one.

Even though you shouldn't be asking for a job or even a job lead during this interview, it is always a conscious goal. At some point, this referral will be in a position to hire someone or recommend someone for a job. You want that person to be you, so you should:

- act as though you were being interviewed for a job.

- be positive and confident about your goals and your background.

- never badmouth your current or most recent position or employer.

- above all, show a genuine interest in your job search and in the meeting itself.

> TIP: If you've read articles that the person has written, or if you've read about his or her accomplishments in a local paper or trade journal, say so. Honest compliments never hurt. Just don't resort to empty flattery.

Take notes throughout the conversation. You want to keep track of any concrete suggestions the referral makes. It's also a good idea to take notes on what questions or comments elicit the best response, advice, or information from your contact. You should use the best methods in other interviews with other referrals.

"Read" the other person for cues, and end the meeting when you think it's appropriate. As a general rule, it's best to keep initial meetings with referrals on the brief side—fifteen minutes to half an hour is usually long enough.

> TIP: Right after the meeting, jot down short notes about it on the contact's file card: date, what you discussed, suggestions the contact made, names the contact gave you, etc. Refer to the card for a quick refresher just before you contact the referral again.

STEP FOUR: FOLLOWING UP

■ **Begin thinking about a follow-up** *during* **your meetings with contacts.**

Keep in mind: A meeting isn't an end; it's a beginning. You should make it possible to remain in contact with the person, even if he or she has answered all your questions for the time being. Before leaving a meeting, ask if you can call again at a later date. Better yet, give the person a definite time when you will call again.

■ **Set up a concrete reason for checking back with your contact—following up on suggestions, names you've been given, companies to apply to, research to do.**

When you have a reason for calling back, it makes it simpler and more logical for you to be keeping in touch. It also guarantees that you *will* follow up.

> **EXAMPLE:** "Ken, I appreciate the suggestions that you've given me on researching the different opportunities available in purchasing. I'll call you next Thursday to let you know how they've all worked out."

■ **After each meeting with a valuable contact, always take the time to send a short thank-you note.**

Networking interviews are similar to regular interviews. You'd send a thank-you note to a prospective employer; you should do the same for referrals and contacts. It's a good way to remind them of your meeting and you.

> **TIP:** Recap a particular part of your conversation—ideally one that highlights a skill or one of your previous jobs, or something especially interesting that the referral had said. A note that is more specific than a general thank-you is also far more memorable.

> **TIP:** Avoid the common mistake of writing a stilted and overly formal thank-you note. The note shouldn't be a form letter that you can send to each and every one of your contacts. *Personalize!*

■ **Regardless of how well a meeting goes, you have to take the initiative to further develop a relationship.**

Don't stop with a phone call or a thank-you note, and assume that the ball is in the other person's court. You *cannot* count on your contacts to keep in touch with you. Maintaining a relationship is far more important to you than it is to them. It's up to you to strengthen the ties that you've begun to establish.

■ **Keep building on your initial meetings with contacts.**

To follow up, you must continually remind people of you and your job hunt. Call them and keep them posted; arrange further meetings when you need or want more help. Don't mistake being persistent with being pushy. It seems obvious, but it's a common mistake. Periodic calls maintain a relationship; constant ones destroy it.

Two of the best ways of following up are:

• calling with a specific question relating to your discussion

• calling to explain how their advice is working out

EXAMPLE: "The articles you mentioned were terrific. I'm writing to the people that were interviewed to arrange meetings with them."

No one is too shy or unaggressive to follow up effectively. If you are uncomfortable on the phone, you can avoid it in the beginning by sending notes as a matter of course—thank-you notes or notes to suggest another meeting. Awkwardness over the phone could come across as diffidence—and that would do more harm than good. But don't avoid following up on your contacts altogether. Instead, turn to other methods of developing the relationship.

TIP: Send clippings of newspaper or magazine articles that might interest your contacts, along with a short note. The clippings show that you've been thinking of them; it's also a diplomatic way of reminding them of you.

TIP: Use other people to follow up for you as well. Have your initial contacts speak to the referrals. Ask them for feedback.

■ **Regardless of how you follow up, the key to making it work is by doing it continuously for the duration of your job hunt, and by modifying your methods as time goes on.**

Don't keep calling people with the same news and the same information. Try to keep your approaches fresh and let your contacts know that you're not sitting still.

> **EXAMPLE:** "At a trade association meeting last week, I ran into an acquaintance of yours, Leonard Carter. He asked me to send his regards when I spoke to you next. He also gave me some interesting leads."

> **TIP:** Some counselors recommend exchanging acquired knowledge with contacts. Job hunters are in a position to learn and absorb a great deal of information about an industry through their research and network. Share it with your contacts.

Above all, fight against feeling awkward. It takes time to find a job. Everyone—including your contacts—knows that. Try to remain as confident and assured as you were at the beginning of the networking process. A positive attitude affects how others view you. People would rather help someone who they think is going to make it—it's human nature. Don't let your contacts see you discouraged. If it looks as though you've given up, they will too.

■ **Keep your network strong.**

As your network develops, start weeding out those people who haven't been helpful. It makes your network smaller, but it also makes it stronger. In later phases, it's pointless to spend time cultivating someone who can't make a contribution to your job hunt, your career, or your personal life.

SPECIAL NETWORKING SITUATIONS

Trade & Professional Associations

■ **Trade associations are a built-in, prefabricated network of industry sources.** *Use them.*

When you research your job hunt, you should compile a list of associations in your field. (As stated in Chapter 3, "Research," check *The Encyclopedia of Associations* to put together a list of associations in your field. Also see the Appendix, "Sources," for a list of the top associations in different industries.)

Most associations have meetings or special events that are open to nonmembers. Call the associations that interest you and ask about conventions, trade shows, and seminars. Have them send you whatever literature they have: newsletters, introductory brochures, and more.

■ Find out if the association has a membership roster or directory.

Most associations publish a list of members annually that can be a real asset to you when you network. In it, members are listed along with their corporate affiliation. Read through a membership directory *before* you go to an association meeting. It's a good way to get a feel for the association, the types of members it attracts, and how useful belonging to it might be.

■ Keep in mind that the chief resource of a trade association is its members.

In general, you should network within an association the same way you would with other people within your established circle of contacts. Start with light conversation and, when you feel the time is right, bring up your job hunt. *Remember:* You are looking for people to add to your network of contacts.

> **TIP:** According to some career counselors, association members often complain about the number of job seekers who are nonmembers attending regular meetings. Be careful about how you approach people. If you're at all pushy, you'll be contributing to the problem.

When you approach people at an association meeting, there are two key concerns:

1. The most important point to get across:
   I'm asking you for information, not a job.

2. The most important question to ask:
   Do you know someone else I might speak with?

■ **Keep your ears open.**

Associations are great places to hear current industry gossip—gossip that might mean a job lead for you, such as which company is starting lay-offs, which picked up a major new client, which is cutting back in one section, which is launching a new product line.

Pay special attention to what seems like cocktail chatter. People often talk about how things affect them personally: "I've been in the office until ten every night for the past two weeks because of the new product roll-out." What you hear may be good ammunition for you in your job hunt.

> **EXAMPLE:** At an advertising club meeting, a woman heard two account executives from a major New York agency chatting about a client and the difficulties they were having with him. Since she had also been involved in business dealings with the same client, she insinuated herself into the conversation and made some suggestions. She gained two valuable contacts, both of whom helped her find a job at their agency.

■ **If you already belong to associations in your field, start making yourself more visible as a member.**

As with the rest of the networking process, the chief objective in being an association member is meeting new people. Capitalize on this built-in network by talking with people about your job hunt. Attend meetings regularly. Join committees. The more active you are, the more people you will come into contact with.

> **TIP:** Join the *membership* committee, which will give you a good reason to contact new people in your field at different companies.

Professional Skills Classes/Continuing Education

■ **Classes, like associations, also provide you with a built-in network.**

Don't just talk with potential employers. It's often useful to trade job information with other job searchers. They may be going through interviews or experiences that you can learn from and can give you the inside scoop on interviewers at specific companies.

In the more casual atmosphere of night-school classes, sometimes professors can be helpful. Often they work professionally in the field in which they teach, and can direct you to people and companies.

Many colleges offer courses that feature industry notables lecturing each week. Many people think these courses are a waste of time. They're not. The lecturers are often more helpful than you'd think.

> **EXAMPLE: A prominent Hollywood director ended his lecture to a film class by telling them that they should feel free to stop by his house and ask him for help when they were looking for work. A woman took him at his word and went to see him after graduation. The director told her that, even though he had lectured dozens of classes and told them all that they were welcome to come to him for help, she was the first one who ever did anything about it. He gave her a job as an assistant on his next movie.**

Networking at Company Hangouts

■ **Through your contacts, find out where company employees go at lunch and after work.**

Typically there is a nearby bar or restaurant where many employees gather. Often that kind of relaxed atmosphere is the ideal spot to meet people from the company, pick up information or gossip, and get a feel for a company or an industry.

> **EXAMPLE: A trade magazine writer who wanted to move into newspapers started going to a local bar where the editors and staff of the local paper relaxed after work. Over several months, he became friendly with many of them and eventually told them of his planned career move. Since they already knew him and respected his skills, they offered to help him break into this very overcrowded field.**

Miscellaneous Methods of Getting Exposure

■ **Winning exposure is important: letting people know what you can do, and finding the right ones to hire you.**

Other methods of getting exposure are:

1. Writing and submitting articles for trade magazines or local news-papers on topics that may interest potential employers, that will show you to be an (employable) expert. *Bonus:* Authorship of arti-cles also looks good on your resume.

2. Working as a volunteer for charity programs that your target com-pany sponsors. Usually, other company employees also volunteer their time, which provides a good, informal setting for making contacts.

3. If you are unemployed and can type, working as a temporary employee at the target company. (See Chapter 6.) Temping is a quick way to get inside companies, and can give you contacts and knowledge of the company before any interviews or applications take place.

Some other helpful sources are:

The International Alliance of Professional & Executive Wom-en's Networks
8600 LaSalle Rd., Towson, MD 21204-3308
301/321-6699

- An association of regional networks for careerwomen.

- Offers seminars, workshops; publishes newsletter and an-nual directory of members.

National Association for Female Executives (NAFE)
127 West 24th St.
New York, NY 10011
212/645-0770

- Sponsors the NAFE network—1,200 career-resource groups nationwide, offering a variety of programs and assistance for career women.

5 Contacting Companies: Letters and Telephone Calls

INTRODUCTION

At this point in your job hunt, you start reaching out for a very tangible goal—an interview.

There are three common ways you can get an interview: through a cover letter, a resume letter, or a phone call.

Cover letters are the most common of the three. At one time or another, virtually all job seekers wind up writing cover letters to accompany their resumes. The trick is knowing how to transform a cover letter from a bland introduction to a strong selling tool that grabs a prospective employer's interest. This chapter will tell you how. It will also explain how resume letters, a hybrid resume/cover letter, can compensate for a problem background and convince employers that you are worth an interview. Last but not least, we will take a look at telephone calls, the most immediate way of reaching a company and possibly the most off-putting. This chapter will demonstrate how to take the terror out of cold-calling—by going step-by-step through proven telemarketing techniques, with sample scripts to guide you.

Each method works better at different times and for different needs. But, with each of them, you are introducing yourself to a company, stating your objective and, if you approach it correctly, you are *selling* yourself into an interview . . . and, eventually, into a job.

COVER LETTERS

■ **Keep in mind what a cover letter actually is:** *a sales presentation.*

Before you start writing a cover letter, think about the roles of the receiver and sender. The prospective employer who reads it is your customer or client; you are the product or service offered. In light of that, avoid dashing off the all-too-typical letter that goes along with many resumes:

> "Dear Mr. Smith. I am interested in securing a position at ABC Company as an accountant. Enclosed please find my resume. You will note that I have extensive experience as a tax accountant, including five years at a Big Eight firm. I would like to apply my experience to a career position in your company. I hope to hear from you in the near future. Sincerely . . ."

A letter like this one says nothing but "here is my resume." It doesn't distinguish the writer from the hundreds of other desperate, dull job seekers. *But it could.*

Most job hunters wrongly view a cover letter as nothing more than a polite enclosure when sending a resume to a prospective employer. It's actually a great opportunity to fine-tune your job hunt and position yourself more precisely than you can in the resume. Instead of composing a broad, generalized letter that just explains your objective and asks for an interview, write about specifics: your qualifications, the job for which you're applying, the company.

A well-written cover letter should:

- direct a reader's attention to your strong points and away from weaknesses.

- highlight and expand upon the facts found in your resume.

- give new, topical information that *isn't* included on your resume.

- show how well you know the company and the industry to which you're applying.

Planning a Targeted Cover Letter

■ **The first step in writing a targeted cover letter is the simplest:** *don't* **start writing.**

Take a few minutes to plan your letter before you write anything down. You'll save yourself time and effort in the long run. Begin by carefully reading your resume. Select at least three aspects of your work experience, achievements, or abilities to include in your letter that will demonstrate how well suited you are for the job. To come up with the strongest points, ask yourself:

1. *Does this example show how much I could contribute to the company?* It should. Choose something that illustrates what you've accomplished for previous employers, thus implying that you'd do the same for them.

2. *Are there concrete facts or numbers I can use to back up my claims?* It's best if you can justify everything you say about yourself with hard numbers, percentages or facts. There's less of a chance that people will think you're embellishing your past work history—and you will come across as more of an achiever.

3. *Is this a subjective claim?* It shouldn't be. Writing that "I bring out the best in my employees" or "I am able to build and cultivate brilliance" tells the reader nothing about what you can actually do. Worse, it sounds as though you have so little to say about yourself, you're resorting to puffery.

4. *Is this skill or quality central to the job I'm trying to get?* The answer always should be yes.

SAMPLE COVER LETTER

123 Elm St.
Canton, OH 44707
May 23, 1988

Marianne Deaver
Director of Marketing
XYZ Toy Company
1000 Rush Street
Chicago, IL 60610

Dear Ms. Deaver:

According to industry sources, XYZ Toy Company is planning to expand into the stuffed toy market. With XYZ's innovative product line and aggressive marketing, there is no question that the company dominates the domestic toy market. I'd like to join such a winning team.

As art director for a small toy manufacturer, I designed and oversaw production of a stuffed toy line that was responsible for 32% of our 1987 profits. This was the first time any one toy line generated such a large margin of profitability. In addition, I developed new packaging for the company's entire product line. Once the new packaging was used, sales to toy stores went up 24%.

I'd like to produce similar results for XYZ Toy Company. With my fifteen years in the toy industry and my hands-on experience in both product and package design, I know I can contribute a great deal to your design department. I will call you next week so we can set up a mutually convenient time to meet.

Sincerely,

Edward A. Carruthers

The Three Basic Parts of a Cover Letter

■ **There are three basic parts to a cover letter: the introduction, in which you state your purpose for the letter; the sales pitch, in which you present your qualifications; and the wind-up and close, in which you aim for an interview.**

Following is an explanation of each of the three parts along with excerpts from a successful cover letter.

Part #1: Introduction

When a prospective employer opens your letter, he or she will have one immediate response—Why is this person writing to me?

Explain up front—you saw an ad, you are interested in the company, you heard that it was expanding. Be exact and accurate. This is the right time to use the research you've accumulated on a company or field. Let the reader see that you are knowledgeable by referring to industry trends, specific events. Mention what the company recently has been involved in: product introductions, new clients, expansion plans, etc. This will demonstrate the level of your interest.

> **EXAMPLE: "According to industry sources, XYZ Toy Company is planning to expand into the stuffed toy market. With XYZ's innovative product line and aggressive marketing, there is no question that the company dominates the domestic toy market. I'd like to join such a winning team."**

Part # 2: The Sales Pitch

The sales pitch is the guts of the letter—the point at which a prospective employer will decide if he or she is interested in reading your resume or meeting you in person.

To sell yourself, tell the employer your qualifications and give examples of your experience. Take care to sound very positive (but not pompous) about your skills and experience. This is no time to be modest.

The same elements that make a resume effective also work here: Use action words. Be brief. Be specific. Write about particular accomplishments to show your qualifications. Use facts and numbers to back them up.

> **EXAMPLE:** "As art director for a small toy manufacturer, I designed and oversaw production of a stuffed toy line that was responsible for 32% of our 1987 profits. That was the first time any one toy line generated such a large margin of profitability. In addition, I developed new packaging for the company's entire product line. Once the new packaging was used, sales to toy stores went up 24%."

> **TIP:** You also can touch on other, less central points: aspects of your background that make you more qualified for the job, but ones that don't require much explanation. This works especially well if you are a recent college graduate or are changing careers and don't have direct experience to prove how qualified you are. Use *any* information that adds ammunition to your sales message.

> **EXAMPLE:** "As you will see on the enclosed resume, I have won numerous awards in graphic design, including a first place medal from the Nevada Department of Tourism for their statewide poster contest."

Part #3: Wind-Up and Close

Be sure to restate *in one sentence* what you can do for the company. Once you've made a strong case for yourself and your qualifications for the job, don't let the letter die down. Wind up your letter as positively as you opened it. Restate how interested you are in working for the company. Don't be coy. Honest enthusiasm comes across. Give them a pithy reason for hiring you, but don't get carried away and oversell yourself at this point.

Close the letter by aiming for an interview with the reader. If you are going for an aggressive or sales-type job, use a direct approach. Take charge of the follow-up by stating a definite time you will call: "I will call next Thursday, April 2, to set up a mutually convenient time for us to meet."

Don't use a direct method if you are uncomfortable with it, or if there is any doubt in your mind that you can effectively follow up on it.

Making commitments does more damage than good if you can't carry them out. Instead, use the common indirect closing line: "I look forward to hearing from you in the near future" or some variation.

TIP: Even though you're putting the ball in the reader's court by asking them to call, be as positive as possible. Say, "I *look forward* to hearing from you," not "I *hope* to hear from you." Sound as though you expect a call.

EXAMPLE: "I'd like to produce similar results for XYZ Toy Company. With my fifteen years in the toy industry and my hands-on experience in both product and package design, I know I can contribute a great deal to your design department. I will call you next week so we can set up a mutually convenient time to meet."

Developing a Cover Letter's Basic Framework

■ One of the hidden beauties of targeting your cover letter to your job objective is that, in the process, you create a multipurpose letter—a basic framework that you can adapt to fit almost any situation.

As soon as you've come up with a strong, workable letter, you can re-use its core contents, and add or subtract from it according to the specific job you're applying for, whether you are answering an ad or making a blind approach to a new contact. The basic letter will be the same, but you can personalize it by highlighting different parts of your background and making references to the particular company you're addressing.

The following two letters should give you an example of how easily you can adapt a basic framework to meet your needs of the moment. They were written under two different circumstances (one as a result of a personal contact's lead, the other in answer to a blind ad in *The New York Times*) but the writer was able to use much of the same material. Note how she made each letter sound unique and how she added more information in Cover Letter #2 to target herself even more precisely.

COVER LETTER #1

[In response to a personal contact's job lead]

55 West 14th Street
New York, NY 10011

February 12, 1989

Ms. Diane Walker
Vice President
National Public Relations Association
800 Third Avenue
New York, NY 10022

Dear Ms. Walker:

Ken O'Brien, the NPRA's director of marketing, tells me that the NPRA has an opening for a public relations writer and promotion coordinator. That's a position I'm very interested in.

[The writer opens with the name of the contact, a sure way to get the attention of the reader. Following with the job and an expression of interest makes the purpose of the letter clear.]

Public relations is an area in which I've a proven track record. Due in part to my direct-mail pieces, press releases, news stories, and brochures, the 1988 Advertising Society of America's Trade Show and Convention was the largest in its 30 years of existence. My releases were picked up by a wide variety of publications, including over 20 international newspapers—which brought in 72% more foreign registrants than before. In addition, print and television coverage of the conference increased substantially.

[In her sales pitch, she gives specific examples of how she helped a similar organization achieve results. The implication: I'll do the same for you.]

That's a little of what I accomplished for the Advertising Society of America. I'd like to do more—but this time for the NPRA.

[She flatly lays out her proposition and restates her interest.]

Enclosed are my resume and several writing samples. If you want a recent reference, feel free to speak with Barbara Baker, the Advertising Society of America's Manager of Public Relations (555-1234). I look forward to hearing from you.

[Because the letter is the result of a personal referral, she gives the name of a reference to check. That gives the reader an immediate action to take, moving the writer one step closer to an interview.]

Sincerely,

Laurel Garrett

COVER LETTER #2

[In answer to a blind ad in *The New York Times*—the position advertised was for a public relations person in a television production company.]

55 West 14th Street
New York, NY 10011

February 12, 1989

Box T1234
New York Times
New York, NY 10108

Your advertisement in today's *New York Times* caught my attention and held it. I've been hoping to see a job opening that would combine my promotion and public relations experience with my hands-on knowledge of television production. This sounds like the one.

[She follows the same pattern as in letter #1—opening with how she heard about the job and stating her interest in it.]

Public relations is an area in which I've a proven track record. Due in part to my direct-mail pieces, press releases, news stories, and brochures, the 1988 Advertising Society of America's Trade Show and Convention was the largest in its 30 years of existence. My releases were picked up by a wide variety of publications, including over 20 international newspapers—which brought in 72% more foreign registrants than before. In addition, print and television coverage of the conference increased substantially.

[Exactly the same as in letter #1.]

The key to getting such a strong press response is knowing what the press wants—especially television. Three years with WXXX-TV taught me a great deal about the press, news coverage, and television production. As associate producer of a news feature show and producer of a special news inserts session, I learned what makes a good story and how to reach the public with it.

[Paragraph added to emphasize television production skills—the other half of her qualifications. She skews the information to stress how a knowledge of production strengthens her skills in public relations.]

Now I plan to merge my public relations and television skills. I accomplished a great deal for the Advertising Society with my press and promotion background. I'd like to have the opportunity to do the same for you.

[Again, a quick summary restating skills and interest.]

Enclosed are my resume and writing samples. I look forward to hearing from you soon.

Sincerely,

Laurel Garrett

Five Rules that Sell You in Your Cover Letter

Rule #1: Know Your Audience

- **You are writing your cover letter for one audience only: prospective employers.**

Each member of your audience receives dozens, if not hundreds, of cover letters and resumes. You want your letter to be the one that grabs his or her attention. The only way to do this is to consciously direct your letter.

The key question in your target audience's mind as they read your letter will be: Is this person worth my time? The answer to their question should be "yes."

- *Talk* **to your reader when you write.**

Your letter is a stand-in for you. You want your reader to feel that you are communicating directly with him or her, not reeling off a sales spiel.

> **TIP: Read your letter out loud to yourself and listen to how it sounds. Does it sound natural, or does it sound forced? Is there too much stilted language or bureaucratese? Remember that no matter what your writing style or the contents of your letter, it should sound natural *to you*.**

- **Use your knowledge to skew your letter** *indirectly.*

If you know that a company is very formal and traditional, avoid using contractions, informal language, or jargon. If a company is informal or if you're familiar with the person to whom you're sending the letter, you can loosen up a bit—but still keep it businesslike. It's better to be a little too formal than vice versa.

- **Create a mental image of your reader.**

Whether your image of the individual to whom you're writing is a correct one or not is immaterial. Use it simply as a device to make your letter more personal rather than dry and dull. You can base your mental image on what you know of the industry and the people in it—anything that will help you get a fix on the type of person you're trying to reach through your letter.

■ **Refer to events in the industry at large that would interest anyone in the field.**

Even if you don't know much about the specific company, you can still present yourself as an expert in the field by mentioning events in the mainstream of things. It also will make your letter seem more personalized.

Rule #2: Create Interest

■ **The best way to get people's attention is to talk about what interests them.**

Open your letter with a sentence that leads the reader in. Instead of writing about yourself, mention an interesting fact about industry trends, a recent company development, or the contributions made by individuals like your prospective employer—anything that you think will catch the reader's eye and make your letter stand out from all the rest.

> **EXAMPLES:** **"Dynamic marketing has made TNC Industries the undisputed leader in the widget field. With the roll-out of the new X-14 widget, TNC has cornered the widget market."**
>
> *Or:* **"As architect of TNC Industries' innovative marketing plan for the roll-out of the new X-14 widget, you spearheaded the company's unprecedented growth."**
>
> **(Of course, the reader knows this already, but he or she won't mind reading it again. A positive, complimentary truism about the company's or an individual's performance works. Just don't gush. Right after this type of opening, get to your purpose in writing and what you have to offer immediately.)**

■ **Referring to published quotes by the addressee is one of the best ways to open a cover letter.**

Quoting your prospective employer shows that you've researched the company and, more important, will appeal to the ego of the employer. Everyone likes to know that their comments have been noted and appreciated.

EXAMPLE: "Your statements in the June 18th issue of *Institutional Investor* about Addison, Thomson and Phillips' long-term investment strategies were most interesting. I was especially intrigued by your views on corporate pension plans. . . ."

■ **Don't mistake being interesting with being overly clever and catchy.**

You want to come across as a professional, not as a professional hype artist. Steer away from inflated opening lines, obvious come-ons, and the clever little gambits you read about in books and articles (the "Here is a dollar bill. I'm not trying to corrupt you, just trying to get your attention . . ." scheme and others). If you've read about these tricks, chances are so has another applicant—or the prospective employer himself.

TIP: *Remember:* **You can grab someone's attention without being super-creative. An effective opening can be as simple as: "Sam DiMatteo suggested I write you," or "I understand you are looking for systems analysts." Your main concern is getting the person to read on.**

Rule #3: Once You Have Their Attention, Keep It

■ **Don't open strongly, then fade out into a bland recitation of your work history.**

You want the reader to remain interested in your cover letter from start to finish. Always maintain a simple and confident style, continually striving to reinforce your strengths and underscore your achievements.

TIP: **Don't phrase everything exactly the same way. Vary your sentence structure and use clauses. Especially avoid the "I, I, I" syndrome—beginning every sentence or every paragraph with "I" ("I am interested," "I have experience in," "I have enclosed a resume," etc.). You come across as conceited or a bore—and either way, you lose.**

Rule #4: Communicate Your Message Clearly

■ **Be sure you are getting your message across—that you want a particular job at this company.**

Always be sure that the reader knows exactly what type of position you're after. It sounds ridiculously simple, but a great many people get vague when it comes to stating their reason for writing. Be specific. Don't say "I am interested in a management position." Say "I am interested in a management trainee position," "a job as a district sales manager," etc. In general, the simpler the better. Omit unnecessary words, flowery language, and convoluted, difficult-to-understand sentences.

■ **Be sure not to lift exact wording from your resume.**

It makes your cover letter redundant, and leads the reader to believe you have little or nothing original to say about yourself. As a general rule of thumb, if you can't expand upon the information you've taken from your resume, it shouldn't be a major part of your cover letter.

> **TIP: Never pad out your letter with nonremarks such as "I'm a people person" or "I have strong interactive personal skills" or other overused, meaningless clichés. You want your letter to be a precisely aimed sales tool. A short letter is better than a puffed-up one.**

■ **Assume that your reader knows nothing.**

Spell out things with descriptive, detailed phrases. Qualify statements: *Not* "I worked in production control for a package goods company," but "I was production control supervisor at the second-largest package goods company in the Southwest."

Rule #5: Keep Hammering at Your Main Objective

■ **Make your examples as pithy and hard-hitting as possible.**

You want to stress how good you are at what you do. At all times the inference should be "I can furnish your company with similar results." Don't force the prospective employer to figure this out by reading between the lines; say it outright.

EXAMPLE: Don't write "I revitalized the sales department" and drop it there. Go on and tell the reader *how* you revitalized the department and what the effects were. "Due to my streamlining of office procedures and introducing weekly staff meetings, department morale improved and productivity increased. We posted a 26% rise in sales the first month after I instituted my new measures."

TIP: Examples that show how you increased profits, cut costs, or brought in more business are always winners. As you did in your resume, use numbers and percentages in your description.

TIP: Use bullets in the body of your letter to highlight your key achievements. They will leap off the page and catch the reader's eye.

Format Do's and Don't's for a Cover Letter

How it looks is almost as important as what it says. Keep in mind the following do's and don't's when you're writing your cover letter.

■ *Do* **keep your letter brief.**

Stick to one page. It is an accompaniment to your resume, designed to pique a prospective employer's interest. It shouldn't be overly explanatory or repeat information verbatim that can be found on your resume.

■ *Don't* **use large blocks of text.**

Break up the cover letter into a minimum of three paragraphs. You want the reader to be able to understand and digest the information in each section.

■ *Do* **use the typical business letter format.**

Even if the letter is informal in tone, the appearance should be businesslike.

■ *Don't* **send photocopies.**

You shouldn't be sending form letters; each letter should be personalized. If you are sending the same letter to hundreds of companies, you shouldn't advertise that fact. Letters should be individually typed or run off on a computer printer.

■ *Do* **use personalized letterhead stationery, on stock that matches your resume if possible.**

Stationery should be white, off-white, cream, or eggshell (the same color as your resume), and the typeface and layout should be standard. If you don't have personalized stationery, use a good quality bond paper in the same weight and color as your resume.

■ *Don't* **address a cover letter "To Whom It May Concern," or "Vice President of Marketing," "Personnel Director," or some other title name.**

Call and find out the exact name of the person to whom you're sending the letter and the exact spelling. Also doublecheck the titles —is it Director of Marketing, Marketing Director, Vice President of Marketing? People are notoriously picky about titles. Be sure to get them straight.

■ *Do* **proofread your letter more than once.**

One typo in your letter, even the most minor, and you've cut back your chances of being called in.

Using a Cover Letter to Handle Special Situations

■ **Sometimes you may need your cover letter to act *defensively* for you—to steer a prospective employer's attention away from rough spots in your background that you can't completely hide on your resume, like gaps in employment, a spotty work record, or lack of experience.**

A cover letter is the only chance you may have to convince a prospective employer that you are worth interviewing, in spite of apparent problems in your background.

■ **To make your cover letter compensate for past employment weaknesses, read your resume objectively.**

Anticipate the objections that a prospective employer might have about you, such as that most of your experience is in an unrelated field; your resume shows that you have been unemployed for the past six months; your experience is limited; you have held a number of jobs for only brief periods of time.

■ **Then choose examples from your background, both abilities and achievements, that *counteract* any objection a prospective employer might come up with.**

Either show how well qualified you are in spite of your drawbacks, or show that your drawbacks aren't really a problem at all by emphasizing specific accomplishments. *Remember:* You have more leeway in a cover letter than you do in a resume, and thus can include information about yourself that is only briefly outlined in your resume (minor job duties, outside activities, hobbies, special courses, associations, volunteer work, etc.).

Common problems that can be handled in a cover letter include:

1. *No or very limited work experience in the field.* Solution: Draw parallels between seemingly unrelated experience and the job for which you are applying. Focus on skills and functions rather than job titles. Expand upon hobbies, outside interests, or memberships that relate to the job.

2. *Re-entering the work force.* Solution: Include examples of what you accomplished while you were out of the work force. It is especially good to mention brush-up courses you've taken or methods you've used to keep abreast of developments in your field.

3. *No previous formal work experience.* Solution: If you are a recent college graduate with only low-level, part-time work experience or none at all, play up educational achievements and extracurricular activities in your letter. Talk about specific courses you've taken that relate to the job, your grades in those courses, any honors papers or theses you wrote. Emphasize skills that any employer wants—efficiency, persistence, hard work.

4. *Series of lateral moves; resume shows little or no upward movement.* Solution: Choose examples of achievements that indicate advancement —if not in actual job title, then in expertise and abilities: you've learned new skills, you've taken on different duties, your respon-

sibilities have increased. Use *action words* that underscore movement and growth.

■ **The one problem you *shouldn't* deal with in a cover letter is unemployment.**

Leave the subject of past or current unemployment alone—especially if you were fired. Going into a long-winded explanation only draws attention to a circumstance that you wish to put behind you. In general, you are better off stressing your qualifications and avoiding comments on the periods of your unemployment.

> **TIP: Functional resume users should be careful. Most prospective employers view a functional resume as an automatic tip-off to trouble: you are hiding a spotty record, you have limited work experience, etc. Even if these are false assumptions, you *must* write a cover letter that counters those suspicions head-on. Everything should stress your stability and depth of experience. *Especially important:* Since time is not mentioned in a functional resume, use time-oriented phrases in your letter: "With my twelve years experience in [the industry or field]"; "After seven years of developing production control methods . . ." You aren't saying how long you held any particular job; you *are* attaching a time frame to general functions.**

RESUME LETTERS

■ **A resume letter is a combination cover letter/resume that takes the place of a conventional resume.**

Like a cover letter, a resume letter targets your background very specifically to a particular job or a particular company. As you would in a resume, you present a prospective employer with a brief sketch of your complete background including employment history, education, and outside activities. But unlike either a cover letter or a resume, the resume letter allows you a great degree of latitude in terms of how to present yourself.

Resume letters work best in these circumstances:

- when you *don't* have the logical qualifications for the job

- when you are changing careers and want to avoid using a functional resume

- when you have little or no related work experience

- when you are a recent college graduate with a skimpy background

- when you have heard about a job opening, but there has been no formal announcement

- when you are testing the waters at a company, but don't want to make a formal application

In these cases—and whenever else you believe a resume would hurt your chances more than help—send a resume letter instead.

The following is a prime example of when to send a resume letter, and *not* a resume. The following resume should never have been sent out. The job hunter is hoping to change careers, but, on the basis of her resume, she will never get an interview, let alone a job offer, in her objective field.

A RESUME THAT SHOULD NOT HAVE BEEN SENT

ANN DELMONICO
123 Main Street, Oxnard, CA 11111 (213) 555-3456

Objective

POSITION IN HUMAN RESOURCES: A job in which I can use my ability to influence others through superior communications skills and imaginative approaches

[An immediate turn-off. This objective sounds ridiculous—pompous and clichéd. More important, what does it mean? This gives you no idea of what the job hunter wants, what she can do, what her qualifications are.]

Experience

- Convinced superiors of necessity to revamp program of instruction and motivational strategies, and was chosen to oversee efforts of four professionals in this project affecting over 300 people per year. Commended for ability to develop rapport and enhancement of working environment.

[How did she convince superiors? What was she doing at the time? What is this program she's referring to? Furthermore, how did she enhance the working environment? Again, this smacks of puffery and exaggeration.]

- Named to supervisory board of one of California's top universities. Persuaded top officers to form financial committee, to which I was appointed, to better plan budgetary matters. Resulted in a four-year wage development and review plan, and a 39% cut in the employee attrition rate.

[More detail needed. This should be tied in with objective and worded much better.]

- With several others, founded local chapter of nationwide organization working against drug abuse, and have given over 75 presentations on that topic at high schools, colleges and other educational and public institutions.

[Good experience, but could be expanded, explained in more detail and tied in to objective.]

- Motivated over 900 people during the past five years. Received awards that reflected my ability to encourage people to achieve beyond what they believed they were capable of.

[Again, much too vague and confusing. Where has she worked? How and why has she motivated people? And the statement "beyond what they believed they were capable of" sounds overinflated.]

Employment History

Teacher in the City of San Diego school system, 1978–present
Instructor, California State University, 1977–1978
Instructor, Centenary Junior College, 1976–1977
Teacher, Immaculate Heart High School, San Diego, CA 1975–1976

[Much too sparse. We have no idea what she teaches or has taught and why that makes her qualified for a human resources position.]

Education

B.A., University of San Diego (English), 1973
M.A., University of San Diego (English), 1975

As you can see, this resume does nothing to sell the job hunter to a prospective employer. The job hunter hasn't presented her background well; she hasn't demonstrated that she has the qualifications necessary for the job. And, regardless of how much this resume is revised, the job hunter still will have to stretch to tie in her unrelated background to her objective. Her best recourse is to write a resume letter in which she can stress her work with people, administrative skills, and interests.

RESUME REWRITTEN AS RESUME LETTER

123 Main Street
Oxnard, CA 11111

June 18, 1987

Ms. Carol Menninger
Director of Human Resources
Western Technical Co., Inc.
555 Wilshire Blvd.
Los Angeles, CA 11111

Dear Ms. Menninger:

In the May issue of *Personnel Management,* I read about Western Technical's plans to expand its human resources department by expanding employee-counseling programs. I agree that counseling is becoming more and more important as mergers and takeovers change corporate culture. The human resources field is changing to accommodate a changing corporate picture, and I am interested in meeting the challenge of these exciting times.

I am especially interested in a position as an outplacement counselor, devising special programs to handle the needs of newly retired or laid-off employees. I believe my background as a teacher, counselor, and administrator is particularly suited for a human resources position with your company. Among my skills and qualifications:

—As a co-founder of a chapter of the nationally known Narcotics Anonymous, I laid the groundwork for existing procedures, set up and implemented public affairs programs, counseled new members, and designed educational presentations for the community at large.

—Over ten years experience teaching at both the high school and college levels has given me the ability to communicate with a wide variety of people. In addition, I have developed excellent organizational, presentation, and training skills.

—I also have experience organizing material and making presentations outside of the classroom. For the past three years, I have spoken to large groups—in local high schools, colleges, and universities—about drug abuse and the various programs available to them.

—Most recently, I have combined my administrative skills and counseling skills while serving as a college instructor at California State University. There, I oversaw the redesign of a business education/motivation program—a program with over 300 participants a year. The two-year project won me a commendation—both for my program design and for the working environment I fostered during its development.

—My administrative skills are not limited to devising educational programs. As an elected member of the supervisory board of CSU, I worked to establish a long-needed financial committee, and subsequently was appointed to serve on that committee. My involvement resulted in a four-year wage development and review plan and a 39% cut in the employee attrition rate.

—I hold both Bachelor of Arts and Master of Arts degrees from the University of San Diego.

With my combined experience as a teacher, counselor, and administrator, I believe I have a great deal to offer to Western Technical's human resources division. The programs you are planning to put into effect sound exciting and very similar to the projects I have implemented in the past. I would like to learn more about them from you and also discuss how I might play a part on the human resources team. I will call you early next week to set up a mutually convenient time for us to meet.

Sincerely,

Ann Delmonico

The rewritten resume letter does it all—and does it better. The writer identifies herself as a focused job hunter with a clear goal, and with clear examples of how her experience relates to her goal. By writing a letter instead of sending the resume, she stresses her strengths, downplays her weaknesses, and sends a forceful message to potential employers.

■ By having detailed information in your resume letter that you couldn't include on a resume (such as outside activities, hobbies, etc.), and *excluding* information you normally would have put into it (such as company names, employment dates, etc.), you can play up only your strongest points and skip over the weak ones.

In a resume letter, you can take a less-than-perfect background and make yourself sound almost perfect for the job. You can even strengthen your sales pitch by omitting mention of certain jobs entirely or glossing over years of unemployment. Despite the leeway you have, a resume letter is actually very similar to a basic targeted cover letter. It has the same three essential parts—an introduction, in which you present yourself and the reason you're writing; a sales pitch, in which you outline your background and qualifications; and a close, in which you give your sales pitch once more, then aim for an interview.

To write a resume letter you should follow these steps:

- Write your introduction like a typical cover letter. Open strong, explain your interest in the company and your job objective.

- Then move into your sales pitch. The simplest way to be sure you are including enough information is to break your sales pitch into two parts. The first will be the main thrust of your letter, the section that presents the key ingredients of your resume (either your work history or education). Pay most attention to giving *detailed* information about your work experience. List jobs or functions and support them with specific examples of your accomplishments.

- The second part of the sales pitch sets out the rest of your background: work experience that isn't as central; education; activities that make you more salable. The information you provide in this part of the letter should roughly correspond to the information you would put further down in your resume.

Remember: Because you're not sending a resume to amplify the statements in your letter, your letter must include anything and everything that will affect your chances for a job. When you write and reread your resume letter, be sure you have covered your entire background and hit on all the key points.

The following sample resume letter is from a career changer who wants to make a career move from legal publishing to a corporate law practice—and who wants to avoid using a functional resume. Note how he uses the more flexible format of a resume letter to emphasize his abilities and downplay his limited experience as a practicing attorney. The associate job he describes is part-time, the private practice is very minor, but he presents them well: making his background appear more substantial, and well suited for a corporate law position.

714 East 14th Street
Savannah, GA 11111

February 15, 1988

Mr. Kevin Bartlett
Vice-President
BTI Insurance Inc.
142 Peachtree Lane
Atlanta, GA 30303

Dear Mr. Bartlett:

I saw your advertisement seeking an attorney to join your legal staff in the June 28th *Atlanta Constitution.*

The position described interests me a great deal. My experience with insurance cases has been from the other side—representing litigants in negligence cases. As such, I would bring to the firm a unique perspective and one that would enable me to work successfully on behalf of BTI.

As a member of both the Georgia and North Carolina Bars and a privately practicing attorney, I have in-depth legal experience. Among my accomplishments and capabilities are the following:

- as a private practitioner, have successfully handled corporate law, domestic relations, and real property cases—and have recently begun expanding my practice to include malpractice and negligence.
- have made court appearances in product liability and negligence cases. In addition, I have handled most other types of litigation, including commercial, landlord-tenant, and real estate.
- extensive experience analyzing current legislation and case law, specializing in corporate issues.
- brief-writing and research on cases involving estates, pensions, copyrights, malpractice, and insurance.

I became a member of the Bar in 1978, upon my graduation from Duke University School of Law. I received my Bachelor of Arts in Political Science from Duke in 1975.

The position you described interests me very much. I look forward to meeting with you.

Sincerely,

Louis A. Russo

TELEPHONE CALLS

■ **Use the telephone instead of a letter any time you think that speed will make a difference.**

There will be times during your job hunt when a phone call will be necessary in lieu of a letter. Usually it's a question of time—you can't afford to wait for your letter to reach a prospective employer and the key strength of calling is immediacy.

More specifically, you should telephone a prospective employer when:

- a want ad lists a telephone number
- a contact gives you a hot lead and you must follow up quickly
- you have been given a personal referral

By using the phone, you can reach prospective employers ahead of other candidates or before a job has been filled. Prospective employers will get a strong impression of you because you are right there on the line.

But being "on the line"—literally and figuratively—is just what makes people uneasy about using the telephone. You are forced to make split-second decisions about how to answer certain questions. You have to know how to get and keep a listener's attention and how to adapt your sales pitch to the immediate situation.

The trick to making effective phone calls is by first planning your sales pitch, then knowing how to present yourself. In this way you are *telemarketing,* selling yourself as a product over the telephone. Your ultimate goal is to give a sales presentation in person or, in this case, to get an interview.

> **TIP: Another way of using the telephone to land an interview is by *cold-calling* prospective employers. As a general rule, cold-calling works *only* if you have a great deal of confidence. You have to sell yourself uninvited to employers and you need a thick skin to handle the snubs, obstacles, and outright rejections you will more than likely encounter. *Translation:* If you feel at all uneasy or uncomfortable about picking up the phone, asking for a specific person and proceeding to ask for a job interview right then and there, don't do it. Stick with letters.**

Selling Yourself on the Phone: Telemarketing Techniques

■ **First recognize what a telephone call actually is: an interview.**

Although the goal of making a telephone call is to get you a face-to-face interview, the telephone call *itself* is a screening process of sorts.

When you call, the prospective employer will have one question in mind: "Why should I spend my time with you?" You have to answer that question—quickly. So you don't waste time on the phone frantically thinking of what to say, you should prepare for the call before you start dialing.

■ **Begin by choosing the selling points that will convince the employer that you are worth the time spent talking, and worth seeing for a formal interview.**

Ask yourself: *What are my qualifications for the job? What aspects of my background will make the prospective employer interested in me? What can I explain easily and concisely about my qualifications?* Select selling points that give the prospective employer a good reason for wanting to meet with you and learn more.

> **TIP:** It might sound obvious, but be sure to choose examples you can *talk* about, not ones that only look good on paper. Always be prepared to substantiate or expand upon any aspect of your background that you bring up.

■ **Once you've chosen your selling points, the next step in making your phone call effective is to figure out how to present them.**

Mentally rehearse the conversation: go over the points you want to cover, the order in which you want to talk about them, and how you will deal with the possible problems and questions.

> **TIP:** If it makes you more comfortable, use file cards to jot down the key selling points that you want to cover. Use these as a kind of script. Do *not*, however, write out an actual script and read it over the phone. You will sound like you're reciting a sales pitch. Worse, you can get too dependent on it and wind up blowing the entire conversation. *A true worst-case scenario:* A job seeker confidently rattled off his strong qualifications, complete with numbers and every conceivable detail that made him sound

right for the job. Everything went perfectly—until the prospective employer asked a simple question that wasn't in the script. The job hunter's reply: "Uhh . . ." *The moral:* Remember that you're going to be involved in a *dialogue.* A dialogue involves two people.

> TIP: Practice your sales call by actually telephoning a friend or colleague. Rehearsing the situation can make the actual phone call more effective.

■ **The final step before placing the actual call is *research*.**

Do as much background prepping as possible—know about the company, the job title, the job's duties, the person you should speak with, and so on. The more you know, the more confident you'll feel —and the better you'll come across.

> TIP: Before you call a specific individual, doublecheck on how to pronounce his or her name. Mispronunciation won't cost you an interview, but it can be awkward. Call ahead and see how the secretary pronounces it. Or ask straight out—just don't say who's calling.

Three Steps to Selling Yourself over the Telephone

■ **The most effective telephone call in a job hunt is one that is patterned after a typical direct-sales call.**

Like a cover letter, a telephone call has three distinct parts: the opening, in which you introduce yourself; the proposition, in which you present your credentials and aim for an interview; and the close, in which you seal the agreement (in this case, to meet).

Step 1: The Set-Up

The best move you can make, and the one that most impresses prospective employers: *getting to the point quickly.* Get directly to your purpose for calling and you will make a good impression from the beginning. This also will set the stage for the rest of your conversation.

Remember: Prospective employers don't know who you are or why you are calling until you tell them, so introduce yourself and state the general nature of your call at once. It can be as simple as "Mr. Baker? This is John Bancroft. I understand you are looking for a new product-control supervisor," or "I am calling in response to your ad in *The Sacramento Bee*." Don't be afraid of no-frills openings. Your aim is to get an interview, not entertain the prospective employer with your gags, or sound as though you're selling magazine subscriptions.

> **TIP: Whenever possible, use a mutual contact's name or refer to an article or ad. References will give your call more weight and credence. This is especially important if you are cold-calling.**

> **TIP: In general, avoid hoaxing your way into meeting a prospective employer. Too many people have tried the "I'm writing an article for the trade paper and want to interview you" approach. Not only is it a bit hackneyed, it can annoy the very person you're trying to impress.**

As when you're networking, make sure the other person has the time and inclination to speak with you at the moment. If you sense a hesitancy, suggest you call again later or on another day. Your pitch won't go over well if the sales target is preoccupied.

> **TIP: If you are cold-calling, *always* try to reach a prospective employer when his or her secretary is least likely to pick up the phone and screen the executive's call. Before eight-thirty in the morning and after five-thirty at night are best bets.**

Step 2: The Proposition

State your proposition flatly: you are interested in seeing the prospective employer in person to discuss a job.

Don't get fancy. You won't gain a thing by sounding like a fast-talking huckster. Plain speaking works better in this situation. But don't stop there and expect a warm welcome. You have to give the person a *reason* for wanting to meet you.

> **EXAMPLE: "I'd like to arrange a mutually convenient time to speak with you about a position at TNC Industries. With my ten years of experience in production control, I'm sure I can contribute a great deal to your company."**

After stating your proposition go directly into your sales pitch, in which you briefly outline the highlights of your background that make you right for the job. Don't be too detailed or overly informative. You *don't* want this phone call to turn into the job interview. It's supposed to be a teaser—deliberately designed to intrigue the prospective employer.

List a few of your strongest achievements, then circle back to your key goal: *an interview.*

> **EXAMPLE:** "To give you a rough idea of my accomplishments, I most recently saved my company—a major cosmetics manufacturer—over two hundred thousand dollars, by designing and putting into effect an inventory control system. I also coordinated and directed the local application of a corporate obsolescence policy. This resulted in a cost savings of over one hundred thousand dollars, the highest regional savings in the company. I'll go into more detail about the programs and tell you more about my background when we meet."

At some point in this part of your conversation, you may have questions fired at you by the prospective employer—especially if you are calling in response to an ad or a formal referral. Answer questions succinctly and honestly, but again keep in mind that your real goal is an interview, not a job offer. In light of that, be as brief and general as possible. Take special care not to box yourself in and avoid saying anything that could *exclude* you from getting an interview.

> **TIP:** Since you can't see the person with whom you're speaking, you can't pick up on body language and hidden cues that would clue you in on his or her reactions. Because of that, stick with safe answers—avoid absolutes and criticisms.

Be *especially* wary when you're asked about salary expectations or salary history.

More often than not, employers ask questions about money to screen out "overqualified" candidates. By answering a salary question with a hard figure, you can be pricing yourself out of the market. You should sidestep these questions by turning them back toward the most important point at hand: setting a time for a formal interview.

> **EXAMPLE:** (*If you're asked what salary you expect*) "I'd like to discuss salary with you after we've met and I have a better understanding of the job and what it entails."
> (*If you're asked what you're making now*) "I'm making a

> **competitive salary here. But salary isn't the issue as far as I'm concerned. I'm more interested in meeting with you and telling you some of the ideas I have for TNC."**

If there's no way out of answering salary questions and you're asked to quote a dollar figure, you can offer a salary range, but never give a single figure. Then drop the subject quickly and move on to something new.

> **EXAMPLE:** **"I'm looking at jobs that pay competitively—in the fifty- to sixty-thousand-dollar range. Of course, I feel you can't measure a job by salary alone. There are other factors that can be more important. For instance, I'm very impressed with TNC's new productivity incentive program . . ."**
> *Note:* **This type of answer also shows that you've done your homework. It reaffirms your interest and sells you once again—four birds with one stone.**

Step 3: The Close

Once you've made your presentation and the prospective employer has asked all the questions that he or she has, it's time to close the conversation. The close should be neat and simple: Restate your purpose, your interest, and your sales pitch, then zero in on getting that interview.

> **EXAMPLE:** **"I'm looking forward to getting together with you to discuss further the production control job at TNC. I'll be in town next week. Are you available next Thursday, or would earlier in the week be better?"**
> *Note:* **By giving the person an option, you avoid a yes-no answer.**

If you're not coming across, and an interview doesn't seem to be forthcoming, stop pushing and close the conversation gracefully. A hard-sell technique won't work to get you an interview—at least, not during your first phone call. Instead of trying to break down a stone wall and get an interview from an unenthusiastic or downright cold prospective employer, thank the person for his or her time and get off the phone. But tell the person you'll send a resume, or find out when (and if) you can call again. That way, the phone call won't have been a total loss.

TIP: *For the very aggressive, confident, and/or thick-skinned only:* It's risky and hard to stomach at times, but sometimes being a pest is a plus. If you can't get an interview or even the ear of a prospective employer, keep trying over and over and over again. People get so sick of hearing your voice on the phone or their secretary announcing your name that they capitulate and let you come in for an interview. It's a defense on their part—it gets you off their backs. But despite the negative way you landed the interview, it can work. Once you're in a prospective employer's office, you can show him or her how qualified you are and he or she will be glad you forced your way in.

Your conversation should be short. Two to ten minutes is usually more than enough time to introduce yourself, make your proposition, and wind up with an interview.

Telephone Do's and Don't's

■ *Do* dress professionally, even if you are calling from home and no one can see you.

Professional clothes make you feel more polished—and that feeling will come across as you speak.

■ *Don't* smoke during a phone call.

While prospective employers can't see you, they can hear you.

■ *Do* sit at the edge of your chair and keep your back straight.

Good posture translates into a good speaking voice.

■ *Don't* do all the talking.

Just because this is a sales call doesn't mean you should rattle on endlessly. Ask questions. Listen.

6 *Tactics: Landing an Interview*

INTRODUCTION

As your job hunt continues, you'll invariably get advice from friends, colleagues, books, and articles about the *only* surefire method of getting an interview. Everyone is an expert and knows the single tactic that works better than any other:

"Don't bother with resumes. Cold-call potential employers."

"Get as many headhunters as you can interested in you."

"Walk right into the company and tell the receptionist you won't leave until you've spoken to the person who can hire you."

The suggestions are endless, but these people are overcomplicating a simple issue. The truth of the matter is that *there is no one foolproof, success-guaranteed way to land an interview.* Anyone who tells you there is either has been very lucky or is lying.

There are a number of different methods that work. The trick is knowing when they work, whom they work best for, and how to get the most from each one you use.

Following are some brief explanations of the most common and most effective tactics. You will probably use at least three of them during your job search.

WANT ADS

■ **Only about 15% of all job openings are advertised in newspapers as "help-wanted" ads. So they aren't the best way to find a job, but don't write them off.**

It's very common nowadays to hear and read that want ads are useless, that the only way to get a job is through contacts or friends, the "hidden job market." *Remember:* Companies *do* place ads looking for job candidates; job hunters *can* get interviews through classifieds; and it only takes a little time and effort. More important, you are probably reading the want ads anyway.

A few tips that can improve your odds and save you time:

• The first (and best) place to look for want-ads is in the top trade publications in your field. The next best places are the Sunday classified section of the major daily newspaper in your area and *The Wall Street Journal* (or the *National Business Employment Weekly*, which compiles the *Journal*'s want ads—including those from the regional editions).

• In general, Mondays and Fridays have the smallest selection of help-wanted ads.

• Don't look only under your job title. Read through other related job headings and even unrelated headings. Sometimes a company (especially a newer or smaller company) lists more than one job in an ad. Also, by expanding your criteria you might stumble across something that you hadn't thought of but that looks interesting.

• Take note of ads for positions *above* yours, such as department heads, supervisors, or anyone who would be your boss. Staff members often are hired or replaced when a new manager comes on board.

Answering Want Ads

■ **You'll answer most classifieds by letter. Make *your* letter stand out by mentioning your experience and qualifications immediately.**

But don't leave out the name and date of the newspaper, and remember to mention the job referred to in the ad.

Avoid opening your letter with the typical and dull "I am writing this in answer to your ad in the June 17th *Baltimore Sun*. . . ." The average employer receives hundreds of replies to newspaper advertisements, and the vast majority of them sound the same. It's better to sound different: more forceful and positive, and more to the point.

> **TIP: To make your letter more interesting, switch your sentence or paragraph around and put the "I" part last: "Your advertisement in the June 17th *Baltimore Sun* calls for a person with strong computer and communications skills. I have both. In my seven years . . ."**

■ **From the outset, set up a specific reason for the reader to read on and be interested.**

Read the ad very carefully. How the ad is worded will give you clues as to how to sell yourself more effectively. Do they use words such as "stability," "integrity," "supportive environment"? Position yourself as a solid employee with a strong and stable work record who wants a career position. Show that you're a traditionalist with proven skills. On the other hand, if the company is described as "on the move," "a dynamic climate," and the position is described as "challenging," be prepared to come up with examples of your own *dynamic* employment history.

> **TIP: Some companies place ads with phone numbers to make it easier for them to screen applicants. Be wary when the first question you're asked is "What is your current salary?" or "What type of salary are you looking for?" This is usually a tip-off that the job is low-level or low-paying.**

As you read the ad, note the main requirements for the job. Be sure your letter addresses each one of them, preferably in the first or second paragraph.

> **TIP: To make your letter read better and look less like a copy of the ad, rephrase the ad. Strike the same notes, but make it sound different. For example, if the ad calls for "an experienced, innovative, achievement-oriented manager," then you're "a forward-thinking manager with a proven record who can produce results." Then give specific examples.**

■ **No matter how interested you are, don't answer an ad on the same day it appears.**

Most people who respond to an ad are sending in their letters and resumes on the same day and the prospective employer will be inundated with mail. Wait a few days before sending your reply. Your resume won't arrive along with that mass of applications—and the prospective employer will pay more attention to it.

> TIP: **The best day to answer an ad you saw in the Sunday paper is the** *following* **Sunday. This might sound risky, but it works. Your letter will stand out.**

> TIP: **If you come across an ad weeks after it has appeared, answer it anyway. You have nothing to lose. Chances are the company is still interviewing applicants (especially if it is a higher-level position or requires advanced technical skills). Or there may be another opening coming up.**

One final note: If you're thinking about placing a "position wanted" ad—*don't.* Ads such as those draw little response and only waste your money.

SAMPLE RESPONSE TO A WANT AD

The ad reads: Executive Administrative Assistant
Join an expanding, prestigious investment bank. Requirements include high flexibility to meet challenges with a personal approach, top-notch communication skills, ability to prioritize and work well under pressure. Interact with top bank officers. Office management experience and excellent computer skills essential. Box 1234

The letter:

123 West Paces Ferry Rd.
Atlanta, GA 30305

Box 1234
The Atlanta Constitution
555 Peachtree Road
Atlanta, GA 30303

The Executive Administrative Assistant position described in your ad in the April 21st *Atlanta Constitution* sounds like a job custom-made for me.

For the past four years, I have been executive assistant to the president of Harper-Blankenship, a small brokerage house. This position entails a wide range of responsibilities—including serving as liaison between the president and other officers, as office manager, and as administrative assistant. I have day-to-day contact with our clients, who are chiefly pension-fund managers for several large corporations, and handle all of my own correspondence, as well as that of the president.

Having final responsibility for all administrative duties—including overseeing a clerical staff of five and generally ensuring that the office runs smoothly—has taught me to make decisions quickly and efficiently. In addition, by working in a fast-paced environment, I have developed the ability to switch gears swiftly, matching my actions to the needs of the moment.

I have a bachelor's degree in Business Administration from the University of Georgia. My hands-on computer knowledge includes experience using WordPerfect and several other word-processing programs, spreadsheet programs including Lotus 123 and Symphony, and specific financial programs.

Working as an executive assistant at Harper-Blankenship has been fulfilling, but it is time for a change and a move to a larger, and more stimulating, environment. This is what drew me to the position you described. Again, your ad was most interesting. I would like to interview with you for the Executive Administrative Assistant position and look forward to hearing from you soon.

Sincerely,

Angela Vezzetti

TARGETED DIRECT MAIL CAMPAIGN

Direct mail—sending job inquiry letters to a series of companies —takes more time and effort on your part, but the chances of success are greater than with most other tactics in a job search.

These are three basic steps:

- First, put together a list of select companies; get the names and company addresses of people to contact from directories, colleagues, etc.

- Then, write a cover letter that is individually targeted to each company in which you express your interest and ask for an interview.

- Finally, follow up by telephone. Call the people several weeks later and ask for an interview.

Compiling a Mailing List

■ **Making a *select* list is crucial.**

Don't confuse a targeted direct mail campaign with a mass mailing job search, where you may send a standardized letter to hundreds of companies. When you mass-mail resumes, you can't target yourself and your letters to the same degree. Sheer numbers prevent it. With a targeted direct mail campaign, on the other hand, you deliberately make your list short and select. The key strength is in having a narrow focus. You'll be selling yourself very specifically to each company you contact.

Some tested ideas on how to proceed:

- Your initial list should consist of ten to fifteen companies maximum. As you go along and get interviews (or rejections), add more companies to your list.

- If putting together a strong mailing list is difficult for you, consider buying a list from a trade publication that focuses on your specific needs. See page 161 for details.

- Research each company thoroughly. For this method to work, you should know what the company has been doing, any trends or recent developments, what they might be looking for.

- *Remember:* You are soliciting the company, not vice versa. There is absolutely no guarantee that any job openings exist. Keep track of industry trends. Which companies are hiring and which are cutting back? While you shouldn't base your list entirely on these factors, you should keep them in mind.

- Don't be overly idealistic when you select companies. Try to be practical about it, choosing the ones that both interest you *and* are reasonable goals. In other words, if you have only a little television experience, you're better off beginning with local affiliates rather than networks.

- Always address your letter to a specific individual, preferably the department head of the area in which you're interested. Get the right name by calling the company and asking. Say you're updating a mailing list. Don't send your letter to the president or CEO (unless you are aiming for a very high-level position). Letters directed too high get kicked down to personnel or tossed.

SAMPLE TARGETED DIRECT MAIL LETTER

Richard Griffin
Sales Manager
Aldus Corporation
666 Bayshore Drive
Palo Alto, CA 94303

Dear Mr. Griffin:

This is an exciting time for Aldus Inc. Under the leadership of the new management team, Aldus has seen unprecedented expansion and remarkable innovation. Now, with the introduction of the Vector System, Aldus is poised to dominate the computer systems universe. I am interested in joining the Aldus team—and helping you reach the market penetration I am sure you want.

For the past five years, I have been district manager for Zephyr Corporation. In this time period, sales in my district have jumped 27%—this, after a previous two-year slump. In addition, as district manager, I have:

- instituted a customer follow-up program that increased consumer confidence and improved market perception of Zephyr
- established new "core values" training for regional sales personnel, resulting in individual sales increases of up to 39%
- increased customer base from less than 4,000 to 17,000+

Prior to my promotion to district manager, I was a salesperson for three years. Among my chief accomplishments:

- won company "President's Award" given for exceeding sales quota by 100%—three years in a row
- took over flagging region and increased sales by 49%

I welcome the opportunity to deliver the same—or better—results for Aldus. I'll call you next Wednesday to set up a mutually convenient time to meet.

Sincerely,

Eric Sullivan

Writing a Direct Mail Cover Letter

■ **Think like a salesperson when you write your letter.**

Remember: The person reading the letter might not have any jobs open, but you want that person to interview you anyway. How can you generate enough *immediate* interest?

■ **Use a tried-and-true selling technique and set up a *needs payoff*.**

Salespeople use this technique all the time. First they show the customer that he or she has a problem, then they show the customer that they have the solution, which of course happens to be the product they are selling.

The best way to begin is by identifying a problem or need the employer has, one that you can meet. Openly state the situation and how you fit in. In other words, show that you know what the company needs and then show that you have the solution: yourself.

> **EXAMPLE:** "In the May 18th issue of *Stores* magazine, I read that the Dawson-Pickett management wants to revamp the store's image and merchandising in an effort to attract a younger, more fashion-forward customer, and turn around sales. Repositioning to capture the junior market is a challenge—and one that I've handled successfully in my twelve years in retail management. Most recently, I combined seasonal promotional activities with a heavy media presence to reposition a chain's established conservative image."
>
> *Note:* By referring to an article or a recent company trend, you also let the reader know this is a personalized letter, not a form letter.

> **TIP:** Career changers usually have a tougher time setting up a needs payoff. In today's tight job market, the tendency is for prospective employers to look only for people with backgrounds that fit perfectly. Take extra care to target yourself for the job. In the first paragraph of your letter, you must prove that you have the necessary qualifications and that your particular experience is what they need.

■ **Lead directly into a sales pitch, highlighting the experience and achievements you have to back up your claim.**

> **EXAMPLE:** "As fashion coordinator for Fashion Connection, a small chain of stores based in Florida, I designed a major promotional campaign timed to coincide with college students' spring break. I arranged in-store fashion shows, special tie-ins with various swimwear manufacturers, and ran advertisements on the Top 40-format radio stations. *Result:* Sales increased 37% for that period. In addition, store visibility went up and we reported a 24% rise in charge-card applications."

■ **Close on an upbeat note: restate both your ability to make a substantial contribution and the strength of your interest—then request an interview.**

> **EXAMPLE:** "These are the kind of results I can produce for Dawson-Pickett. I would like to get together to discuss my plans with you. I will call you next Thursday to set up a mutually convenient time."
>
> *Note:* Because the letter is unsolicited, it's best to take charge of the follow-up immediately and say you'll call for an interview, rather than say "I look forward to hearing from you."

Following Up by Telephone with a Direct Mail Campaign

■ **By following up with a phone call, you *more than double* your chances of getting an interview.**

Follow-up is the part of a direct-mail campaign that many people forget or deliberately avoid. Few people want to pick up the phone, call prospective employers, and sell themselves cold. It can be difficult, it can be frightening. But there is a very compelling reason why you should steel yourself and take the time to follow up: if you don't follow up, you drastically cut down your chances of having your mail campaign work. You will have wasted a huge amount of time and effort.

■ **Have a rough idea of the key sales points you want to make before you call.**

Start by prepping yourself. Keep a copy of the letter in front of you so that you know what you wrote and when you sent it. Decide what you want to emphasize during your call.

■ **Give your name and ask for the prospective employer in a direct, authoritative tone.**

Your first major hurdle will be reaching the right person. Typically, you will speak with a secretary whose job it is to run interference. To get around him or her, don't let on that you are a job hunter. If pressed for a reason for your call, tell the truth but not the whole truth: "I told him I would call," or "He is expecting my call," is usually effective.

> **TIP:** One job hunter got around cautious secretaries by referring in a brisk, businesslike way to the key point of his letter: "I'm calling with the marketing plans for XYZ's new product line." This was the absolute truth: the job hunter *did* have some plans about how to market the new product line; he had referred to them in his letter. But this presentation made it sound a shade more official. It almost always got him through to the right person.

> **TIP:** Although it's important that you reach prospective employers, don't go overboard in your efforts. *A few ploys to avoid:* Pulling people out of meetings; claiming you're calling on urgent, personal business; lying about who you are. You'll probably get the person on the line, but speaking to an irritated potential employer isn't your goal.

■ **Once you have reached the prospective employer, immediately refer to your letter.**

To make your call effective and to take advantage of limited time, don't merely say "I sent you a letter on such and such a date." Instead, refer to a specific aspect of the letter and resell yourself by repeating your strongest point.

> **EXAMPLE:** "Mr. Smith? This is Barbara Billings speaking. I wrote to you about my experience in updating images of fashion retail stores. In my letter of May seventeenth I mentioned how I increased sales for Fashion Connection. . . ."

■ **Briefly touch on the main points of your letter. Then get to your main objective: setting a date for an interview.**

> **TIP:** Don't quote your letter verbatim. You'll sound as though you're reading the letter or reciting from a prepared script. Instead, recap your letter with different wording.

EXAMPLE: "Some of the plans I put into effect for Fashion Connec-
tion would work well for Dawson-Pickett. I think you'd
be interested in seeing them, especially the ones that
captured the youth market on a small budget. What
would be a good time for us to meet—next Tuesday? Or
would Wednesday be better? I'm free either day."
Note: This tactic works especially well when you give
yourself a *reason* for arranging an interview by offering
to show something to the prospective employer (in this
case, the promotion plans).

■ **Be prepared for a hard sell.**

This prospective employer never asked you to call. You're the
instigator. As such, you must continually prove that you are worth
his or her time. Expect some employers to fend you off, and be ready
with comebacks. Don't get antagonistic, whatever the temptation.

Following are three typical telephone put-offs, and how to handle them.

1. "I don't recall the letter."

Refresh the prospective employer's mind *briefly* by referring to one
or two specific examples you mentioned in your letter. Don't rehash
the entire letter. If you still don't strike a chord, judge the situation
carefully. Either telemarket yourself into an interview or offer to
send another letter (never a copy!) or (best) do both.

EXAMPLE: "I discussed the promotional campaign and tie-ins I put
together when the store wanted to attract a different customer. One of them was a spring break promotion."
[The employer still doesn't remember.]
"I'll put another letter in the mail today that outlines my
background and a few of my successful campaigns. I'm
sure you'll be interested in hearing about the plans that
attracted the teen- and college-aged customer you're
after. Why don't I come in and show you the promotional
package I developed? I'm free next Tuesday—or would
Wednesday be more convenient?"

2. "I haven't gotten to the letter yet."

Make sure he or she actually has the letter, then offer to call back at
a later date.

> EXAMPLE: "I'll give you a call when you've had a chance to read it. Would Wednesday be all right with you? Or would Thursday be more convenient?"

3. "We're not hiring right now." (or we're cutting back, laying off, etc.)

This is difficult to handle. There's always the strong temptation to say "Fine. Thanks for your time," and hang up quickly. If you can, fight it. Get something out of your efforts. Tell the person you don't want a job, you want an interview—even just an *informational* interview. Once you're in his or her office you might be able to turn it around into a job or a job referral.

But if you're *truly* aggressive and sales-oriented, push on with your phone call. You can brazen it out with "I have some ideas I'm sure you'll be interested in that will help your company save money," and the like. As one large employer said, "We always have jobs for the right people, even if officially we're not hiring."

■ **No matter how well you sell yourself or how polished your techniques, you will still get rejections.**

While a targeted direct mail campaign is a strong tactic, it isn't failproof. If you do get rejections, work at not being bothered by them. *Remember:* With each rejection, you have a better idea of what employers want in a candidate; you are continually adding to your salesmanship. You are moving closer to getting an interview.

> TIP: If you consistently get rejections, rethink your strategy. Ask yourself: *Am I picking companies that are out of my league? Are my letters well-targeted? Am I reaching the right person in each company, or should I redirect my letter? Am I proving my qualifications?*

RESUME-BLITZING

■ **Resume-blitzing is a widespread, shotgun approach to a direct mail campaign.**

With this method, you use an extensive mailing list consisting of hundreds of companies in your general field of interest, and mail cover letters (usually called broadcast letters) along with resumes to all of them.

Many job hunters automatically think this method of papering the town with their resumes is the only logical way to land a job. The more resumes that go out to more companies, the better the odds, is the reasoning behind it. Consequently, it is one of the most common methods of job hunting. But you should think twice before you do this. *Take into account the following:*

> **Fact #1:** The typical Fortune 500 company receives over a quar-ter of a million *unsolicited* resumes a year. Yours will be just another one joining the slush pile.
>
> **Fact #2:** The average success rate of a mail campaign, i.e., get-ting a call for an interview, is 2%.

The success rate isn't as high as a targeted direct mail campaign for a very simple reason: *focus.* Because you are sending letters to hundreds of companies, by necessity, you are forced to send a form letter. You won't have time to write or send anything else. *Result:* You can't set up a specific needs payoff that grabs a prospective employ-er's interest.

Another disadvantage is that mass-mailing can cost quite a bit of money. Printing and mailing hundreds of resumes adds up. And if you purchase a mailing list, the cost mounts even higher. In addition, follow-up is difficult and time-consuming—when it's possible.

Conclusion: In most cases, launching a resume blitz isn't worth the time, cost, and effort. If you want to do a resume mailing, you're much better off with a targeted direct mail campaign.

Consider resume-blitzing only if:

- you're a recent college graduate seeking a management trainee or entry-level position

- you can sell yourself to a broad range of companies because your job target is so basic

- your job objective is so unique and your experience so well-matched, you don't need to target yourself

If you fit into any one of these categories, if you don't have the time or energy to do a targeted mail campaign, and if you are pre-pared for a large number of rejections or no replies, a resume blitz can be worthwhile.

Blitzing does have one selling point for all of its drawbacks: it isn't a complicated method to master. You have to concern yourself with three steps: setting up a mailing list, writing a letter, and managing and tracking the campaign.

Setting Up a Mailing List for a Resume Blitz

■ **To set up a mailing list you have two basic options: put a mailing list together yourself or buy a preexisting list from a publication in your field, or from a mailing-list company (see page 162).**

The mailing list is the heart of a resume blitz. To compile your own list, use the library as a start-off point. Your main sources will be reference directories and trade publications. If you are planning a job hunt that will focus mainly on Fortune 500 companies and the like, you can put together a list in the library with little trouble. (See Chapter 3, "Research," for specific information, techniques, and sources.)

> **TIP:** Virtually every industry publication puts out a special issue that lists the top companies in the field. Check for those "round-up" or "top 500 companies" issues: they are excellent sources for addresses and often list the names of executives. For example, *Advertising Age* puts out a Top Media Companies issue.

> **TIP:** A best bet for free mailing lists is trade associations. Check the associations in your field. Most professional groups put out an annual membership directory or roster, listing member names, affiliations, addresses, and phone numbers. *Asset:* Because associations have a widespread membership mix, the chances are good you'll get the names of people you want to write to. *Drawback:* Lists are often arranged alphabetically by member name. You have to rely on the index to find the appropriate companies.

Recent college graduates and MBAs should check the following publications, which are specifically designed to help them look for a job:

Peterson's Business & Management Jobs
Peterson's Guides
Princeton, NJ 08540
—lists employment opportunities at over 400 companies; listings include name, address, profile, contact name and phone number, starting salaries, requirements

Peterson's Guide to Engineering, Science and Computer Jobs
—lists employment opportunities at over 1,000 manufacturing, research, consulting, and government organizations

If you can afford the expense and *aren't* planning a general Fortune 500-type of company search, buy a preexisting mailing list. What you spend in money, you make up for in terms of time and effort saved.

Mailing lists are available from a number of sources: commercial mailing houses specializing in lists, newspapers and magazines, credit card companies, direct mail houses, and more. Compare prices and lists to find the best deal for you. At the end of this section we've included the names of the larger mailing list companies.

Before you buy a list, be sure it meets the following criteria:

- It is targeted to your area of interest. (Although you want an extensive list, a list that is too general is a waste of money.)

- It is current. (Lists over a year old often have outdated addresses, phone numbers, and executive names.)

- It includes the names and titles of the company executives who would hire you. (Many lists have only top corporate officers included, names which are useless for resume mailing purposes.)

- It is indexed for cross-referencing purposes. (You can arrange your list according to geographical location, company earnings, however you choose.)

■ **The best source for a preexisting mailing list that meets the necessary criteria is trade publications.**

Most trade publications sell their subscriber lists. These lists are ideal for a resume mailing because they are aimed directly at your targeted group of prospective employers. Usually the circulation department breaks out the lists into different classifications: job title, chief responsibilities, type of business, company products or services, geographical locations, company size, salary level, and more. Because of the numerous categories, you can make your mailing list as general or as specific as you want. For example, you can put together a list of marketing managers of mid-sized sporting goods manufacturers in the Midwest. Or you can make a general list of all managers in sporting goods companies across the country.

For information on other mailing lists that are available to buy, check the following directories:

Direct Mail List Rates and Data
Standard Rate & Data Service
3004 Glenview Rd.
Wilmette, IL 60091
312/256-6067
—over 50,000 mailing lists of business people and companies, consumers, etc.
—title and description of lists, name, address, phone number, name of contact

The Polk Mailing List Catalog
R. L. Polk & Company
2001 Elm Hill Pike
Box 1340
Nashville, TN 37202
615/889-3350
—over 900 listings

Writing a Broadcast Letter for a Resume Blitz

■ **The letter you write for a resume blitz is called a broadcast letter because it broadcasts your availability to a large audience.**

While you cover the same ground in a broadcast letter that you do in any other job-hunt letter (stating your job objective, highlighting your qualifications, requesting an interview), a broadcast letter has to be designed to appeal to the greatest number of prospective employers possible.

The best part about this method is that you only have to write the letter once. That one letter will be duplicated and sent to your entire mailing list. But you *don't* want this to be obvious. Employers, like everyone else, prefer letters that address their particular needs and desires, not some general "To whom it may concern" mailing. This is why you should know the tricks that will make your letter read as though it were written for an audience of one, not hundreds.

■ **Your opening paragraph is crucial in making your letter *appear* as personalized and specific as possible.**

Remember: Avoid overly canned openings, especially ones that read like advertising copy: *"No one thought I could do it—but I did. Generated profits in a business that had been losing money for ten successive years, that is . . ."*

Openings like this are catchy, but they communicate one thing more than anything else: "This is my formula sales pitch letter that tells you how great I am, which I'm sending to everyone and anyone." Even if this might be true, don't let prospective employers know it.

Instead try to personalize your letter by focusing it as much as possible. You won't be able to write about specific developments at each company on the list, but you can opt for the next best targeting mechanism: *industry* trends. Zero in on your job objective by discussing your area of interest and what's been happening in the field, and then state your qualifications.

> **EXAMPLE: "As corporate cutbacks become more and more common, the role of a human resources manager is becoming more and more challenging. Outplacement counseling, in particular, has become a vital function, and an area in which I have special expertise."**

SAMPLE BROADCAST LETTER

542 Lowe St.
Ridgewood, NJ 07450

Mr. Oscar Gordon
Vice-President of Production
The Heinlein Company
100 Caltech Drive
Pasadena, CA 91106

Dear Mr. Gordon:

American companies need tight-fisted, cost-cutting professionals to streamline inventory procedures and compete more effectively.

As corporate budgets get tighter, the role of a cost-conscious scheduling supervisor becomes more and more vital. I know this from extensive experience. Over the past five years as a Supervisor for Production Control with a Fortune 500 company, I have slashed inventory budgets and streamlined operational procedures. More specifically, I have:

· saved company over $100,000 by introducing and overseeing new obsolescence policy on local inventories.
· introduced new inventory handling procedures reducing inventory costs by 5% per year.
· selected from management training team to be sole office representative for feasibility study of "Just in Time Inventory" program review.
· awarded three Manager's Certificates of Outstanding Achievement.

I have a bachelors degree from Dulwich College, and am currently completing course work for my Master's in Business Administration at Fairleigh Dickinson University.

I'd like the opportunity to apply my skills in inventory management to a market leader such as your company and look forward to your call. I have many specific ideas on how to effectively cut inventory costs that I would like to discuss with you.

Sincerely,

John Lerner

■ **The remainder of your letter should be the same as any other cover letter you've written: a sales pitch and a close.**

Managing and Tracking a Resume Blitz Mass Mailing

■ **Divide your list into workable units: an "A" list, "B" list, and "C" list.**

To make a large direct mail campaign work harder for you, roll it out in stages: in this case Stages A, B, and C. This allows you to track the success of the mailing and modify your approach as you go along.

■ **Start by sending your letter and resume to the companies that are specialists in your area or those that particularly interest you: your "A" list.**

> TIP: Don't concentrate only on large "name-brand" companies. Often smaller to mid-sized companies that are less well-known turn up stronger responses because the competition for jobs is less. One job hunter did a resume blitz with two distinct letters and lists: one for well-known companies, the other for those that are less known.

> TIP: Address your mailing to the people who would be your supervisors, not to the personnel, training, or employment department. If you aren't sure of the right name or title, call and ask the switchboard operator or receptionist for the name and title of the person who heads up the appropriate department.

Because your "A" list consists of your primary targets, give it priority. After your first mailing, wait a week or two, then follow up. Don't wait for the companies to call you, call them.

> TIP: Use your mailing list to keep track of your mailing. Beside each company name, note the date you sent out the letter, the date of your follow-up call, the date you received a response, and anything that happens. Even jot down the times when you've tried calling, but have spoken with a secretary and couldn't reach the addressee. This is especially handy when you speak with the people you've sent letters to—you can refer to specific dates and information.

▪ **Make follow-up phone calls.**

You can bring your success rate up to 10%, which is far better than the normal low 2% rate.

In your follow-up call, refer to the date you sent the letter, briefly touch on the contents, and restate your job objective and desire for an interview. If you can't get an interview, ask for further information about the company or the names of other people to whom you should write. Don't let the phone call end your campaign. Use it for referrals to add to your list.

▪ **Send out your "B" and "C" list mailings when you start getting responses from your original mailing.**

If you are having no luck getting interviews, consider changing your letter or adding to your list. Continue tracking responses and making additions to the list.

Blitz Do's and Don't's:

- *Don't* send photocopies or obvious form letters. Although this is a large mailing, you should be hiding that fact as much as possible.

- *Do* use a computer to run off your letters, instead of having them professionally set. A typeset letter looks better than a photocopy, but it's expensive and ends up saying the same thing: this isn't unique.

- *Don't* send more than one copy of your letter to the same company. You never know who will pass your letter around and who will wind up seeing it.

- *Do* match resume and letter stock. And use a simple, readable typeface and layout.

TEMPORARY WORK

▪ **If you have the time (if you are currently unemployed or have only a part-time job), seriously consider working as a temporary employee as a way of eventually getting a permanent job.**

"Temping" *isn't* what many people think it is. It can be one of the best ways to position yourself for a job—whatever your job objective. It isn't simply secretarial work and it isn't just interim employment that can help pay the bills while you're looking for a job. Temping (or free-lancing, consulting, contract work, or special project work) *is* a successful job hunting tactic—if you know how to make it work for you.

> **EXAMPLE: A systems analyst was laid off during a slump in the high-tech field. He sent his resume to several companies and was called back by one computer manufacturer. No full-time jobs were available, but they needed someone to work on a short-term, special project. A two-month job wasn't what he wanted, but he took the project anyway and did his best. When it was finished, he moved on, but his efficient work was remembered. A month later, he got a phone call and was offered a permanent job at the computer company.**

Because the number of temporary workers and the range of available jobs is growing at such a fast rate, you can find or create a temp job in virtually any field: not only in office staff positions, but also in technical and managerial positions. Financial consultants, accountants, engineers, computer systems specialists, publicists, lawyers, even doctors, are hired on a temporary basis.

Temping is especially recommended if:

- you have little or no experience in your targeted field.

- you are seeking an entry-level job in a "glamour" profession, such as advertising, publishing, broadcasting, film, and the like.

- your target company isn't hiring.

- you are a career changer, student or recent graduate, or are reentering the labor market.

A few initial guidelines:

- The simplest way to start temping is by going through an agency. Speak with a number of employment agencies to find out what type of companies they handle. Ask for specific company names: the more you know about an agency's clients, the better you can judge its potential to help you get a job.

> TIP: Check to see if the agency is a member of the National Association of Temporary Services (NATS), which establishes guidelines for the temporary services industry.

- Pay particular attention to agencies with specialties: they work especially well for people seeking nonsecretarial work. For example, New York-based Accountemps specializes in placing accountants; Chicago-based LAW/temps places lawyers.

- Move beyond agencies once you've started temp work. Spread the word that you are available for free-lance work. Create your own temp network of clients. This is often the best way of getting temp positions that will lead to bigger and better things.

Following is a discussion of some of the best uses of temping.

A "Back Door" Method of Landing a Job

This is the most valuable way to use temping. By getting inside a company and meeting prospective customers face-to-face, you avoid the problem of having to openly contact a company with the standard resume/letter. You can sell yourself in person rather than on paper.

It is ideal for people seeking entry-level positions, especially in the "glamour" industries. Since industries such as advertising, film, and broadcasting are continually flooded with resumes, your best bet for winning an interview is by getting inside the company *first*—in any capacity.

> EXAMPLE: All three television networks were in the midst of a hiring freeze. A woman who wanted to work in casting took a job as a temporary secretary at one of the networks just to get her foot in the door. Her strategy worked. She impressed people with her skills, talked about her extensive experience in the film industry, and got offered a full-time job—*while the hiring freeze was still on.*

> TIP: If you are offered a temp job at a company you want to work for, but in the wrong department—take it anyway. Once you're inside, you can learn more about the department you want to join.

To make a temp position lead to an interview for a permanent job, *you must make sure that people know about you, your qualifications, and your ambitions.* No one at the company will be aware of your goals until you begin to tell them. Speak up, volunteer for extra assignments and, in general, show that you are ambitious, dedicated, and focused on your goal. This is no time to be shy. Find out who can hire you and make certain you introduce yourself to those people.

It's important to remember that temp jobs are just that: *temporary.* You have to take advantage of whatever time you have.

> **TIP: A good, subtle way to impress prospective employers is by doing your work accurately and efficiently, no matter how low-level. Don't make the mistake of thinking temp work is beneath you or unimportant. Doing a good job on even the most minor task is often noticed.**
>
> ***Better yet:* Do a little extra work—and make sure the right people know about it. Stay at the office an extra five minutes to type a letter or finish a project. It will make you look like a committed, hardworking employee—the kind of employee a prospective employer would want to hire.**

Learning Inside Information About a Company or Industry that Will Increase Your Salability

Temping gives you the opportunity to see *exactly* how to target yourself in a resume, letter, or interview. Instead of immediately setting yourself up as a potential job candidate, keep your eyes and ears open, and scout out a company or industry.

> **TIP: Don't be overly selective about the companies you work in, particularly at the beginning. Temping anywhere in your field can pay off: you'll still get information about the industry, discover the types of jobs available, and so on. In addition, sometimes working for a competitor is the best place to hear gossip about the company in which you're most interested.**

Listen to office talk for insights into what is happening at a company. Many times the grapevine is the best place to hear about upcoming events, what jobs may be opening, what managers are leaving the company, and so forth. Pick up clues about the corporate culture. Even small things can help you sell yourself: Is the atmosphere casual, informal? Does management expect people to work late hours or on weekends? Apply whatever you learn to your cover letter and interview techniques.

> **EXAMPLE:** When a young woman temped at a magazine, she learned that the company was very bullish on corporate sporting events. Later, when she sent them a targeted cover letter, she made sure to mention her involvement in different sports: specifically, how she coached a company softball team and ran in a city-wide corporate-challenge race. She got an interview, and a job offer. The interviewer commented on how well she would fit into the company.

Adding to Your Skills and Qualifications

Temping is especially helpful for people reentering the work force, career changers, and those with little formal work experience.

In effect, let temping train you and make you more employable. Working as a temp allows you to fill out your background *before* and *during* your job hunt. Pinpoint the areas where you have gaps or trouble spots and look for temp positions that will help diminish them.

> **EXAMPLE:** A career changer was having no luck switching from government work to publishing because he had no experience in the new field except for a few college courses he had taken years before. After months of fruitless searching, many targeted mailings, and following leads through networking, he decided to take free-lance work as a proofreader and copy editor. *Result:* His free-lance assignments gave him credibility. After listing publishers he had worked for in cover letters, and mentioning his work to contacts, he soon landed a full-time position at a large New York publishing house.

> **TIP:** If you are changing your career, reentering the work force, or have little experience, be sure to include temp jobs that relate to your job objective in your cover letter. You don't have to identify them as short-term jobs. Instead, emphasize functions, duties, and accomplishments.

Increasing Your Network of Contacts

The people you meet through temping make excellent contacts, especially those people in upper and middle management positions. Even if you don't get a job at one particular company, recognize that the people you meet there are potential sources of job leads and referrals.

Ask people about job opportunities at their company and in the industry in general, and if they can suggest other contacts or offer some general advice. Cultivate the people who are in jobs similar to your objective and those who directly supervise them. Both groups can give you the most insightful tips.

For more information on temporary work and agencies:

National Association of Temporary Services (NATS)
119 S. St. Asaph Street
Alexandria, VA 22314
703/549-6287
—establishes guidelines for member agencies
—publishes an annual directory that lists member agencies, and other informational brochures and booklets about temporary work

Prominent agencies with offices nationwide:
ADIA Personnel
64 Willow Place
Menlo Park, CA 94025
415/324-0696

Kelly Services
999 West Big Beaver Rd.
Troy, MI 48084
313/362-4444

Manpower
5301 North Ironwood Rd.
Milwaukee, WI 53217
414/961-1000
Mailing Adddress: P.O.Box 2053
Milwaukee, WI 53201

Uniforce
1335 Jericho Turnpike
New Hyde Park, NY 11040
516/437-3300

Western Temporary Services, Inc.
301 Lennon Lane
Walnut Creek, CA 94598
415/930-5300

EXECUTIVE RECRUITERS

■ **Executive recruiters (also called executive search firms or head-hunters) are hired by corporations to find them the "right person" for a *specific* job opening.**

Executive recruiters differ from regular employment agencies in that they usually handle higher-level positions requiring very specific experience: you don't just walk through the door and wind up with four interviews.

In addition, the positions that search firms handle are ones that aren't advertised in the media or broadcast throughout a company or industry. Often these positions are the top jobs in a field. Typically, they are in mid- to upper-level management, commanding a minimum salary of roughly $50,000. If you are seeking a job that pays less than that, odds are you should go to an employment agency (see page 177) rather than expect a call from a headhunter.

There are two different types of executive recruiters: general firms, which handle positions across a range of professions, and specialist firms, which focus on a specific field or industry.

■ **If you currently hold or are seeking a job in mid- to upper-level management, you should try to get your resume on file with several executive recruiters that specialize in your field.**

It is one of the best ways of landing interviews for jobs that you might never hear about in the so-called "hidden" job market. An added plus—you don't have to do the initial selling of yourself. It is the recruiter's job to sell you into an interview situation, then it's up to you to sell yourself in person.

■ **Your chief concern with executive recruiters is getting one interested in you.**

The top executive recruiters receive over 10,000 unsolicited resumes a year. Only a small percentage of these resumes stays in the firm's files. The rest are thrown away.

Remember: Executive recruiters are not in business to find people jobs. They are hired by corporations to find people to fill specific positions. That makes for a small, select pool of potential candidates that search firms will contact. *You* have to work to get yourself into that pool.

Attracting Executive Recruiters

■ **The most foolproof method of being actively sought out and promoted by headhunters is the simplest: already having a job that is similar to the ones the recruiters are trying to fill.**

In light of that, it's a good idea to cultivate a relationship with a recruiter *before* you start an intensive job search. Most middle managers get about two to four calls a year from executive recruiters. The next time one calls you, talk to him or her even if you don't want the position offered. Find out what other openings the recruiter has or may have in the future; mention that you are interested in moving to another job; sound out the prospects.

One of the best moves you can make is to position yourself as an *information source*—give the recruiter names of potential candidates, tips about your company, possible openings, and other people to contact who might be interested in changing jobs.

> **TIP:** To attract executive recruiters, join trade associations and professional organizations. Search firms often use them as resources and ask members for referrals. As an attention-grabber, write articles for trade journals or association newsletters.

> **TIP:** Re-contact any recruiter who has previously called you. If he or she has been interested in you in the past, chances are you can get him or her interested again. Explain that you are now actively job hunting and suggest a brief meeting.

■ **If the phone *doesn't* ring, or if you don't have the time or patience to wait for recruiters to contact you, it's time to take a more active role and directly solicit the recruiters themselves.**

Frankly, your success rate in attracting recruiters will depend a great deal on blind luck and good timing, for instance, whether a recruiter gets your letter the same day that he or she has a job opening requiring someone with your exact background. But you can create your own "luck" by knowing the right notes to hit with a recruiter.

A few guidelines on choosing which executive recruiters to approach:

- Ask people in your field for suggestions of recruiters to contact. Often they will be your best and most objective source.

- Have a friend or colleague who is regularly contacted by recruiters mention your name and suggest that the recruiter contact you. *Or:* Ask if you can use your friend's name as a reference when you call the recruiter. A personal reference can increase your chances of getting the attention you want.

- Recruiters are assigned to different specialties within a search firm—even if the firm is focused on only one industry. Always find out who is responsible for your specific area of interest at the firm and address your letter accordingly. There is less of a chance that your letter will be tossed aside.

- Be selective. Don't send a letter and resume to hundreds or even dozens of recruiters. It isn't worth your money or time.

Selling Yourself to Recruiters

■ **Convince recruiters that you are worth their attention by sending them a targeted cover letter with your resume.**

A cover letter to executive recruiters should be similar to any other letter you write during your job hunt: as specifically targeted to the reader as possible, emphasizing your strongest points, and closing with a brief summary and request to meet.

However, unlike typical cover letters, this one isn't an attempt to "tease" a headhunter into wanting to know more about you. Instead, prove to a recruiter that you fit the firm's criteria, that you are the type of person the firm's clients would want to hire.

To write a cover letter that will sell you to recruiters:

- Spell out *why* you are the type of candidate they already recommend to clients. Leave little to the reader's imagination. Be clear, concise, focused, and thorough. Catchy openings and clever phrases are absolutely out. Explain what you're looking for, why you are interested in a new position, and what your qualifications are.

- Unlike other cover letters, a letter to a search firm *can* include your target salary range. Let the recruiter know you fit the firm's range.

- Let recruiters see how they can sell you to their clients. Give recruiters the ammunition they need by listing specific examples of your salable achievements in the second or third paragraph of your letter. Choose more examples than you would in a typical cover letter. Lift details from your resume. Bullet the examples to make them leap off the page.

- Keep in mind: Headhunters search for people to fit very specific jobs, so often your best chance of making a match is by having a *unique* blend of qualities, abilities, and experiences. Make yourself stand out from other people in your field or position. Try to come up with *unusual* characteristics or abilities that will peg you as more of an individual.

> **EXAMPLE: An ex-government employee was having problems switching careers to finance. As a last-ditch effort, he sent to recruiters letters that mentioned his MBA but strongly highlighted his negotiating experience and his ability to speak two dialects of Chinese fluently. Three headhunters contacted him, each for financial sales positions that required a fluency in Chinese.**

Following Up with Recruiters

■ **Don't call recruiters to follow up on your mailing.**

This is one time when follow-up phone calls are just a waste of your time. The reason is simple: recruiters can't help you unless they have a position that matches your qualifications. If no such position exists, you won't gain a thing by trying to push yourself into their office.

■ **If you've heard nothing four to six months after you've contacted a recruiter, try again.**

After a reasonable period of time, send out another letter and resume. This time the recruiter might have an opening you match.

Interviewing with Recruiters

■ **Typically, your first encounter with an executive recruiter is on the phone. He or she calls to tell you about a job opening, and in doing so is *screening* you for a possible interview.**

Recruiters will first tell you a little about the job, check to see if you're interested and qualified, then ask you questions about your employment history, achievements, and objective. This is the time for you to ask questions as well. While you can't expect the recruiter to tell you the company's name, you *can* expect to find out other information that can help you determine if it's the right job for you.

> **TIP:** If you get an unsolicited call from a recruiter, make certain the firm is legitimate and useful to you by asking what type of firm it is, where they got your name, and the kind of companies the recruiter handles. *Don't* agree to send in your resume until you are satisfied that the firm and offer are legitimate.

> **TIP:** Always doublecheck about confidentiality if you're currently employed.

■ **If the screening interview goes well, you're on to the next step: a face-to-face meeting with the recruiter.**

The recruiter will want to go into more depth about your accomplishments when you see him or her in person. But you should also be prepared to answer more philosophical questions, ones that are designed to help the recruiter understand you and see if you'd mesh with the client company. Expect questions like: What kind of corporate culture do you prefer? In what work environment do you produce your best efforts? What has given you the most personal satisfaction—both in work and in your nonprofessional life?

A few general tips:

• You're better off being completely straightforward when you deal with recruiters. Lying about qualifications, or even your interest in a particular job opening, won't help you and, in fact, will probably hurt you in the long run.

• Be candid about *your* requirements for a job: from salary to corporate culture to responsibilities. This information will help recruiters decide if you're suitable for the opening they have in mind. The more guidance you can give them, the more accurately they can assess your needs.

- *Remember:* You want to cultivate a relationship with an executive recruiter. Even if you aren't asked to interview with a client, you've moved ahead in your job hunt by establishing ties with a recruiter. As suggested earlier, maintain these ties by becoming a valuable source: offer inside information about your field, suggest candidates for openings, etc. Keep up the relationship even after you have found a job.

To find names and addresses of executive recruiters, check the following:

Directory of Executive Recruiters
Kennedy & Kennedy, Inc.
Templeton Road
Fitzwilliam, NH 03447
603/585-2200
—This is the definitive directory, listing over 1,800 recruiters complete with addresses, principal names, specializations and minimum salaries.
—It also includes helpful information on how to use recruiters (from both the client and job hunter points of view).

Executive Employment Guide
American Management Association
135 West 50th Street
New York, NY 10020
212/586-8100
—Lists executive search firms, employment agencies, job registers and career counselors.
—In addition to name, address, and phone number, entries include specializations, types of jobs handled and minimum salary ranges, policies on resumes and interviews.

Association of Executive Search Consultants (AESC)
151 Railroad Avenue
Greenwich, CT 06830
203/661-6606
—Publishes a list of member search firms.

EMPLOYMENT AGENCIES

- **Employment agencies, like executive recruiters, are contracted by companies to find candidates for job openings. Unlike recruiters,**

agencies usually deal with a wide variety of positions, from secretarial to middle management.

There are basically two kinds of employment agencies: *general employment agencies,* which normally handle entry-level, secretarial, and non-management or lower-management positions in the $25,000 to $30,000 salary range; and *specialist employment agencies,* which handle anything from entry-level up to and including middle-management positions. Specialist agencies are a better bet for anyone seeking a position above entry-level or secretarial slots, and cover a large number of fields from publishing to accounting to engineering.

■ **Unless you are aiming at an upper-level management position, it makes sense to sign up with at least two to four agencies.**

Because employment agencies generally don't handle the upper-management positions or the highly exclusive spots that executive recruiters do, they are easier to contact and use in a job hunt.

Contacting Agencies

- Avoid general employment agencies if you have a lot of previous work experience. An agency that specializes in your field will probably have many more opportunities available to you than one that's more generalized.

- Ask friends and colleagues for recommendations of specific agencies, perhaps ones they have used for their own job hunt or ones they have used through their company. Be sure to get the names of individual counselors to contact.

- Call the personnel departments or office managers of companies in your field and ask them which agencies they have used. This will give you a good sense of which agencies work with which companies.

- Whenever possible, contact agencies directly by phone and save yourself some waiting time. If you don't have the name of a counselor, ask for the person who handles jobs in your specialty area.

- Avoid contacting agencies on Sunday, Monday, and Tuesday. Because of the number of ads that are run in the Sunday classifieds, agencies are busiest on those three days. Wait until Wednesday to call. You'll be given closer attention and won't be slotted as another desperate job seeker.

When You Get to an Employment Agency

- Ask the counselor questions to be sure the agency will work well for you. Find out the names of the companies it works with; whether it has successfully placed other candidates with backgrounds similar to yours; and the types of jobs it usually handles.

- Carefully read any contract you're given. You should expect to pay nothing for job-placement assistance: agency fees are normally paid by the companies. Be on the lookout for hidden costs tacked on for extra services, such as resume-writing and reviewing, job-counseling, etc. It's better to see an independent career counselor for those services.

- Beware of agencies that ask you to sign contracts immediately, demand money up front, guarantee placement, or boast of placement rates upward of 90%. There has been a recent increase in the number of fraudulent agencies that prey on desperate job seekers with such practices and stories; most reputable agencies report far lower success rates and don't push you into signing up.

- If you want a nonsecretarial position (entry-level or management trainee) but are still asked to take a typing test, think twice before working with that agency. The agency may be trying to pass off secretarial jobs or dead-end administrative assistant positions as trainee positions when they're not. *A major exception:* Entry-level positions in the communications area (television, radio, publishing, advertising, etc.) usually require typing skills. In addition, taking a low-level secretarial job may be the best way to break into these "glamour" professions.

Once You've Signed Up with an Employment Agency

- Don't be intimidated by a counselor who tries to push you into having job interviews that don't fit in with your job objective. If you find yourself being pressured into them, consider switching agencies or asking for a different counselor.

- If a position comes up that isn't exactly what you want, but is in the right field or company, have the interview anyway. Use it to practice your techniques. Afterward, you can ask the counselor for feedback: what did the employer think of you, what problems arose, is there any one area of your presentation that needs work, etc. You then can apply this information to more important interviews.

- Don't wait for the agency to contact you. Make it a habit to check in periodically and see what's happening. It refreshes the counselor's memory and increases your chances of being remembered when something suitable comes in.

- Consider switching agencies if you have no results after a few weeks. Counselors often start easing up on their efforts to place you if they haven't done so in a short time. If you sense this is the case (the counselor is unavailable to meet with you; no interviews are forthcoming; you rarely get through to speak with the counselor), you are better off starting fresh with a new agency than sticking with the old.

For further information, check with:

National Association of Personnel Consultants (NAPC)
1432 Duke Street
Alexandria, VA 22314
703/684-0180
—Publishes *Access,* a directory of member employment agencies that is organized by specialty and geographical location.

RECRUITING DATABASES

■ **Using computer databases and going online with your resume is the newest method of looking for a job.**

In general, it's a good idea to find out about the available recruiting databases. The process is relatively new, which makes it difficult to determine how successful it is, but the costs and effort on your part are minimal and the outcome might well be a job interview.

■ **There are three basic services offered by recruiting databases: resume-listing, job-listing and a combination of the two.**

With *resume-listing services,* you send your resume to a recruiting database, they put it online, and prospective employers search through the listings to find potential candidates. While you have no control over the number of prospective employers who will read your resume, it's an excellent idea to have your resume seen online. It gives you good exposure and costs little, if any, money or time.

If you have access to a computer, consider searching a *job-listing service.* Essentially these databases are computerized help-wanted ads. Job openings are listed online and you browse through the want ads as you would flip through a newspaper's classified section. *One drawback:* In many cases, these databases get their information from ads in newspapers, trade journals, and other publications, so the information may be dated—and the jobs already filled.

Some databases offer both services: you can list your resume with them, as well as search through available job listings.

To find a database that might work for you, be sure to check:

- which companies use it
- the sort of positions it lists or fills (A great many recruiter databases are still focused on technical and computer jobs.)
- the cost
- the number of resumes on file
- how many successful job placements it has made

Some of the more prominent recruiting databases include:

Adline
Business People, Incorporated
100 North 7th Street
Minneapolis, MN 55403
612/370-0550
—Listings of want ads from high-tech employers; no fee
—Can browse through the ads, then connect with a company's personnel department and transmit your resume

Career Placement Registry
302 Swann Avenue
Alexandria, VA 22301

703/683-1085
800/368-3093
—Resume-listing service; resume is listed for six months, a year for college seniors
—Cost is minimal—from $12 for students to $45 for people in the $40,000+ salary range
—Roughly 400 companies a month request resumes

CSI Career Network
Computer Search International Corp.
7200 Rutherford Rd.
Baltimore, MD 21207
301/664-1000, 265-1020
—Job-listing service used primarily by executive recruiters
—Pools resumes and job openings from about 500 search firms
—Resume submissions are accepted for possible inclusion at no cost
—Subscribers to The Source can scan job openings

Delphi
General Videotex Corporation
3 Blackstone St.
Cambridge, MA 02139
800/544-4005
—A popular system that offers a combination service listing both situation-wanted and help-wanted ads
—For a one time $49.95 fee, you can place an ad and browse through openings
—A wide area of fields covered, including: finance, sales and marketing, hotel/restaurant management, engineering

Online Careers
Information Intelligence, Inc.
P.O. Box 31098
Phoenix, AZ 85046
602/996-2283 or 800/228-9982
—Lists job categories in the information systems field

7 *Interviews*

Everything you've been doing in your job hunt—putting together the strongest possible resume, researching companies, setting up a network of contacts, writing cover letters, and trying out different selling tactics—has been leading to this point: the interview with a prospective employer that lands you the *job*.

The interview stage of your job search is the most crucial. You can make or break your chances of being hired in the short amount of time it takes to be interviewed. With so much at stake, many people lose their winning edge. They may have been successful up to now, but put them in a chair opposite a prospective employer and all is lost.

It doesn't have to be so difficult. *Anyone can learn to interview well.* Most mistakes that are made can be corrected, most techniques can be learned.

Interviewing effectively means commanding better interviewing skills; listening to suggestions that others may have; reading about interviewing; going back over past interviews in your head and analyzing what you did wrong, then thinking of ways to improve your performance; and, most important, *going out on as many interviews as you can to practice and refine your technique.* The more interviews you go on, the better your odds at getting the job offers you want. It may not be easy, but it's the best way to achieve interviewing success.

GENERAL GUIDELINES

Before we talk about how to interview, let's consider a few facts about interviewing itself:

- You can get a job without a resume, but you can't get a job without an interview.
- The interviewer often makes the conclusive decision about you in the first three to five minutes of the interview. However "open-minded" he or she may try to be, the rest of the interview is often spent simply justifying that first impression.
- The interviewer is more influenced by your negatives than your positives. If the recruiter changes his or her mind about you during the interview, it's usually for the worse.
- Your interpersonal skills are more important than your background, experience, or education.
- Most people don't talk enough during an interview. Instead of taking charge of selling themselves, they allow the interviewer to ask all the questions, and content themselves with just answering them. They *respond*, they don't *initiate*.

Before you create your own interviewing style, keep in mind what the following facts mean:

1. *The best interviewees do it fast.* They set the tone of the interview in the first few minutes, then spend the rest of the time enhancing what they've said. This requires that you have a strong idea about what you're going to say before you say it, which can only be accomplished through preparation. You must practice your presentation, and learn as much as you can about the company, interviewer, and position before the interview.

2. *An interview is in some ways unfair.* Who can figure you out in five minutes? Or even two hours? Instead of worrying about it, let it work for you. Don't let interviews intimidate you—at best they're an imperfect way of accepting or rejecting an *impression* of you, not who you really are. So you should create a strong, straightforward, first impression. If you're shy and meek—no problem. Just try to make a less shy, less meek first impression. Work on gradually improving yourself—and you will succeed. Effort counts.

3. *Think about your negatives before the interview, and have answers ready that will explain them sufficiently if they're discovered.* Unfortunately,

people pay more attention to negatives than to positives. The trick is to either keep them hidden or be able to explain them away.

4. *Recognize what an interview is and what it isn't.* It is not a rehashing of your resume, nor is it merely an opportunity to answer questions that an interviewer may pose; interviewing is salesmanship. It is *selectively presenting the facts in an organized, confident manner* so that you can sell yourself into a job. This means that *you* must take control of your interview. The people who get job offers are the people who do the talking. Quiet, passive people *do* get job offers, but assertive people get more. They come across as effective and likeable. And they can present the interviewer with clear and cogent reasons why they should be hired.

5. *The objective is always to be a brief, target-oriented interviewee.* Take interviews step by step. Step One is *preparation:* researching and preparing an effective presentation, planning what to wear, what to bring. Step Two is *practice:* going over what you're going to say, and working on keeping a strong, positive attitude. Step Three is *the interview itself:* making certain to concentrate on the major aspects of yourself and your background that will sell you.

STEP ONE: PREPARATION

■ **If you prepare for an interview, you'll be calmer, more organized, and sound better during your actual presentation.**

Before you are interviewed, learn about the company, the position, and if possible, try to find out something about the interviewer as well. Read annual reports, trade magazine articles, and company literature in order to come up with questions to ask the interviewer. You should also prepare yourself for any possible questions that he or she may ask you. *Always* be on the lookout for information you can use to make yourself sound more knowledgeable, more interested, and *better* than the other applicants. (Reread Chapter 3, "Research," for suggestions on where to get the right literature.)

■ **Think of ways your background and experience might fit in with what you've read.**

For example, many companies today stress being "entrepreneurial," and their literature is full of references to their need for self-starting employees. If you are interviewing at such a company, start thinking *before* the interview of items to mention that will highlight your own entrepreneurial past.

> **TIP: For best results, review your research at least three times before the interview: a week before, the night before, and a few minutes before you go in. By the third time you should be able to remember the important facts you've accumulated, easily and without straining. When reviewing in order to memorize, the trick isn't how *long* you review, it's how *frequently* you do it. Information is more accurately recalled if you review it many times for a few minutes, instead of one time for an hour.**

> **TIP: Jot down key ideas, figures, or points you want to make on a 3 × 5 note card. Stick it in your pocket and review it right before the interview begins.**

> **TIP: Read the newspaper or watch the news before interviewing. Many companies, in a policy effort to hire "well-rounded" people, want applicants who can discuss current events. This is particularly true in publishing, public relations, advertising, television, and government.**

What to Wear on an Interview

■ **Play it safe and dress on the conservative side.**

Even if you are interviewing for a highly creative position, you can't lose with a professional look. You are selling your professionalism—not your innovative fashion sense.

> **TIP:** *The rule of thumb:* **Wear the same type of clothing as your prospective boss. People are automatically drawn to those who are like themselves. It's human nature. Take advantage of this fact whenever possible.**

■ **Dressing conservatively doesn't have to mean looking like a "corporate clone" who has internalized every dress-for-success rule.**

Remember: You want to come across as confident, successful, and professional. And you can do that by wearing something *other* than a pin-striped suit. In fact, if you ordinarily avoid conservative styles, you *shouldn't* dress too conservatively for an interview. You'll end up feeling uncomfortable, stiff and unnatural. Instead, adapt a classic outfit to fit your personality.

Don't use the day of your interview to try anything new.

Don't test a new hairstyle, break in new shoes, or wear a new outfit for the first time. You'll already have more than enough on your mind, so guard against having any distractions. The last thing you need is pinching shoes or petty concerns about your appearance. If you are intending to wear new clothes, try them on the day before. Get accustomed to the feel of them. If you have new shoes, break them in a week earlier.

> **TIP: Little touches can make a difference: shined shoes, manicured fingernails, neat hairstyle, and a good leather attaché or briefcase will all add to your overall appearance and contribute to the first impression you create.**

Specific Pointers on What to Wear

For men:

- *Do* wear a well-tailored suit, not a blazer or sport jacket and slacks. The best suit material is wool. If it's warm, wear a tropical-weight wool. Avoid polyester. Successful people spend money on natural fibers—and you want to look successful.

- *Don't* wear a suit that is brown, black, or brightly colored. Navy-blue and gray are the preferred colors. As for patterns, a pinstripe in white or a muted color is fine. Plaids, houndstooth checks, tweeds, and other patterns are out.

- Your shirt should be cotton or cotton blend. The best color choice is white. The next best is cream. *Don't* wear a patterned shirt. While some thin-striped shirts work, it's simpler to avoid the whole issue and stick with solids.

- *Don't* think your tie is a chance to prove your individuality. Be an individual *after* you get the job. During the interview, stay away from bow ties, bright colors, extreme widths, splashy prints. Stay with the basics instead: either a small, foulard-type print or a regimental stripe always looks good. As for colors: red, yellow, maroon, forest green and navy work best.

- Wear well-polished dress shoes; black is best, but you can also wear brown or cordovan. Be sure your belt matches your shoes.

- *Don't* wear a pocket square or silk handkerchief in your breast pocket. Some people think they look sophisticated; others think they look foppish. Some say they should match your tie; others say they shouldn't. It's simpler to leave your breast pocket empty.

- *Do* wear thin, dark-colored dress socks in a shade that matches your suit. An over-the-calf length is your best bet: when you cross your legs, there's no gap between the bottom of your pants and the top of your socks.

- *Avoid:* Ornate jewelry, heavy cologne, shirts with contrasting collars, ostentatious monograms.

For Women:

- *Do* wear a tailored dress with a jacket or a softly tailored suit. Both are interview favorites—from both sides of the desk.

- Always wear a jacket—whether you are wearing a suit, a dress, or a skirt and blouse. But don't think you have to wear a female version of a man's suit: dark blue, super-conservative, white blouse, foulard tie. Surveys show that too man-tailored an outfit is as much a turn-off as too feminine and frilled a dress.

- The best skirt length is at the knee or just below the knee.

- *Don't* wear pants—not even well-cut trousers or a designer pantsuit. Even if you already know that staff members wear pants, wait until you've landed the job.

- *Don't* wear anything too trendy or ultra-fashionable. Again, whatever the position, you are safest erring on the side of conservatism. One woman interviewing for a buyer position at a major fashion-forward department store wore an above-the-knee skirt, long jacket with shoulder pads, chunky earrings and brightly colored opaque stockings. An up-to-the-minute fashion statement, she thought, but the interviewer explained that the store wanted people "who dressed like executives."

- The best shoes for an interview are basic pumps in black, brown, beige, or cordovan, on a mid-high heel. Over two inches is *too* high. Don't wear sandals, even in the summer, and steer clear of bright colors and styles that are too casual.

- You can't go wrong with panty hose in a neutral shade. Beige or taupe are best, but you can also wear darker colors. Don't wear brights, opaques, or overly fussy patterns. Lace is definitely out, as are seams; pinstripes and other subtle textures are all right if you're going for a nontraditional position.

- As a fallback, bring an extra pair of panty hose in your handbag or briefcase. Stockings run when you least expect it—and this way, you'll be prepared.

- *Do* wear jewelry, but keep it simple. Stud or button earrings, a few good rings, pearls or a simple necklace: all are fine. But stay away from an armful of bangles, dangling earrings, huge hoops, anything that looks distracting or unprofessional.

- *Avoid* anything too lacy or girlish, low-cut necklines, anything too clinging or see-through, heavy perfume, too much makeup.

Before you leave for the interview, doublecheck yourself from head to toe in a full-length mirror. Be as critical as you can: this is your last chance to perfect your appearance. Are your shoes polished? Suit brushed? Do your socks match? Don't overlook even the smallest details.

What to Bring on an Interview

■ **Bring along appropriate reading material; at the very least, it will refresh your mind and get you ready for the interview.**

Bring trade magazines or *The Wall Street Journal* to read while you wait in the reception area. Even better, bring specific newsletters or trade magazines that relate *specifically* to the position and the company. In this way, you can establish yourself as an expert before the interview, if the interviewer notices what you're reading.

> **EXAMPLE: An applicant for a financial position at a limousine company took to his interview a photocopy of a newsletter about the limo business. The founder and president of the company, who had never read the newsletter, asked him about it before the interview had begun, and talked about the plans he had for expanding his business. The applicant, in effect, got a job offer before the formal interview ever took place.**

You should also bring the most important information you've gathered on the company, in case you quickly need to review it.

> **TIP: Carry key points on a card in your purse or vest pocket. On unexpectedly tough interviews, where you find yourself being grilled on information that you know but can't remember, excuse yourself to go to the bathroom, and look over your notes. You've got nothing to lose.**

Always bring extras copies of your resume. The interviewer may ask for another.

STEP TWO: PRACTICE

■ **Practice can mean just going over what you plan to say, or it can mean actually going out and interviewing somewhere else *first* as a rehearsal for a more significant interview later.**

A practice interview is most useful if you haven't been job-hunting for a while, and it's also a good way to work out flaws in your style. Apply for a job you don't really want, but plan to go on the interview anyway, as if it were just as important. Be aware of how you're doing and how the interviewer is responding to you. Do you sound confident? Are you organized? Does the interviewer seem interested—or is he or she falling asleep?

After the interview, think about what you did right, what you did wrong, and how to improve. Ask the interviewer for advice if you feel comfortable doing so. Then go on another interview and see if your improvements really help.

One danger: Some people do better on a "safety interview" just because they know it doesn't matter. Then they get nervous and do badly on the important one.

> **TIP: Even if you don't think you need the practice, *arrange* your interview schedule so that you visit the least desirable jobs first, and thus can work out any problems with your interviewing technique *before* you see the best companies. Save the best for last.**

■ **Never stop practicing, and never stop seeking and going out on interviews.**

Again, the more interviews you go on, the better you'll get. Don't make the mistake many job hunters make and hide out in the library or behind a typewriter banging out cover letters. It's an easy way out:

"I can't go on interviews today because I'm too busy working. Besides, the job was too low-level. . . ." *Any* interview is a start. And as we stated in Chapter 4, "Networking," all interviews are good ways to meet people who may become potentially valuable.

■ **Rehearse the interview yourself, or with a friend acting as an interviewer.**

This second form of practicing is essential. Plan in your head what you're going to say, how you'll answer tough questions, how you'll sell yourself. Be certain your friend acts as an interviewer, and not as a friend, and be certain you think of your friend in those terms. Have your friend critique you, and then try again.

> **TIP: Go over your interview in your mind while commuting to and from work, and during other "in-between" times. With almost no conscious effort, you'll have many answers on the tip of your tongue.**

■ **Work on developing an upbeat, positive attitude during your interviews.**

A common problem is the difficulty of projecting an optimistic attitude during the strain of an interview, or after a slew of job rejections.

> **TIP: Don't kid yourself into believing any false claims about how easy and fun interviewing can be. It's difficult for almost anybody: sitting in front of a stranger who is asking you personal questions about your background. If you accept that interviewing will be hard, it becomes easier to make it *less* stressful.**

■ *Knowing* **all you need to know beforehand makes interviewing easier and less nerve-wracking when it actually takes place.**

Research and practice are essential, but even with the right preparation, interviewing jitters and worries can crop up, particularly if you've been unemployed for a long time and really need a job.

Five other key ideas to keep in mind:

1. *Think of an interview as just a game.* If you win, you get the job. In this way, you can focus on the positive aspects and put off worrying until later.

2. *Think of all interviews as learning experiences.* If things go badly, you'll still be successful at having learned how *not* to interview, and can concentrate on how to avoid similar problems in the future.

3. *Don't get intimidated by a single interview.* There will always be another.

4. *Try an old sales technique: count rejections.* To avoid the sting of not being hired, tell yourself you'll probably get fifteen or more turndowns before you get an offer. Try to find out the average number of turndowns for job hunts in your field. Think of each "no" as getting you closer to a "yes."

5. *Don't let fears clog your mind.* Turn your attention to thoughts of success. If you find yourself getting bogged down in "what if" scenarios, do something active or gently concentrate on positive things.

> **TIP:** Read upbeat books and articles when not working or researching for the next interview. There is a definite link between this type of positive reinforcement and confidence during an interview. According to one bookstore owner, prominent businessmen are the primary buyers of Dale Carnegie and Norman Vincent Peale. Don't be embarrassed if you want or need encouragement.

> **TIP:** For a quick "psyche-up," just before the interview think back on the most successful interview or meeting of your life. Review it in your mind, and let that confident attitude flow into your interview. In fact, do this at *all* times when you're tempted to rehash your "failures."

■ Be honest about your interviewing style.

One counselor noticed that every client who was coming to her for interviewing assistance was either too proud and arrogant, or too much of a shrinking violet. You should stay *between* what she calls the "twin pitfalls of arrogance and excessive humility." If you seem to have either of these characteristics, work hard with friends or counselors to change how you come across.

■ Make certain you are interviewing for the right job and career.

Sometimes the problem may be the job itself; poor interviewees for one job may blossom into confident, dynamic interviewees for another.

STEP THREE: THE INTERVIEW

■ **Whether you're interviewing for a position as a banker, an astronaut, or a sewer worker, interviewers want to know about three basic things: your experience, your interpersonal skills, and the reasons they should hire you.**

Whatever type of interview you're having, your strategy should be the same—to sell your way into a job. Only the formats and styles differ.

■ **There are only two parts to an interview: the first five minutes and the rest.**

In the first five minutes you should sell your *attitude* and personality. Show you're a winner by your stance, your confidence, and your demeanor. During the rest of the interview you should prove how the interviewer's first impression of you is correct. Highlight your skills and background and why you are right for this job.

Just Before the Interview

■ **Always arrive early.**

Arrive at the office building at least ten minutes early. Give yourself at least that amount of time to avoid any last-minute mishaps. Wait in your car, or walk around the block, and arrive at the interviewer's receptionist a few minutes before the appointment.

TIP: Go to the location of the interview the day before. The next day you'll be less worried about getting there and finding the place, and more able to concentrate on what you'll say during the interview.

TIP: For nervous interviewees it's a good idea to arrive even earlier and get an orange juice or coffee near the office. It's a good way to relax. Even for anxious types, *one* cup of coffee or tea may cheer you and make you sound more confident. For smokers, it's a good place to stoke up on the last few cigarettes unobserved before going in.

■ **Have something pleasant to say to the secretary or receptionist when you arrive at the interviewer's office.**

Secretaries do as much or more work than the executives, whatever executives may say to the contrary. Don't overlook them. In all companies, a secretary has the power to mis-type, mis-direct, or forget your application. Many times a secretary can provide the little extra push that gets you hired.

> **TIP: Don't confuse being friendly with being patronizing, or with pestering. One busy employment counselor's secretary complained of "nervously friendly applicants who try to joke with me while I'm typing or on the phone." A pleasant comment or two and a smile are usually enough.**

In general, never ignore anybody on an interview. You never know who *really* makes the decisions.

■ **Try to get a *feel* for the office and the environment.**

While waiting to be called, look around the reception area and look at employees at work; this will give you an idea of what kind of organization it is, and whether you think you'd like to work there.

Impressions: The First Five Minutes of the Interview

■ **Start the interview with a warm but professional tone, and maintain it throughout.**

Be confident and businesslike, but also friendly and personable. The first five minutes are very important, but don't take that too literally and try to get everything over with quickly. The key is to create the right *impression* of yourself. It's not what you say, it's how you say it, and how you look.

Concentrate on the following:

• a firm handshake

• looking the interviewer directly in the eye

• a pleasant smile

• good grooming and dress

- upright posture

- a strong but not overbearing voice

> **TIP: Smokers and coffee drinkers: Don't forget you may have bad breath. Take a breath mint before going in. A surprising number of interviewers mention smoker's or coffee breath as turn-offs.**

■ **Smile warmly, offer your hand and, if it seems natural or appropriate, make a *light* joke or observation.**

Most of the time it's to your advantage to take charge of the conversation by saying something first. Show the interviewer that you're not going to be a passive dud during the next hour, that you're not going to just respond to his or her questions; that, in fact, you have something to offer. There's no need to get too creative in opening—just say something.

> **EXAMPLE: If it's raining badly, comment on how bad the traffic was because of the rain. It's not particularly fascinating (in fact it's dull), but it will get the interviewer chatting. Or, comment on the offices. Say something specific about them.**

The Rest of the Interview: Selling Yourself as a Basic Strategy

There are eleven basic attitudes and techniques for putting yourself across correctly in an interview.

1. Sell Yourself

■ **Turn everything you do or say into a reason or a means of getting yourself hired.**

Think of the interview as a sales call. Constantly ask yourself: *Is what I'm saying helping me to get a job?*

Tailor the interview to your job objective. Surprisingly, many people don't. Instead of selling themselves on specific points, many applicants get lost in defending their resumes, explaining their backgrounds, discussing their motives, or just chatting with the interviewer. Don't waste *your* valuable interview time on these things unless you feel that they're helping you; there's no reason to linger on topics or ideas that don't sell you. *Don't forget:* The only reason you're talking with an interviewer is to get a job.

> **EXAMPLE: An interviewer mentions a bad gap in your resume, when you were unemployed for seven months. Don't get defensive and talk about the poor economy, rotten luck, problems in the industry, etc. Even though it'll make you feel better, it doesn't sell you. Interviewers hear excuses every day.**
>
> *Instead:* **Give a reason that exonerates and *sells* you at the same time. "Yes, I was job-hunting for seven months after my position was eliminated when my company was taken over. As you can see, being unemployed gave me time to upgrade my financial skills: I took two courses at the local college and completed a degree. So I was able to put myself in a better position that used those skills as well, which is why I think this position suits me extremely well. . . ."**

■ **You should be flexible and ready to *change* your approach, even if it means departing from a "normal" interviewing style.**

Don't get stuck in an interviewing rut just because you think you have to emphasize certain aspects of your resume. *Remember:* During the interview you're not only selling your skills and job background, you're selling yourself.

> **EXAMPLE: An unemployed man who was interviewing for a plant manager's job had started explaining his resume, experience, and schooling when he noticed that the interviewer (and president of the small company) kept switching the topic to an upcoming football game. The applicant stopped and switched topics, highlighting his hobby of working as a high school referee and explaining how his experiences on the football field had helped him as a manager. He got an offer over more experienced applicants because he sold *himself*.**

2. Link Yourself and Your Background to the Job

■ **Link what you're talking about with why you should be hired.**

When discussing your background, don't just state what you did, explain how it would be useful to the company. If your background doesn't exactly fit the job description, be creative. The best-qualified applicants don't always get the offers. Very often, it's the most confident and inspired individual who wins, the person who can *make* his or her background sound right.

> **EXAMPLE: In an unusual case of salesmanship, a secretary talked her way into a brokerage job: "Being a secretary for ten years has been excellent preparation for this position as a stockbroker, better than being an analyst or an MBA. Brokers may rely on experts for the technical aspects of their job, but the crucial part is selling. As a secretary, I've learned how to get through to and talk with top executives and others with substantial assets."**
> *Note:* **She was hired over more seasoned brokers.**

■ **Don't make the mistake of merely reciting your job history or education.**

Amplify your past in a way that sells you to the interviewer. Extracurricular activities can be helpful.

Highlight your current job skills and duties that are applicable to the new job. Many people make the mistake of giving equal weight to *each* of their current job responsibilities. Don't waste your valuable selling time explaining things that don't matter: a brief mention of your more minor responsibilities is all the interviewer needs to know.

3. Emphasize Specific Accomplishments

■ **Don't just talk about what a good and loyal employee you are, give examples that *demonstrate* how you increased sales, improved staff morale, or recovered missing funds.**

Be specific. Interviewers want to hire people who can do things, not simply warm a seat and talk.

> **EXAMPLE: "In 1986 I was responsible for a sales staff of ten. My team increased sales by thirty-five percent, which was fifteen percent above the average store-wide increase. I accomplished this by streamlining customer ordering procedures in my department, and top management has now adopted these for the company as a whole."**

4. Professional Tone

■ **Always maintain a professional posture and tone.**

Look directly at the interviewer while talking, just as you would when speaking to a friend, but don't overdo it. A common mistake many applicants make is to stare at the recruiter, which looks hostile and challenging.

> TIP: **Pause intermittently as you speak to see if the interviewer is still paying attention. Before embarking on any long explanations, briefly sketch out the basics, then ask the interviewer if he or she wants more details.**

Smile if appropriate, and avoid a monotonous style. A *light* sense of humor is almost always helpful.

> TIP: **A career counselor advised her female clients who were going for "stuffy jobs" such as banking, big business, and accounting, to avoid smiling too much when interviewing with men. Women have a tendency to smile more, and men interpret this—wrongly —as a passive gesture. Some women find this advice useful, others don't.**

■ **Occasionally break into a topic that's slightly personal: psychologically it's harder to reject and easier to hire someone who has a distinct personality that goes beyond a resume.**

Don't talk about dull generalities, talk about yourself and why *you,* personally, want the job. Political analysts all agree that President Reagan was a master of this technique, no matter what they thought of him otherwise.

> TIP: **Talk positively of personalities you've encountered in the workplace: a particularly tough but always fair and supportive boss, top-notch co-workers, etc. Speak of your past and try to help the interviewer *picture* it. Don't use jargon.**

> EXAMPLE: **"I particularly enjoyed working as an operations clerk at Merrill Lynch—the toughest job I ever had. I was in at six A.M. and out at 10 P.M., but I learned how to process stock transactions better than anyone."**
> *Avoid:* **"I worked as an analyst at Merrill Lynch, which was a challenging position that expanded my ca-**

reer horizons." Sentences like this make you sound like a robot. Or worse, a boring robot.

5. Pick Up Cues from Your Interviewer

■ **Tailor your style to fit the interviewer.**

Be yourself during the interview, but don't overdo it. If the interviewer is a joker, tell a few jokes and laugh along with him or her. If the recruiter is a serious type, *don't* tell a few jokes. Keep the conversation straight and professional.

■ **A quick glance around the office and a few minutes of discussion can give you an indication of what the interviewer is like.**

The best job applicants are sensitive in reading signs that reveal the interviewer's personality. Look for personal items to give you a clue. Again, be careful of overdoing it; for example, avoid praising photos of children: it sounds fake.

TIP: **Often the interviewer is as shy or as nervous as you are. Putting the recruiter at ease is an effective way of getting hired. Try to see through gruff or impersonal interviewers. Very often, they are new and awkward in the role.**

■ *Listen* **to the interviewer and pick up on cues for subjects to discuss.**

If the interviewer talks about the stresses of work in general, you should emphasize your ability to handle stress.

TIP: **Try to read how the interviewer is reacting to what you say. If he or she looks bored, stop and ask if you've covered the topic adequately.** *React* **to the interviewer. Many overly arrogant applicants ignore subtle cues and blithely keep on talking their way through the interview and out of a job.**

6. Believe in Your Own Myths

■ **Being the ideal candidate means acting and thinking about yourself as you are at your best.**

Talk about your triumphs; don't weaken yourself by mentioning your failures. If your failures come up, acknowledge them, refer to them as what they are, and how you learned from them. Then turn the conversation back to what you have to offer. Remember, you're selling yourself, not telling your life story.

> **EXAMPLE:** "In nineteen eighty-eight I was the top salesman in my office—and I could do even better at a firm like yours. . . ."
> *Not:* "Although I did pretty badly last year, I'm sure I could perform a lot better at your firm."

> **EXAMPLE:** If asked about a failure directly, answer in the following manner: "Yes, I was laid off in nineteen eighty-eight. I was low in seniority. It was unfortunate, because I feel I had a lot to contribute, and I got along very well with my fellow employees. But there was one advantage to having that hiatus: I had the time to develop a career game plan, which is why I've applied for this job. It *fully* meets my skills and career expectations."

■ **Even though estimates are that up to one third of job applicants lie during interviews, it's usually a mistake to lie or hide mistakes or failures from prospective employers.**

If you're ever found out during or after the interview, you definitely won't get the job. Admitting to failures won't necessarily hurt your chances as much as you may think. Surveys consistently show that most failures, such as being fired or failing in a private enterprise, don't matter much to interviewers. In today's erratic business climate, being laid off or losing at a new business venture no longer carries the weight it once did. What *does* matter is how you've dealt with it and how confidently you've taken things in stride.

7. Don't Apologize

■ **Interviewing apologetically is a common mistake, made most often by people who feel they're too young, too old, or over- or underqualified for the job they're seeking—which covers just about everyone.**

People often get negative ideas about their qualifications from reading or hearing about the average age or experience levels in the positions they seek. So they start the interview with an apology: "I know you normally hire younger [or older, or more qualified, etc.] applicants but. . . ."

No but's. Say why you're good and stick to it. If it seems that the interviewer has some objections, figure out what they are and communicate the *advantages* of hiring someone your age and with your level of experience.

> **EXAMPLE: "My thirty-five years of on-the-job experience would be a real advantage in this job, because I know how to publish this type of local paper with my eyes closed. I don't need a lot of supervision. . . ."**

> **EXAMPLE: One man in his sixties brought a magazine article to the interview which reported that senior citizens have better attendance, less sick time, and greater productivity than younger men. He was hired.**

None of this is to say that overcoming such obstacles is easy. But it's always better to face a problem squarely and confidently than to apologize for what you are. (Even though there are age discrimination laws, it's better to convince an employer of your worth, rather than threaten legal action.)

8. Never Say "Maybe"

■ **Always sound positive during the interview.**

Never let weak and mealy-mouthed words such as "maybe," "kind of," or "hopefully" clog your speech. Lukewarm words make you sound lukewarm, and make it less likely you'll be hired. Be direct.

> **TIP: If asked whether you plan to stay in this career, say "Yes!" instead of "I think so," even if you aren't certain. You can always change your mind later and, in the meantime, you sound positive rather than weak and vacillating.**

■ **Don't worry about seeming more arrogant or pushy than you usually are.**

Unless you've been told you're too arrogant, the odds are that you're not firm *enough.* Many interviewers criticize applicants for being too shy and reticent. An interview is no time to be demure and polite about your accomplishments.

9. Summarize

■ **Summarize your main points periodically.**

After each "section" of the interview, or after each long question, briefly summarize what you feel is important for the interviewer to remember, and how it fits in with the position you're applying for. The objective is to keep impressing upon the interviewer's mind the factors that make *you* the right person for the job.

> **EXAMPLE:** After describing your last job for a few minutes, summarize and repeat your most significant accomplishments: "So I feel my biggest accomplishment during this period was supervising one hundred employees in the largest company warehouse construction project, which is why I was so interested in your ad. . . ."

When it becomes obvious to you that the interview is winding down, start summarizing the main points you've been making. Do this only if the interviewer gives you the chance—not if he or she wants to chat about something else. But if the interviewer asks whether you'd like to add anything, you should always answer "yes," and then quickly re-list your accomplishments.

> **EXAMPLE:** "So, all in all, my background points to a strong interest in publishing as a career. As we discussed, because of my college degree in Transylvanian Literature and my internship with a literary magazine, I feel . . ."

> **TIP:** A good trick to sounding professional is to *number* your accomplishments: "There are three major reasons why I feel this job is right for me. One . . ." Statements like this make you sound organized and intelligent. This advice is frequently given by career, media, and political consultants. Henry Kissinger often does this during interviews on television—"There are three elements to a coherent foreign policy: one, . . ."

10. Close the Interview

■ **Closing an interview can mean asking for the job, especially if you're applying for a sales or sales-related position.**

In these cases, treat the end of an interview as you would if you were closing a sale. If it seems as if the recruiter has settled on you as his or her first choice, end the interview by affirming that you have been hired. If it's a first interview or it's obvious that the interviewer can't or won't hire you, then close by highlighting your attributes and establishing an exact date for your next meeting.

> **EXAMPLE: Salespeople at the Xerox corporation advise sales force applicants to ask questions toward the *end* of the interview ("Is there any reason you wouldn't hire me?"). If there are objections, you have a chance to rebut them, and then *close* with a confirmation you're hired or an agreement to meet again.**

■ **In most cases, it's better to wait for the interviewer to indicate he or she is ready to end the interview.**

If you're applying for a nonsales job, you don't need to close the interview with a hard sell. Instead, thank the interviewer for the meeting, and repeat how much you are interested in the job and how well qualified you think you are for it. People often forget to do this or are too embarrassed. Do it anyway—it definitely helps. It brings home the message that you are a person who firmly believes that he or she is right for the job.

> **EXAMPLE: "Thanks, Mr. Jones. I appreciated this opportunity to talk about my qualifications. I'm looking forward to talking with you further about the job; as I've said, I'm very enthusiastic about it and know I could make a significant contribution to your company's new marketing drive."**

11. Be Yourself

■ **If you interview with a false front, you may lose by *getting* the job.**

Create your own interviewing style, but don't confuse selling yourself with being fake. You could end up mismatched, working at a job that genuinely doesn't suit you.

> **EXAMPLE: A woman imitated a friend's bold interviewing style at an interview with an entrepreneurial computer company. She got the job, but was laid off several months later: she couldn't maintain the tough, street-wise act she had put on during the interview.**

The key to successful interviewing is interviewing at *your* best, not someone else's.

TYPES OF INTERVIEWS AND ASSESSMENT

No one interview is ever like another, of course, but there are certain types of interviews that share particular characteristics and that should be treated accordingly. In what follows we've sketched out the most common of these, ranging from group interviews to in-basket tests. Expect to face at least one of these during your job search; the days of having only one-on-one interviews are long gone.

Group Interviews: If You Are Interviewed *with* a Group

- **If you are interviewed with a group of other applicants, your objective is to show that you're a team player who can effectively lead as well as work with others.**

Group interviews are usually organized with five or so job applicants seated around a table. There are various types of group interviews, but all are designed to test your interpersonal and negotiating skills.

Sometimes each applicant is given a separate handout outlining a company program, and he or she is expected to defend this program to the group. Since all programs can't be accepted, the group must then decide which ones should be used, and work together to arrive at a consensus. This method is popular with the Foreign Service of the U.S. Department of State, among others.

In other variations, the group as a whole is given a problem to solve and is expected to arrive at a joint conclusion. Several major retailers like to use this interview technique. In some cases, a group interview can turn into a full-fledged simulation of a business, in which applicants are asked to come to an agreement on production schedules and budgets. Sometimes an interviewer will announce in mid-session a complete change of agenda; in this case your ability to cope with spontaneous decision-making is being tested as well. In every instance the applicants talk, while several evaluators are sitting on the sidelines, taking notes.

■ **Group interviews can be very tough: you have to interact with five or more people you've never met, and withstand having several people watching and evaluating you.**

The very nature of this test is stressful. You have to show that you are a leader, but so must everyone else. Somehow, you've got to compete with these people without appearing to be overbearing and prove that you're the true leader in the group, or at least one of a few true leaders. Many people suffer from a modified form of stage fright in these circumstances.

■ **The longer you wait to take a major role, the greater your anxiety, and the harder it will be to participate.**

The key is to jump in early. Assume the role of *moderator* as soon as you can. Open the discussion, suggest an order of presentation, *ask* the others what they think. Instead of arguing your points, try to mediate between the others. *Remember:* You are being evaluated for leadership, and effective leadership often comes from not being too aggressive. You must act as a team player, one who is capable of getting along with others and leading them to *one* objective. It doesn't have to be *your* objective as long as it is obvious that you've been instrumental in getting the group to agree on one or more major issues.

■ **Show yourself to be a patient, persistent, people-oriented leader with enough flexibility to negotiate among many kinds of people.**

Offer creative solutions to problems. *Don't* jump to conclusions, browbeat others, or speak only when spoken to. Don't flaunt your knowledge. Instead, demonstrate your ability to get people to work well together.

> TIP: Inevitably, there will be a loud talker who tries to monopolize the conversation. You can win supporters by calling on other people to speak.
> *For example:* "That's a good point, Mr. Loudmouth. How do you think that will affect the plan, Mr. Quiet?" This will quickly gain you gratitude from the quiet ones, who will then turn to you for leadership. This technique has been used successfully by a number of candidates during the U.S. Foreign Service exam.

■ **Take responsibility for *closing* the meeting.**

Summarize what the group has decided, mention the opposing viewpoints, and announce conclusions.

> **EXAMPLE:** "Well, we've established that programs one and five will be adopted, and part of program four. Are we all in agreement? [Look to see if there's a response.] We're all in agreement then. . . ." (Turn to the evaluators and tell them your team has finished.)

> **TIP:** In some of the more aggressive retail chains, take a correspondingly more aggressive tack. Here, you may be better off firmly taking charge and not letting up. A woman in New York retailing was told after her group interview: "We hired you because you didn't shut up or give up. In this business, you've got to deal with salespeople the same way."

> **TIP:** In some cases you will be asked to evaluate yourself after the session. Be realistic. Your evaluation will be matched against those of the assessors, and if it differs significantly you will lose points for not judging yourself accurately.

Group Interviews: If You Are Interviewed *by* a Group

■ **Being interviewed by a group tests how well you can deal with the public and customers in a stressful setting.**

This type of interview has become increasingly common, and is almost always tough. Group interviews are used most often by government employers, universities, banks, and consulting firms, and for higher-level private industry positions.

The best way to do well is to be calm, organized, and relatively brief. There are too many people involved for you to be giving long-winded answers.

■ **The chief difficulty is having to confront three or more people, all of whom are firing questions at you before you have the chance to catch your breath.**

One trick is to rephrase the questions after they are asked to give yourself more time to think of an answer. Don't be afraid to pause and think before speaking, or openly ask for more time.

> EXAMPLE: "How would I handle the marketing of Nutsy Nuts in Albania? First . . ." OR: "That's an interesting question. Let me think about it for a minute . . ." Taking a moment shows that you're not intimidated by the group-interview process, and are able to take charge of the situation.

■ **Having more interviewers usually means facing more technical questions.**

You must be well prepared. Typically, each interviewer will have a specialty or concern that he or she feels is essential. One danger is in thinking that you have to answer all their questions. If you don't know an answer, say so! *Remember:* These interviewers are testing how you'd interact with the general public, so attempting to bluff your way out of something is far worse than just admitting your ignorance.

■ **Don't worry about the "feel" of the interview.**

Because more people are involved, a natural flow is lost and you may think that things are worse or more awkward than they are. Keep in mind that many of the people present are untrained as interviewers and can be extremely uncomfortable with the entire interviewing process.

> TIP: Don't ignore *anyone*. One applicant to a company which had a reputation for being tough and hard-driven treated a question asked by a young, frail-looking observer sitting in the corner very lightly. He wasn't hired. That observer was the very quiet, very studious, very delicate personnel director.

■ **Most important, don't hesitate to make the points *you* want to make.**

Many people go through group interviews passively: they just respond, they don't initiate. Be brief, but don't make the mistake of letting the interview proceed as though it were an interrogation in which you simply allow the interviewers to grill you. Instead, treat the group interview as if it were a regular interview. Don't be intimidated because there are so many interviewers; ask questions, make your points, and sell yourself.

All-Day Interviewing or Multiple Interviews

■ **Particularly at large companies, an all-day assessment is a formal process, used for entry-level and mid-level applicants.**

All-day interviewing usually occurs after an initial screening interview with one interviewer. If you pass this first hurdle, you are called back a week or so later for a series of six to eight individual interviews with managers of various ranks.

The day starts with a meeting with the original interviewer, who sells you on the company and goes on to explain whom you will be meeting. Lunch is spent with a manager who is usually closest to you in rank, and the day often ends with an interview with a high-level manager, quite possibly your projected boss.

Within the week following your all-day assessment, all the people you've seen will arrive at a group consensus as to whether or not they want to invite you back. If so, you are called for a final interview with your direct line manager. Sometimes you're being considered for more than one position, in which case you will meet with two or more line managers.

■ **Part of the screening process is to see how well you react to the rigors of an all-day interview.**

A whole day of interviewing can be very grueling. Don't worry about being repetitive. Each interviewer will want to know the same things about you, so tell him or her the same things you've been saying to everyone. Varying your format occasionally will help to reduce your fatigue. Don't overdo it—by the end of the day some applicants have talked about so many different things that their interviewing style begins to suffer, and they forget to include the major points. Keep reminding yourself to sound fresh and somewhat spontaneous. Interviewers often turn down applicants who sound overly rehearsed with their presentations: this was frequently mentioned as the biggest turn-off by interviewers at a large package-goods corporation. The problem is that, as the day goes on, it becomes harder and harder to sound spontaneous and unrehearsed, particularly when someone asks you for the third, or worse, the sixth time, "What are your strengths?"

TIP: Keep your ears open for unusual or difficult questions in the first set of interviews, and start formulating good answers. They will usually crop up again.

TIP: Use what you've discussed in earlier interviews during your later ones. *For example:* "In the last interview, Tom Goetz said that he's set up quality-control circles in his division with excellent results. He said that he got the procedures from you. How has this idea worked in your division?" Supplementing your interviews with insights from other employees keeps the conversation going and implies that you and the previous interviewers got along well.

TIP: One successful applicant at a Fortune 500 firm suggests that new applicants should have some tough *questions* about the firm and its business in reserve. By the end of the day, when you're tired and can't think anymore, ask the interviewer these questions. This will establish your intelligence, and while the interviewer is busy formulating answers, you can get some rest and time to reformulate your own answers.

TIP: One interviewer at another Fortune 500 firm says that an applicant should be ready for a nonbusiness-oriented interview: "I like to throw off candidates at the end of the day by discussing hobbies, politics, cultural events and other nonresume items. It tests their ability to deal with the unexpected, and allows me to see how easily they can handle the public and their co-workers."

■ **Bring at least ten resumes.**

Inevitably, someone will want an extra copy. Also, you may have to supply a copy of your resume to people who are called in to interview you at the last minute.

Luncheon Interviews

■ **The purpose of a luncheon interview is to assess how well you can handle yourself in a social situation.**

Almost no one *likes* lunch interviews; almost everyone feels nervous and unnatural during them. But, for some reason, many interviewers insist that they are a good way of judging candidates.

■ *Rule of thumb:* **Stick to the middle ground during a luncheon interview.**

When ordering, choose middle-priced dishes; if asked to select a wine, pick a middle-priced brand. Steer away from controversial topics, difficult-to-eat food (lobster, spaghetti, chicken) and heavy drinking. In conversation, follow Benjamin Franklin's old credo: "Never contradict anyone."

> **TIP:** Don't assume the interviewer is psychoanalyzing every move you make. Some career counselors go so far as to advise applicants to taste food before putting salt or pepper on it—otherwise the interviewer will assume you are impulsive. Most important, try to *relax*. If you're too self-conscious, it will be an awkward and difficult lunch.

> **TIP:** Common advice is to *avoid* drinking alcohol, even if the interviewer drinks. The reasoning is that it's better to look good, and to keep your mind fresh. Better advice from an interviewer who drinks: If you drink, go ahead and have *one*. Sometimes one drink establishes you as "one of them" and not a prude.

■ **When it comes to conversation, let the interviewers take the lead.**

Luncheon interviews are primarily social events, so a hard sell can look unprofessional. But *do* sell yourself. Bring up hobbies and special interests that reflect your character and show you're the right type of applicant.

> **TIP:** Even if you hate sports, it's a good idea to scan the sports pages a few weeks before the interview. Often the conversation will turn to sports, and it's helpful to be able to at least *mention* a key player or two, before trying to change the subject. If you don't follow sports at all, don't make the mistake of thinking you can wing it through an entire discussion without getting caught.

■ **Avoid politics.**

If asked your opinion on a controversial topic, make a minor point that won't offend anybody. If at all possible, link your answer to what concerns you most: the industry you work in and the job you want. More forceful people can say the truth: they don't like to discuss politics in social situations or at work.

> **EXAMPLE:** *Interviewer:* "That senator is a complete incompetent. I blame him for the mess we're in with the Nicaraguans. What do you think?" *Applicant (for a grain-trading company):* "What interests me most about the whole affair is the economics. I'm concerned over the precedent an embargo might set in relation to our business. Did the senator suggest an embargo?"

This turns the question back to the interviewer and keeps things technical, noncontroversial, and boring, thus avoiding any personal conflicts.

TIP: If you want to be sneaky, try to turn the question around so you can find out the interviewer's opinion before expressing your own. *Danger:* The interviewer may just be testing you, or others at the table may disagree with your opinions.

Telephone Sales Interviews

■ **Telephone sales interviews are sometimes given to applicants who are obviously expected to do a large amount of telephone selling.**

These test situations are supposed to simulate the "real" work as much as possible. They are often conducted by outside testing firms, but are given at your prospective employer's office. Stockbrokers, magazine advertising salespeople, and financial salespeople are typically asked by large firms to come in for this type of assessment after a successful first interview.

The test begins when you are seated at a desk with a telephone and given memos, some phone numbers, and a paper detailing your duties for the next hour or two. At a stockbrokerage, for instance, you may be given four different, partially incomplete call sheets with the names of investors or potential investors. You will have to cold-call the potential investors and try to sell them on the firm's investments. The people you call are actually employed by the testing firm, and will later evaluate your performance. Often, you'll be asked to make a call to a supposedly irate customer, and you will have to inform him that an investment you recommended lost money. In all cases your job is to fill in the blanks on the call sheets, and try to get the people interested in making new investments that the firm is selling.

■ **Be a little more aggressive and persistent than you would be on a real sales call.**

Be ready beforehand with your best sales attitudes. Use your creativity. In a test interview, you've only got an hour to demonstrate what a dynamic salesperson you are, while in an actual job you could always call back or try again the next day.

In-Basket Tests

■ **In-basket tests are usually given by large bureaucratic firms as a way of determining your managerial aptitude.**

In-basket tests are corporate games of make-believe. They're not interviews, since they only involve you and a stack of paper. But they usually occur after an interview, or as part of an all-day assessment.

Generally, you're given a desk for an hour or two and told to act as if you were a manager temporarily replacing someone else, who has left an in-basket full of memos, notes, and files requiring action. You may also be given some reference material such as an office manual or job description, but basically you're given a minimal amount of information about the job and its priorities. You've got to figure things out on your own and take appropriate action in the next one to two hours.

■ **The best (and only) way to take the test is to act as a good manager would and go through everything in the basket first.**

The tried-and-true trick that most companies use in these tests is to put memos at the bottom of the in-basket that supposedly were written later and therefore contradict earlier memos. One meticulous person didn't understand this and did things in order; he wasted a half hour writing a detailed memo on a project only to find a later memo that said the project had been shelved. He panicked and didn't finish the test. These tests can get like that—the tension builds up as the time limit approaches.

■ **Beat the time problem by going through the in-basket and making "to do" lists; put memos and papers in a prioritized order.**

There's often not enough time to do everything; and it will go against you if you don't get the important things done first. As time winds down, go through as much of the low-priority material and quickly jot down notes so a secretary or assistant can take action later. This shows that you can delegate authority and that you have a handle on most of the work.

■ *Remember:* **The in-basket tests show how well you behave as a manager.**

You'll have to write brief letters, write follow-up instructions for a secretary or administrative assistant, and answer letters. Judgment decisions will crop up as well: Do you take action yourself, or do you wait and talk to the division head? Do you answer a complaint from an important client who demands an immediate answer, or do you wait and write an action memo to the company lawyer, who's out of town and won't be back for a week?

SPECIAL SITUATIONS DURING INTERVIEWS

The unexpected always comes when you least need it or want it —which means during your most important interview. Below are some of the most common surprises and problems that can occur, ranging from arriving late to facing down an interviewer who is making more than the usual fuss over your spotty employment record. You may also be asked to undergo pre-interview testing. These tests are becoming increasingly common, and more and more people are unpleasantly surprised when their interviewing day begins with a multiple-choice personality test. The rest of this section is designed to reduce the shock of these rude awakenings as much as possible.

If You Are Late to the Interview

■ **Personal experience and recent surveys show that being late to an interview almost never hurts you.**

If you are late, apologize briefly but sincerely for causing a problem, and express the hope that you can go on with the interview anyway. Virtually every interviewer will still want to see you, and almost all say it won't affect your job prospects. If you are very late, call ahead and explain the situation. Have a reasonable excuse: your car broke down, the train was late, etc. *Don't* give an excuse that makes you sound irresponsible, such as saying you overslept. Whatever you do, don't panic or get flustered. Don't let being late set a negative tone for the entire interview.

If You Are Asked to Take an Intelligence or Personality Test

■ **Companies that offer these tests most often *require* them as a part of their assessment process: if you don't take the test you won't be considered further.**

In general you're best off taking these tests, even if you disagree with the notion philosophically. If you don't pass them with flying colors, you can always explain during the interview that you do badly on standardized tests and go on to highlight your qualifications. A good interview and your personal attributes could outweigh any test results. You may get the job over someone else who tests well but makes a bad impression in person.

Intelligence tests vary with the company and the testing service they use. Many are simply IQ tests, with questions designed to test reasoning skills. These include word analogies, number or letter patterns (what is the next letter in the series s m t _ ?), and mathematical reasoning questions.

■ **Review the basics of the business before going in.**

Some firms offer *aptitude* tests based on their business. One nationwide investment firm, for example, gives an assessment test that lasts one to two hours and covers twenty-five reading comprehension questions and twenty-five mathematical questions. Both sections deal primarily with investment. The reading comprehension test has a passage dealing with a merger, and questions relating to the passage deal with the ramifications of the merger. The mathematical section focuses on your reasoning ability, with reference to investment specifics. Questions may describe a hypothetical portfolio, with investments in bonds at a certain percentage, or monies in Certificates of Deposit paying at another percentage, and income at another specified level. The applicant may be asked to calculate the total income, or evaluate the present value of the investor's portfolio. These questions tend to be algebraic, often requiring you to solve for two variables. Those who pass this test are called in for interviews and further assessment.

The major problem with these tests for most people is that you can't use a calculator. People accustomed to pushing a button to add a column of figures or to compute the present value of an investment must now use pencil and paper.

TIP: Before taking a test, practice your basic mathematical skills. Most people find themselves surprisingly rusty even with simple multiplication.

Personality tests are more difficult to assess. Some companies offer multiple-choice tests that examine personality in a seemingly facile way. ("How would you rather spend a Friday afternoon: watching TV, reading Shakespeare, or playing tennis with a friend? Do you agree or disagree with this statement: 'I enjoy going to parties and meeting new people'?")

The best way to answer these questions is to ask yourself: *What kind of person does the firm want to hire?* Think about the particular industry and the sort of people who are successful in it. In general, your answers should show that you are an energetic, outgoing team player. Obviously, if the position is detail-oriented, play up your liking for detail; if you're interviewing for a service position, choose answers that indicate you enjoy helping people.

In a similar vein, psychologically-oriented firms may have candidates draw pictures and explain them. Successful applicants have reported doing simple line drawings quickly and decisively, and interpreting them briefly and in a light tone.

▪ Be ready for tests that judge your honesty.

Here you'll probably face a lie-detector test or a series of true-false questions that ask some very basic questions about attitudes. Over 25% of major U.S. corporations use lie-detector tests for some employees; half of all supermarket chains require them. A few firms require handwriting (graphology) tests; these are especially common in Europe, as one shocked upper-level manager learned when he was told that his interviews had all gone well but that he had to submit to handwriting analysis before he could be hired.

▪ And now there is another test that is becoming increasingly common: drug-testing.

Many large firms now routinely administer drug tests, (usually urine tests), despite the public controversy over whether they're legal. A recent Gallup poll reported that 28% of large corporations (5,000 or more employees) screen applicants for drugs. The percentage is expected to increase, particularly for jobs where safety is a prime factor.

A word of advice: Don't take drugs before an interview, of course, but also refrain from taking cough syrup, drinking gin, or eating poppy seeds (such as you would get on a bagel, for example). In some sensitive tests, the chemicals in these foods may show you as having used illegal drugs. Not a great way to open an interview: "No, I don't use drugs, but I just *love* poppy-seed bagels. . . ."

If the Interviewer Is Hostile

- **Sometimes "stress interviews" are given by companies in highly competitive industries that want to test how tough you are.**

Occasionally you may come across an interviewer who is out for blood. The first consideration you must face is that this person represents the company; so, do you still want to work for it? *Remember:* There is no rule that says you *must* sit through an abusive interview. But if you choose to stay, *don't* lose your temper and don't argue with the interviewer.

- **Stay cool and respond to your interviewer's criticisms with calm, rational statements that highlight why you are well qualified for the job.**

The purpose of hostile interviews is to see how well you handle stress. Don't take things personally and don't react negatively—don't let them fluster you.

> **EXAMPLE: After the interviewer says that, in his opinion, your academic credentials aren't worth a damn, say: "Some people think that practical experience counts for more. If you look carefully at my experience, you'll see that I learned as much on the job as I did at school, and in fact, my last promotion was due to my success at . . ."**
> *Note:* **The applicant acknowledged the objections, but explained that she also had useful hands-on experience. She didn't bother arguing with the interviewer about the value of her degree, but neither did she agree that it was worthless.**

- **Ignore any hostile remarks and concentrate on what the interviewer is looking for in a candidate.**

As with all interviews, concentrate on selling yourself. If the interview gets too hard to take, or the interviewer seems against you personally, quickly wind down the session and leave on a calm, upbeat note.

If You Get Trapped in a Lie

■ **Telling the truth is not only morally better, it's *easier*.**

Lying is a bad tactic: most applicants get caught in the contradictions of a lie, or sound so nervous while they're trying to lie that any possible advantage is lost. Still, many people will lie during interviews, usually on the spur of the moment, in response to an awkward or difficult question about their past.

> **EXAMPLE:** *Interviewer:* **"So, you've only changed jobs twice in the last five years?"**
> *Nervous applicant, who actually changed jobs three times:* **"Yes, only twice."**

In cases like this, don't give the interviewer a chance to catch you in a lie. Correct yourself briefly. But don't make an issue of it; just go back to your main discussion.

> **EXAMPLE:** **"Excuse me, I meant to say I changed jobs three times. And, as we were discussing, all those jobs gave me skills that I can put to work immediately. . . ."**

If the interviewer catches *you,* correct yourself and keep on going. Treat it as a minor mistake, one which you made because you were so absorbed in the discussion at hand.

> **EXAMPLE:** **"Oh, yes, you're right, I changed jobs three times. I meant to correct myself earlier. But the point I'm trying to stress is that my experience . . ."**

If the Interviewer Makes Suggestive Comments

■ **If the interviewer is making sexually suggestive comments, the normal and usually correct approach is to look the person in the eye and say that you expect to be treated as a professional.**

Usually the person is too embarrassed to persist, or will say he or she was only joking. If the person continues to offend you, walk out. If, however, the interviewer asks more vague, "personal" questions that seem inappropriate, politely remind him or her that you are here to discuss business-related topics. If you feel strongly about the situation you may want to notify the individual's superior at the company, and/or the appropriate civic or government group.

If the Interviewer Harps on Your "Spotty Resume"

■ **Most people have gaps, false starts, periods of unemployment, and new career directions in their pasts.** *Problem:* **The more changes you've been through, the worse you look to a prospective employer.**

Lay-offs, career-changing, and an uncertain economy have all made "normal" career paths obsolete. Almost no one can say he or she started in one career, advanced steadily in one firm, and now is looking for the same type of job at a different company.

There's no easy way to get around this problem, but there are some good strategies. Earlier, we explained how to tailor your resume, when to avoid mentioning unemployment gaps, and when to *explain* unemployment periods and different careers. Use the same approach during your interviews—show how all the jobs in your past have led you to this career and this interview. *Remember the key concern of an interviewer:* Will you stay with this job if you're hired?

■ **Stress that your job hopping has given you experience and the knowledge that you needed to have to be absolutely certain about what you want to do now.**

Refer to this job or career as the capstone of your career, as a permanent move for you. Be as strong and determined as possible. The interviewer will be suspicious of your motives if you're a proven job hopper; you must forcefully convince him or her that you are sincerely interested in the job. Talk about what you have learned. But don't dwell on the past. Direct the conversation toward the job and the future.

> **TIP: Try to anticipate this problem** *before* **the interview. Successful job hoppers rely on better preparation, personal introductions, and good planning.**

> **EXAMPLE: One man in his mid-thirties applied to a large trading firm, after having had brief stints as a paralegal, news-**

paper manager, and graduate student. The interviewer looked at his record with mild disgust: "Who asked you to interview here with *your* record?" he asked. "The senior vice-president," the applicant replied, much to the interviewer's surprise.

The applicant had made a point of anticipating the problem by networking with line employees first, *before* the formal interview process. Armed with the "unofficial" backing of the SVP, he was hired.

If the Interviewer Asks About Chronological Gaps in Your Resume

■ If your resume shows that you had periods of unemployment, or the interviewer discovers it, explain how even during those periods you were involved productively in other activities.

Talk about fund-raising groups, clubs, volunteer work—anything you did that shows you are a hard-working person who always keeps active. Try to show how these activities will make you a better employee *now*, and link your activities to your goal of selling yourself into this job.

> EXAMPLE: "Yes, I was unemployed for six months. Rather than sit back, make phone calls, and send out resumes, I organized my time so that I could work part-time as a clerk to pay the bills and still volunteer to help my town's fund-raising efforts to get a new school built. I actively campaigned door to door, and received a record response—which is why I know I could be very effective in your sales department. Even during my own unemployment, I achieved a sales record. . . ."

If You Had Low Grades in School

■ Don't worry about grades after your first job; worry even less if you have an MBA. Employment surveys show that having good grades is among the *least* important factors in getting hired.

Employers look at grades in only one context: How will this affect the employee's job performance? Don't volunteer that you had low grades, but if asked, tell the truth. The odds are that a firm won't check, but if they do, you can be fired for something that doesn't make much difference anyway. Make certain to show how your other skills will make you a valuable employee.

■ **Stress *reasons* for having had low grades that explain how other vital activities took away study time.**

For example, you could explain that earning your way through college or having to attend night school prevented you from getting high grades. Play up extracurricular activities in which you had a *leadership* role. Never sound upset or apologetic. You're not stupid or lazy, you just didn't have enough time to study. You were too busy supporting your mother, raising children, etc.

> **EXAMPLE: "My GPA was 2.0—but as you can see from my resume, I had one part-time job and one full-time job during college. These jobs taught me quite a bit, particularly about how to juggle responsibilities and handle high amounts of stress. That's why I'm interested in this job. . . ."**

8

The Most Common Questions Interviewers Ask

INTRODUCTION

Behind every question an interviewer asks is one other: "How well can you do the job for me?" Or, more bluntly, "Why should I hire you?"

When you sit across the desk from an interviewer, he or she already has a mental checklist of skills, personality, and experience that together adds up to the right employee, the right person for the job. Interviewers know whom they want to hire. You have to demonstrate that *you* are that person.

This is where preparation and anticipation come into play. If you already know (or have an idea of) what you're going to be asked, you can make certain that every answer you give adds to your sales pitch.

Here are fifteen of the most common questions interviewers ask, along with suggestions, hints, and tips on how to field them. You should tailor the answers to fit your personality and specific job requirements, but in each case you can and should be *selling yourself*.

1. Do You Have Any Questions? (When Asked at the Beginning of the Interview)

This is a favorite of so-called "behavioral" interviewers who want to avoid canned responses by getting you to take the initiative at the very beginning of the interview.

Of course, you should always have something to ask. But don't be typical and ask just anything. Instead take advantage of the hidden sales opportunity and ask questions that immediately position you as a strong job candidate—questions that highlight your potential role *with* the company and show how knowledgeable you already are about the business.

To sound informed and up-to-date, concentrate on current news you've picked up in trade magazines or professional journals, not the basic run-of-the-mill information every other applicant usually uses. And, whenever possible, incorporate an example of your own expertise into your question.

> **EXAMPLE:** "**I was interested to read in last week's *Widget Age* that your company captured fifty percent of the widget market last quarter. It reminded me of *my* work with widgets at XYZ Inc. We were trying to expand our market share, so I launched a campaign specifically targeted to the teen market. We didn't have a large budget, so I concentrated on local print and some radio. What were the key elements to your success?**"

Be sure not to ask anything about benefits, salaries, or personnel policies. You want to show how knowledgeable and achievement-oriented you are, not how greedy you are.

> **TIP: Do *not* make suggestions on how to manage the interviewer's company or ask leading questions that end up with you explaining how you would run things. Some people make this mistake, particularly MBAs, as a way of indicating how useful they would be to the company. Maybe they would be—if they got an offer. Most interviewers cite this as a major turn-off.**

If you have no experience in a relevant area, ask questions about planned expansions or operations in the department or area where you want to work, making sure to show off your knowledge of the company at large.

In other words, if you can't talk about yourself, show off your knowledge about the company. Then ask how the company's proposed changes will affect your department. This way your questions won't look frivolous, and they will communicate to the interviewer that you've done your homework.

This approach works particularly well when interviewing with line managers (versus professional human resources people). Managers tend to be uncomfortable during interviews anyway. This type of question gives them the opportunity to discuss what they know best: their own work in their own department.

> **EXAMPLE:** "I was impressed with the way the firm has kept its strong service record in the face of rising labor and parts costs. What measures have you taken to maintain your record?"
>
> *Added bonus:* Questions like this keep interviewers talking and make you sound smart at the same time. A young officer once interviewed with General Douglas MacArthur, and asked him one slightly flattering question. MacArthur kept talking for an hour, never giving the officer a chance to say a thing. Later, he praised the officer as a "fascinating conversationalist"—rare praise from the general.

2. Could You Tell Me a Little About Yourself?

This is the open-ended question that scares the most people. It shouldn't. Use it as a low-key way of selling yourself into the job and overcoming anything that may seem to be a problem on your resume.

Remember that the interviewer doesn't care about *you*, but what it is about you that can solve his problems and fill an open position. In light of this, avoid launching into a life history. Instead, give only the information that supports your credentials for the job. *Briefly* outline your background: past job history, goals, schooling, even hobbies or memberships, always relating it to the position you're interviewing for.

For example, point up parallels between your work experience and the requirements for this job; mention courses you've taken that make you more qualified; touch on outside interests (in most cases, virtually any sport is ideal), and link them to your leadership qualities and ability to get along with people.

Don't be afraid to stretch things a bit, but don't lie. Just present the jobs and experiences in your past so that they form a coherent pattern—even if you didn't have the foggiest notion at the time that you were building a foundation for your career.

> **EXAMPLE:** A recent college graduate in history, interviewing at a bank, highlighted his after-school job and the one or two economics courses he had taken. He explained how his

interest in banking had developed during his job, where he learned how to keep books and manage a small enterprise. He discussed how this led him to realize that banking would be the right career choice, *enhanced* by his liberal arts degree, "since banks require people who are generalists with perspective, who are able to deal with many kinds of people and situations." His reasoning convinced the interviewer and he got the job.

Note: The real reason he wanted to go into banking was that he couldn't think of anything else he could do. But it's unlikely he would have gotten the job offer if that's what he had told the interviewer.

Everything you say about yourself should fit together to form one cohesive message: I have unique qualities that make me the right person to fill this particular position.

EXAMPLE: A laid-off marketing manager from a large firm, who interviewed with a smaller company, emphasized her past work responsibilities in a way that showed they could easily be applied to a smaller company: broad control over a single campaign, tight budgeting procedures, leadership of a small team. Who cared that she'd be coming from a larger company? She demonstrated how everything she did there would help her do an even better job at a *smaller* firm.

TIP: According to a G.E. engineer, "Even if you are interviewing for a purely technical position, strongly stress your interpersonal skills. Few scientists or engineers work alone; unless you are unquestionably brilliant, interpersonal skills are important. Always talk about wanting to be a team player."

3. Why Did You Pick That Job (or that Company, or that College)?

This is another open-ended behavioral question that floors some applicants. The key to answering it: Consider the factors that led you to past choices *before* the interview. In all cases, show that whatever you've done, you chose to do for practical, responsible reasons. Avoid the most common beginning response to such questions: a long, drawn-out "Uhhh. . . ." Have your reasons ready, so you can be direct and to-the-point during the interview.

EXAMPLE: "I worked at that firm because it offered me the best opportunities for growth. I began the job as an account manager, and ended by supervising the entire Southwest region. It was an excellent experience."

EXAMPLE: "I picked State College for two reasons. It had a strong Economics program and, frankly, it was less expensive than Private University."
Note: No one can fault you for being frugal.

If the company or career decision you made was obviously a bad choice, don't waste time discussing it. Briefly state why you made your decision, stressing the rationale for doing it at the time.

EXAMPLE: "I accepted the offer because the company was poised for substantial growth, which was substantiated by articles in *The Wall Street Journal* and the trade magazines. The market collapsed a year later, of course, and things changed. But given what I knew and what the experts were saying at the time, it was the right decision. As it happened, I learned quite a bit while I was there that is applicable now. For example . . ."

4. Have You Received Any Other Offers?

If you have other job offers, it's usually best to say so. It shows that someone else thinks you're good enough to hire, which ups your chances at the current interview. Add, of course, that this is the job you're most interested in—even if it's not.

5. Are You Interviewing Anywhere Else?

There's usually no harm in saying that you are. Just don't say where. To do so might hurt your chances for an offer, particularly if the other firms are more prestigious or pay higher salaries. If asked, just say you'd prefer not to say.

If this is not your first-choice company, *don't* tell the interviewer this. Interviewing is like proposing marriage: no one wants to be told that he or she is the number-two choice. According to job counselors and recruiters, a surprising number of applicants do admit to this. For example, commercial bank recruiters in 1986 reported being told by many MBAs that their first choices were investment banks, and that they were interviewing at commercial banks "just in case." Even when they didn't say so openly, they clearly implied it by talking about investment banks the whole time. Needless to say, these people were not offered positions.

Never admit to interviewing for jobs in another field—even if you are. If you're asked, say no or avoid the question entirely. Who wants to hire someone who is not even sure what he or she wants as a career?

6. Is There Anything About Your Personal Life That May Affect Your Performance in This High-Travel, Demanding Position?

Employers are prohibited by law from asking anyone if their family will interfere with their job. This, then, is the "legal" way around an illegal question, usually addressed to women.

The answer is "no."

> **TIP:** In general, interviewers cannot ask about your personal life: sexual habits, children (their ages, your plans regarding them, and how you take care of them), religion, age, weight, whether you own or rent a home, possible criminal record, military background. Divulging such information is subject to certain restricted limitations depending on the sensitivity of the position. The Pentagon, for example, very often goes into all aspects of a candidate's personal life for security-related jobs; expect the same from all jobs that require security clearances. Even with private firms, these questions will often be hinted at, and the more you can ease the interviewer's mind, the better off you'll be.

7. What Are Your Strengths?

Mention *specific* attributes that you have, which your employer *needs* in the job. If you're a detail nut and you're applying for an auditing job—great. Talk about it. But give examples: explain how you found the missing million in the Billings account. Interviewers, like all people, remember specifics, not generalities.

> **EXAMPLE:** *For a managerial position:* "My greatest strengths are my ability to supervise and my interpersonal skills. Last year I won the company's supervisor award, but more important, I think, was an employee poll that voted me the best supervisor of the year. I believe that good operating results come first and foremost from good employee relations."

Avoid being dull or using clichés. Don't say that your greatest strength is your attention to goals, that you are "motivated by challenges" and are a "perfectionist"—unless you have memorable examples to prove it. Do you realize how many "goal-oriented perfectionists" walk through employment office doors every week?

8. What Are Your Weaknesses?

This is a dangerous and quite frankly stupid question that can hurt you more than it can help you. If you confess your true weaknesses, interviewers may respect your honesty, but they won't hire you. Two major mistakes are common and should be avoided at all costs. The first is the gut-honest answer: admitting to your major weaknesses. Don't. Most interviewers recognize that you won't, and don't expect you to do so.

> **EXAMPLE:** **For incurably honest types who cannot tell a lie, remember one interesting fact reported in *Harper's* magazine. Forty percent of all astronauts suffered from motion sickness in space. Zero percent admitted that in public. There's nothing wrong with holding back certain information.**

The second common mistake is to give a canned response that sounds rehearsed. You're not at an interview to act, you're there to sell yourself. Pick a fault that you have that isn't too horrendous, and that in fact may make you sound even more employable. Turn the question into a way of selling yourself. To make it sound *real* and unrehearsed, and to make you stand out, give brief but specific examples.

> **EXAMPLE:** **Almost every dedicated employee worries too much about work, and overworks. So . . ."My biggest weakness is that I can't relax when I'm working on a big project. During our last public relations campaign, my friends [or husband, wife] complained that they barely saw me. Since then, I've set aside at least two hours a day, and one full weekend day, to spend with them. Unless, of course, something major comes up. . . ."**

To repeat a point: Be sure to give examples that *sell you*. Your objective isn't to discuss your weaknesses as much as it is to discuss how and why even your weaknesses make you an ideal candidate.

Whatever weakness you bring up, briefly stress how you've taken steps to overcome it. Self-improvement shows that you can not only see a flaw, you can act on it. Be careful not to mention any faults that could in any way impinge on your position. Don't mention nervousness, sloppiness, carelessness, poor organizing skills, or anything else that might make you seem like less than an ideal employee.

9. Why Do You Want This Job? OR Why Should We Hire You?

This is the best opportunity you'll have to sell yourself. Use it.

Explain why this is a logical position for you; sum up your work history and reemphasize your strongest qualities and achievements; most important, let the interviewer know that you will be an asset to the company.

Many interviewers report that candidates *don't sell themselves strongly enough*—at all levels. Avoid the problem by stating flatly and openly why you want the job: because you're convinced that you have the right skills and background to make you the right candidate. Then move into your sales pitch, explaining why and how you can contribute to the company. Give specific examples.

> **EXAMPLE:** "I know this business, and I know your company's excellent record. I started as a clerk with a smaller company in production control, and I worked my way up. This position as supervisor in one of the largest and best-run firms in the business is the culmination of my accomplishments. My background, experience, and enthusiasm make me certain that I'm the right person for the job. For example, you've stated that you need someone with strong managerial skills. My years of experience, and recent success . . ."

> **EXAMPLE:** "This position combines my talents and skills and uses them very effectively. As we discussed, prior to my current job I was a copywriter. Soon after, I had overall creative responsibility for a small account. This position puts both experiences to work in a product category I know well and have many ideas about. I've already explained how I turned around a flagging product line. I know I can accomplish even more here with your already successful line. For example, I have extensive experience in broadcasting. We could put together a new television campaign. . . ."
> *Note:* Saying "we" strikes a positive note and implies that you already envision yourself as part of the team.

10. Why Did You Leave Your Previous Job?

The best answer is usually the easiest: you left your previous job for more responsibility and a substantially higher salary. Avoid any suspicion on the interviewer's part that you had problems with your former employer. Usually, that *is* the case, but if at all possible, stress the reasons that make you look like a responsible but somewhat ambitious employee. You left because you were seeking better growth potential, a unique business challenge, and a higher salary.

If the interviewer knows you had problems with your previous employer, don't lie or struggle to change the subject. This often occurs in small towns or close-knit industries where everyone knows what everyone else is doing or can easily find out that information. Acknowledge your previous difficulties at work, stress that they were unique to that situation, then talk about the *positive* aspects of the job, what you learned, and how that experience can be helpful in this job.

Whatever the temptation, don't bad-mouth your previous employer. Don't forget that the interviewer looks at things from a different angle. You may someday leave this job, too. If you did, what would you say about them? Negative gossip makes you look unprofessional.

Be careful. Some interviewers may lure you into making negative judgments about ex-employers. Even if the interviewer genuinely seems to feel the same way you do about your previous employer, avoid being conspiratorial about your opinions.

> **EXAMPLE:** Several people have reported that interviewers encourage them to make negative statements. One interviewer started by being very sympathetic: "That company is a real pressure cooker." The applicant agreed, and the interviewer made a more negative judgment, to which the applicant also agreed, and so on until the applicant was telling all.
> *Note:* This is a common pitfall with younger or less-experienced applicants.

> **TIP:** Don't lie or defend your previous employer either. If your previous employer was tough or unfair, try to concentrate on what was good about the job (you learned freight-forwarding procedures, etc.) and how you can apply that experience to *this* job.

The same principle applies if you've switched careers. It's always best to take the positive approach: your previous career was fine, but you've always wanted to work in this field. Avoid the temptation of talking about how bad it was being a paralegal, etc. Save that discussion to have with your friends. You never know what background experience may be of interest to an interviewer, and what you might lose by downgrading it.

> **EXAMPLE: A would-be refugee from "big-city" life applied to a "down-home" mail-order house specializing in camping gear. The interview was excellent until the applicant began criticizing his current employer for its rigid, corporate, urban way of retailing. The interviewer's face dropped, and the interview was soon over without an offer. It turned out that the interviewer was looking for a candidate who could update ordering and handling procedures. By expressing his dislike for his competitor's ways, the candidate talked himself out of a job in a small town.**

11. Where Do You See Yourself in Five Years? In Ten Years?

When interviewers ask you to project your career into the future, give a bland reply. Say you see yourself at the same company in a position of greater responsibility. Talk about the *job*, not the title, unless the company is an openly aggressive up-or-out organization. By concentrating on the position itself, you establish your commitment to the work, as opposed to being overly ambitious and fixated on money or title.

Be brief. Talking about the future isn't as productive as talking about the present and why you're a good candidate for the job. Moreover, since you don't know the company's plans for the future, you might say something that could disqualify you.

> **EXAMPLE: "I expect to still be involved in financial services, with a solid client base that I'd develop with you at XYZ brokers."**

> **TIP: Avoid making an overly glib and ambitious statement such as "I see myself in your job" or "I see myself as president of the company." Although it may make you seem like a go-getter, in today's uncertain economy it also sounds threatening—or foolish. Who wants to hire someone who's openly gunning for his or her job?**

> **TIP: Sometimes honesty works best of all. Several employers in extremely high turn-over industries such as stock-trading have**

preferred applicants who answered "I don't know"—at least they were being honest and weren't trying to snow them.

12. What Salary Range Did You Have in Mind?

Don't say. If the numbers you pick are too high or too low, it may put you out of the running even before the interview is over.

Almost always, people will respect you if you say that you'd prefer to discuss salary later. In some cases, however, the interviewer will insist on discussing it then. First, try to get the interviewer to set the range. Turn the question around: "What salary range has the firm been considering?"

If you still have to give your price first, think back on your research and come up with a figure that meets the standards within the industry and is reasonable in light of your background. Choose a figure that's a little on the high side: it's better to look valuable than cut-rate. But stress to the interviewer that it's the *job*, not the potential salary, that particularly interests you.

Especially with entry-level positions, but also in fields where competition is tough and applicants are many, you may be told a salary and asked if it is suitable. If it falls within a reasonable range, it is best to say yes, but beyond that be as noncommittal as possible. Chances are, the job is probably an easy one to fill. If you say no, you'll be cut out of the running. By saying yes and curtailing further discussion, you keep them interested in you, but you also reserve the opportunity to negotiate a better benefits package, or vacation arrangement, after an offer is made.

13. Sell Me on My Company or Product.

Asking you to give a spontaneous sales presentation is a quick way for interviewers to weed out applicants. This tough task is commonly presented to people who are applying for sales jobs, and is increasingly used by banks and brokerage houses. Most people aren't prepared for it and answer by stumbling and stammering their way through a very amateurish monologue that is embarrassing to them and painful (or amusing) for the interviewer to hear.

Be ready beforehand. Before any interview, go over the product or services, and practice being on a sales call. Be thorough in your research, but don't worry too much about it: the fact that you are prepared to give a measured and coherent answer is what's important.

Make a point of saying you welcome this opportunity. After all, that's why you're interviewing here: to get the chance to represent the company and its product. Then proceed as if you were on a sales call, highlighting the advantages of the product or service.

> **EXAMPLE: "Yes, I'd like the chance to show how I'd sell your product. After all, that's why I chose to interview here, because I believe in the company and what it sells. I'll begin with the top-of-the line product, which is the best of its kind. . . ."**

> **TIP: Use props to underscore your salesmanship. One young bank applicant photocopied an advertising article on the bank's new cash-management service, and used it during his sales presentation. Don't be afraid to copy this technique: it shows resourcefulness and a strong sales mentality.**

14. Can You Think of Anything Else That You'd Like to Add?

The answer to this question is always yes.

If the interviewer neglected one critical area that further qualifies you, mention it now. Even if nothing critical was omitted, use this opportunity to re-sell yourself. Combine points from your resume into a logical, understandable reason for hiring you.

> **EXAMPLE: "Yes, we were talking about your inventory control system. I understand that it's not a principal function of the job, but I'd like to add that I've had several months of experience as an inventory control clerk. So, together with my experience as a manager, I feel that I've got a uniquely appropriate background for this job; I could quickly and effectively take charge. . . ."**

If the interview has gone badly, use this time to counter all the negatives that the interviewer may have mentioned. *Don't* bring up your weak points unless you feel fairly certain that the interviewer is going to make a negative decision: repeating the negatives can be counterproductive. You may wind up, at the very end of the interview, *reminding* the interviewer of reasons not to hire you. But if you have had a bad interview, a forthright stand on the relevant issues can sometimes turn the interview around. You have nothing to lose.

EXAMPLE: "I can understand your objections to a candidate who has switched careers three times in ten years. But I'd like to add that by hiring me you'd be employing a man who is now *determined* to make this one work. I've demonstrated my firm dedication to this career by taking the night courses I mentioned, and working very hard. My references will all corroborate how excellent my skills are, and what a real advantage they'd be in this job. You'd be getting all my experience and ability at a far lower cost than you'd normally have to spend. And you won't find such dedication in anyone else. . . ."

9 *Follow-Up*

INTRODUCTION

After you've finished an interview, you just can't relax and wait for a job offer. The minute the interview is over—sometimes even *during* the interview—you should start thinking about follow-up. What can you do to further convince the interviewer that you are right for the job? The answer is the all-too-often forgotten follow-up letter, or, in some cases, phone call.

Don't make the mistake many job hunters do and dismiss the idea of follow-up as a time-consuming nicety, something that makes you look polite but doesn't accomplish much else. Follow-up is too important to be pushed aside.

FOLLOW-UP LETTERS

■ **While thanking the interviewer is technically the reason for a follow-up letter, what you actually are doing is taking advantage of a sales opportunity.**

A follow-up letter is often your *last chance* to convince a prospective employer that you are the right person for the job. Writing one effectively often can make the difference between a job offer and a polite "we regret to inform you that the position has been filled. . . ."

■ **The sooner you write a follow-up letter and send it, the better.**

You will come across as interested, aggressive and courteous—all positive signals when it comes to landing a job.

> TIP: To make the best impression, write and send a thank-you note on the same day as your interview; or send it the following day but date it the same day as your interview.

How to Write an Effective Follow-Up Letter

■ **Since this is ostensibly a brief thank you, keep your letter short: one page or less.**

This is more than enough space to (1) remind the prospective employer of your interview, (2) sell yourself one more time, and (3) recap—which are the three essential sections of a strong, well-organized follow-up letter.

Section #1: The Basic Reminder

■ **Start simply. Unlike any other type of letter you send during your job hunt, a follow-up letter *doesn't* have to grab the reader's attention from the outset.**

All you want to do in the opening of your letter is remind the interviewer that you were interviewed for the job and that you're very interested in it. A basic, no-frills "Thanks for your time today. I enjoyed discussing the position" is fine to begin with.

> TIP: The letter's tone should match the intended audience—the interviewer. If he or she was casual, make your letter a bit looser and more informal. If the interviewer was very traditional, stick with a formal business letter.

Next, restate your interest in the job, being sure to mention the exact position you discussed. If possible, give your "interest" statement a double value: write it as a mini sales pitch that introduces your strongest qualifications and thus leads directly to the next section.

Section #2: The Sales Message

■ **To back up your qualifications for the job and remind the prospective employer of your interest, repeat the highlights of the interview.**

In this portion of the letter, you should continue the sales pitch you began during your interview. Refer directly to specific points you discussed. Be sure to mention several examples of your qualifications, ideally those which the interviewer appeared most interested in. *Remember:* Your aim *isn't* to come up with a new way of presenting yourself. Instead, you should be building on the foundation you already established during the interview.

This is a good place to give the interviewer additional information that will strengthen your case. If you've learned more about the position or the company and realize you should expand upon your qualifications, do it here.

Note: If any misconceptions arose during your interview, or if the interview went poorly in general, this is where you should straighten things out. One important exception to this rule: If a problem came up during the interview (your qualifications weren't right; you didn't have enough experience, etc.) and you dealt with it successfully then, *don't* bring it up again in a thank-you letter. Leave well enough alone.

Whichever tactic you focus on, you should be constantly hammering home one point: "I am the person you should hire."

Section #3: Recap

■ **Close your letter as concisely as you opened it.**

The last paragraph in the letter should be essentially a repeat of your opening: thank the interviewer again for his or her time; restate how interested you are in the position and why you are qualified.

> TIP: *For aggressive types:* **Set up a reason to have another interview and say you'll call to arrange a definite time.**
> *Example:* **"Based upon our discussion, I have outlined a series of training programs that should work well for AMB Enterprises. I will give you a call early next week to set up a time in which you and I can go over them."**
> *Note:* **This approach can either force the interviewer to make a quicker decision *or* strengthen a weak interview.**

SAMPLE THANK-YOU LETTER

Mr. Mark Conrad
Executive Vice President, Human Resources
MegaBux Incorporated
666 Sixth Avenue
New York, NY 10022

Dear Mr. Conrad:

Thank you for meeting with me today to discuss the Director of Training position. I was especially interested in your comments about the need for expanded employee education in light of MegaBux's rapid growth and latest acquisitions.

[A basic opening; nothing flashy, but the writer has hit all the right notes. By referring to a specific aspect of the conversation, he nudges the interviewer's memory and makes himself stand out. Even better, he leads smoothly into his sales pitch in the next paragraph.]

As I mentioned during our conversation, I have a proven track record in the development and implementation of training programs. Most recently, I designed and oversaw a series of intensive sales training seminars for Alta Industries. The proof of their effectiveness was dramatic: sales increased 23% and the sales staff reported better understanding and higher morale.

[He immediately repeats his strongest selling point—one that matches the job opening. Again, nothing flashy, but it works.]

Again, many thanks for your time and attention. There is no doubt in my mind that developing a corporate-wide system of interactive employee education programs for MegaBux would be a rewarding challenge—the type of challenge I know I can meet successfully. I look forward to hearing from you in the near future.

[A utilitarian close; he thanks the interviewer again at the bottom, repeats how interested he is in the job, how confident he is that he can do it, and gets out of the letter gracefully.]

Sincerely,

Lawrence Putnam

FOLLOW-UP TELEPHONE CALLS

■ **One hard-and-fast rule applies to using the phone:** *don't* **use a phone for follow-up if it makes you uncomfortable.**

But there is a major exception to this rule. If your interview was a few weeks ago, you've already sent a follow-up letter and you still haven't heard back, swallow your discomfort and pick up the phone. If the worst is true and the prospective employer has hired someone else or decided you weren't right for the job, you have absolutely nothing to lose.

On the other hand, you may also discover that your fears were unfounded. In that case, your phone call should turn into a small sales pitch.

Consider using the phone for follow-up if:

• your interview went badly and you want to aim for a second interview

• you've gotten another job offer and you need to know where you stand at this company before you make a decision

• you have new, important information to share with the interviewer—and you want to be sure he or she gets it immediately

How to Make Follow-Up Phone Calls

■ **As you would with a follow-up letter, keep it short and to the point.**

As with other phone calls you may make during your job hunt, you should answer any questions the person on the other end of the line might pose *before* he or she has to ask them. Explain who you are, why you are calling, when you were interviewed and for what position.

> **EXAMPLE: "Mr. Brown? This is Sandra Kinney. We met two weeks ago, May seventeenth, to discuss the marketing assistant position that's available at Magitech. . . ."**

Be straightforward when you ask about the status of your application. You want to know if you're still in the running. Again, it's up to you to bring up the subject. Depending upon the exact circumstances, you might mention having other job offers, give the employer new information, or try to close in on a job offer.

> **EXAMPLE: "I wanted to know if you've reached a decision yet. I've received another job offer, but before I make a decision, I need to know about the position at Magitech. . . ."**
>
> *OR:* **"As I'm sure you realize, I'm very interested in the position. Since we met, I've taken the time to draw up several sample marketing plans to show what I have in mind for Magitech. When could I come in to show them to you?"**
>
> *OR:* **"Is there anything else you need to know about me before you reach a final decision? I'd be glad to stop by. . . ."**
>
> *OR (for the confident, aggressive sales personality only):* **"I'm looking forward to working at Magitech. I think I can contribute a great deal to the marketing team. Could we meet to finalize your decision?"**

Another method that works, especially if you're calling because you've heard nothing, is to be honest and direct. Ask what is happening—no tricks, no gimmicks, nothing but curiosity. "I was hoping to hear from you and decided to call to see if you've made a decision yet." Follow *that* up with a reminder of your interest and top qualifications: "I'm enthusiastic about working for Magitech. As I mentioned during our interview, my five years experience in marketing widgets . . ."

■ **When you call an employer to follow up, you must be prepared for rejection.**

An employer may tell you flatly that you weren't right for the job; someone else has already been hired. Hearing even the most polite rejection, the "I'm sorry, but . . . ," isn't easy, and it certainly isn't pleasant, but it also isn't the end of the world. If you have the temperament, ask the employer what the problem was—it's possible that you may be able to overcome his or her objection. At the least, you can find out what (if anything) you can improve upon in future interviews.

■ **Recognize that many rejections aren't your fault and can't be avoided.**

Keep reminding yourself that there are other positions out there, other interviews you'll be having, and other follow-ups. Stay optimistic. Each day—and each rejection—brings you closer to a job.

10 *Assessing a Job Offer*

INTRODUCTION

You've been offered a job; now comes the hard part. Do you accept it immediately or do you wait? Do you start negotiating for better terms or do you accept the total package as is? Is the salary competitive? What about benefits? How do you assess the job you've been offered and decide if you need it or want it?

As with the rest of your job hunt, the best way to handle these questions is in a step-by-step manner: methodically and carefully looking at each question and problem. In most cases, try to resist the temptation to accept an offer immediately and throw the consequences to the wind. This is especially hard if you are unemployed, but you'll be far better off in the long run if you look before you leap.

Before accepting a position, break the offer down and analyze it.

The three basic steps to take are:

1. Assessing the company

2. Assessing the position

3. Assessing the salary and benefits package

If everything looks good, accept the job. If certain aspects look bad, consider *negotiating* a better package. If all aspects look bad, ask yourself: *"Why the hell did I interview for this job in the first place?"*

GENERAL CONSIDERATIONS

■ As a rule, don't accept an offer on the spot.

In the first flush of success, particularly if you've been unemployed for a while, your natural inclination will be to accept and forget the potential consequences. But you should realize that the consequences can be severe, ranging from a lower than normal salary to a slow career track to bad working conditions. In other words, you might not know what you're getting into.

Tell the interviewer you need a week to think about and assess the offer. This will give you time to analyze the company, the position, the salary, and the benefits package. Most companies *expect* you to take at least a week.

> **TIP:** *First warning flag of a bad job offer:* **When the interviewer presses you to make a decision immediately. This suggests a problem with the quality of the company or the offer. The position may be one that the company is having difficulty filling, or the company itself may be having problems that the interviewer doesn't want you to find out about.** *Ask* **the interviewer why he or she needs a quick decision, and look at those reasons suspiciously.**

There are a few exceptions. Sometimes, you'll have to make a fast decision for all the *right* reasons. Entrepreneurial companies, which pride themselves on being fast-moving, may want someone who can make a decision on the spot. This is particularly true when the founder of the firm makes an offer. He or she is used to gutsy, seat-of-the-pants decision-making, and expects such behavior from subordinates. If you want the job, you may have to say yes quickly.

With lower-level positions in highly competitive industries, an immediate acceptance or reply in a few days is also sometimes the norm. In the words of one interviewer: "They need us more than we need them. If they can't decide quickly, they can walk out without a job." It's usually easy to tell if your firm and/or offer falls into this category. The salaries in such firms are low, benefits are standardized, and employment officers, rather than line managers, are the principal decision-makers. Even in this case, you usually can negotiate for an overnight delay or a delay of a few days.

STEP ONE: ASSESSING THE COMPANY

Business Record and Finances

■ **After holding back from accepting the offer, start your next day by analyzing the company and its business.**

It may take only a few hours to research and analyze a company or institution, but the benefits of doing this can affect the rest of your career.

Ask yourself: *Where is the company going? Is it gaining or losing market share? Would I be working in a strong division? If not, would the rewards be worth it?* Analyze nonprofit institutions and government positions in the same manner. Is the area or function receiving adequate and increasing funding? Are the functions of the position well supported and respected by the profession or the rest of the institution? In other words: *Is this company a good place for my career?*

> TIP: *Advice from an older but wiser middle manager:* **If you are offered a high-paying, high-visibility position in a division that needs to be "turned around," think twice before you get enticed by challenges, above-average salaries, bonuses, and visions of yourself on the cover of *Forbes* magazine as "The Turn-around King." In today's cost-cutting atmosphere, entire divisions can be sold off, and managers as quickly dumped, by the new owners. Or the "turn-around" division may be impossible to turn around, leaving you looking like an ineffective manager who has wasted several years.**

■ **Check library references and personal contacts for a reading on the company and its future.**

Read between the lines and make certain to go beyond surface impressions, particularly with smaller, less-known firms. Don't rely merely on credit reports from *Dun & Bradstreet*. Many disreputable or even failing businesses maintain strong credit ratings to the very end. Instead, ask if you can speak to your potential co-workers in the firm. Get a reading from what they say—or *don't* say—about the company. Speak with friends or acquaintances in competing corporations and read the trade magazines to get a feel for the company and its place in the industry.

EXAMPLE: *A worst-case scenario of a newly-minted MBA who accepted a job with a trading firm that had plush offices and an impeccable credit rating:* The interviewer explained that the company traded "consumer electronics goods and other items" to certain nations. The MBA didn't press to find out what the "other items" were when he accepted the very generous offer. He did check a credit source that rated the firm A+. He found out a lot more after a few weeks on the job, when FBI agents knocked on the door. They were investigating shipments of arms to the Middle East. The MBA quickly applied to another firm, offering a unique reason for having left his previous job: "I didn't find gun-running compatible with my long-term career plans."

TIP: For major firms and industries, check *Value Line* to get a quick fix on your potential employer. See Chapter 3, "Research," for other ideas on how to find out more about your company.

Company Culture

■ **Check if you are compatible with the firm.**

Are you and the corporation compatible in terms of working and social styles? If you prefer bureaucratic management, you might be very unhappy in a small, hard-charging, entrepreneurial company. Or vice versa. Pick up clues from the interview itself: How did they treat you? Did you feel comfortable during the interview? Did you like the people?

Compatibility with your new firm isn't a minor consideration. Never presume that "I'll just get used to it." Maybe you won't. Besides, unhappiness with your work often means a slower career track and less money or advancement down the road. Job satisfaction pays practical career dividends, while *you* pay for your career dissatisfaction.

EXAMPLE: One woman made a "successful" job switch to another firm in the same business. She got more money, but lost on everything else. Her first firm was entrepreneurial, friendly, and casual. And she was on the fast track. Her new firm was a giant in the field, slow-moving and bureaucratic with employees seated quietly in their cubicles all day. For a few thousand extra dollars she traded away her happy and productive work environment—and suffered from depression and problems on her new job. Was it worth it? Only if three thousand dollars extra for *one* year was the only factor in her decision.

■ **Compare your prospective employer's management style with that of the rest of the company.**

Openings often occur when a manager is in trouble with senior management: the manager's employees may be leaving so as not to be part of a losing team. Make certain you're not *joining* that team.

■ **See how well the combination of your style and your employer's style would mesh with the company as a whole.**

Managers hire people who either match or complement their style. However, if your employer is a very different type of person from the company norm and he or she leaves, you might be forced to leave as well, even if you're just *perceived* to be similar.

EXAMPLE: This happened to a man employed in the materials-processing center of a large fragrance manufacturer and marketer. His immediate supervisor was a nontraditional, seat-of-the-pants administrator with a messy desk and sloppy procedures who was also bright, fun to work with, and somehow got the job done brilliantly. But he was completely at odds with the conservative, slow-but-steady style of upper management. Shortly after the man was hired his supervisor was forced to leave, and the employee had a problem. He was associated with the old manager and was viewed suspiciously by the new, tough, no-nonsense manager, who quickly brought in his own people from his old division to shake things up.

STEP TWO: ASSESSING THE POSITION

■ **Ask for a job description and do some other checking; don't just *assume* you understand the position.**

The most important part of assessing your offer is the most obvious and, for that reason, the most overlooked: the position itself. See where the normal career track lies, and estimate how long you are expected to stay in the position. What are the job responsibilities, and are they clearly spelled out? Again, talking to your predecessor can be very valuable and can give you a good sense of what you're accepting if you take the job.

> **TIP: If you have nagging doubts about the management, get a *written* job and responsibilities description.**

■ Review the history of the position.

What happened to the person before you? One man thought his position looked very attractive until a brief investigation showed that the average tenure in the job was one year. Three previous employees had each held the position for one year and then were fired. This doesn't necessarily mean that the firm is disreputable or the position is wrong for you. Many sales-oriented companies and stock broker- ages maintain strict "up-or-out" policies; if you can't sell or make money, you're fired. But you should *know* this in advance, and be prepared.

It's the same case at lower levels with large "management trainee" classes—where many aspiring Fortune 500 banking and fi- nancial people get their start. Find out how many management train- ees are kept on after the year or so of classes is over, and what happens to the average trainee after training.

> **EXAMPLE: Certain larger banks use the trainee position as a way of observing a candidate's performance, so they can later "weed out" the lower-than-average performers. Others, like the Morgan Bank, maintain a strong commitment to *all* trainees and expect them to remain. Don't make the error of assuming that all large corporations treat entry- level employees the same.**

■ Another major consideration: How does the position you've been offered fit in with your short- and long-term career plans?

A low-paying, high-stress job actually may be better than any alternative if it is the only way to break into a new business or indus- try. For example, "glamour fields" such as television or entertainment typically offer anyone who is not experienced or well-connected low- paying, unprestigious jobs. If you accept this as the cost of getting your foot in the door, then you can work your way up.

> **EXAMPLE:** One mid-level, ex-government employee who wanted to break into television news learned this the hard way: he was offered a low-paying network news job, but he arrogantly turned it down, figuring that with his experience he should be earning far more. He realized later that he had made a mistake. His job hunt was still in progress when one network froze its positions and others started having major layoffs, so he found himself without any news job at all.

This approach should also be considered by career changers and unemployed middle managers who are forced to switch fields. Sometimes the only way to get the right job is by taking the *wrong* job first and accepting low level, low pay, and low prestige. In many cases it's better to take a step backward *now* rather than suffer the consequences of long-term unemployment. But always look carefully at career paths: Does the position offer opportunities for career growth? Or is it a dead-end administrative assistant job?

> **TIP:** Unemployed managers and recent college graduates should be particularly careful when going to employment agencies. Less reputable firms may offer "high-growth administrative assistant" positions that, in reality, are dead-end jobs.

STEP THREE: ASSESSING THE SALARY AND BENEFITS PACKAGE

- **The definition of a good salary and benefits package is: "It all depends . . ."**

It all depends on industry or professional standards, your position, your experience, your background, your goals. Salary and benefits packages vary widely among different industries, and among different companies *within* the same industry.

The best way to assess a benefits package and salary is to determine:

- if it meets or exceeds what others are getting for the same position at the same level of skill

- if *you* feel comfortable with both your salary and your benefits

Salary

■ **Check industry standards for salaries at your level in the industry.**

The best sources for information about industry standards are want ads and articles in trade publications, annual salary surveys published in newspapers and magazines, and word of mouth from friends and acquaintances in the field.

> **TIP:** *From a career expert:* **When a colleague tells you how much he or she is making,** *reduce* **the amount by 10%–20% to get the real salary. If colleagues tell you the "average" salaries in their field without mentioning their own,** *add* **10%–20%.** *Reason:* **People want to think they make more than the industry norm for their position, and stretch the facts to fit their version of the truth. They're not necessarily lying to** *you,* **they're just finagling a bit in their heads: "After all, I really am getting $45,000 a year, or I would be if I hadn't been fired that time, but that wasn't my fault, and if you throw in my bonus and the company car, I'm getting $39,000, which is close. . . ."**

■ **Warning flags should go up if the salary you're offered is much higher or lower than the norm.**

If the salary is much higher than usual, don't just be flattered and accept. Look for problems with the position, or the company, or both. They may be offering more because no one will take the job at a lower salary due to bad working conditions. Or, the company could be in precarious shape. If the salary is much lower than usual, look for problems in their perception of *you.* You should be worth what the market is paying, or there should be very good reasons why you're not being offered a market salary.

■ **Check the firm's bonus policy, if any.**

There is no hard and fast rule about bonuses: some firms are very generous, others offer next to nothing. One manager received a Christmas turkey at his automobile dealership; in his next job he negotiated a bonus of 10% of his total salary. Performance bonuses are increasingly common in certain industries at the mid to upper levels. Middle managers typically receive 10%–15% of their total compensation; higher executives receive more. Financial firms commonly offer very generous bonuses depending on their performance in the financial markets and on individual merit. Finance is one of the few fields in which lower-level employees, including secretaries, can receive bonuses in the thousands of dollars. Sales jobs typically give bonuses based on your sales performance. If you've been offered a sales position, you may want to negotiate your bonus in advance based on your previous sales record and what you think others are getting.

In general, more and more companies will stress profit-sharing, and productivity-based *incentive* increases. Salary increases for white-collar workers averaged 4%–6% in 1988, but increasingly companies are cutting back on across-the-board, standardized, yearly salary increases. Instead, yearly raises are linked to personal and corporate productivity.

Benefits Packages

■ **A good benefits package can be worth 20%–40% of your salary.**

When assessing the salary you've been offered, be sure to factor in the fringe benefits as much as possible: the full range of *medical, dental, pension,* and *disability* benefits. Although it is difficult to give dollar values to certain benefits, try to determine their worth by reading through the company's printed material on the subject. Many people don't even glance at the written plan because it's too technical and boring, or they're intimidated by the accounting terms and "legalese."

It is even more difficult to *compare* and choose between two benefits packages that are offered by the same firm. The difficulty of understanding one, let alone two, complex pension plans, for example, can be so frustrating that you end up damning the day you decided to work for a living. But take the time to wade through the basics of the benefits package. You should be looking for omissions and signs of bad management. If you see problems or discrepancies, take your concerns to a qualified accountant or lawyer. Typically, the larger the company, the less the odds of there being anything unseemly about your plan. It also works the other way: with smaller firms, it pays to look carefully at the full range of benefits.

When you are looking at different benefits packages, don't let the relative differences between two plans outweigh the opportunities afforded you by the position itself. In general, the older and more experienced you are, the more important your benefits are—and vice versa. If you are young, consider the *experience* and *exposure* the job will give you well ahead of any benefits package.

■ **Benefits packages vary widely, from standard packages with only a little flexibility to pick-and-choose "cafeteria style" flex plans where the employee can design his or her own package from a variety of options.**

Many employees have become very enthusiastic about these flexible benefits programs, since they allow them to tailor their benefits to fit their specific situations. People who worry about disability may opt for higher disability insurance, for example, while others may prefer to put more money into a solid medical plan. With these types of programs, there are only a few requirements and a lot of freedom. Usually employees are required to sign up for some form of medical, life, and disability insurance, but can select among varying coverage levels and deductibles. They can then shop among other options, which may include child care, legal services, and extra life insurance, as well as additional medical, life, and disability coverage, up to a certain level. Employees also have the option to pay extra and *add* coverage to the plan, using their pre-tax salary dollars. The advantages of flexibility are many, and these plans are becoming increasingly common. Ask about them after you've had an offer.

Below are some of the principal elements of a good benefits package; what to look for—and what to look *out* for.

Pension Plans

■ **First check to see if you are being offered a pension plan.**

Pension plans and other forms of retirement income vary widely by company and by industry. Added administrative expenses have prompted some companies to ease out of offering such plans. Although new federal regulations have required companies to give much the same pension benefits to lower-level employees as they do to senior management, some corporations have taken the easy way out and dropped their pension plans altogether.

■ **Check the *vesting period* of your plan, i.e., when you are eligible to acquire your pension benefits.**

Federal regulations require that the *maximum* vesting period for most employees be five years. Before 1989, vesting periods were often as long as ten to twenty years.

▪ *Ask* **for a rough estimate of pension benefits that will come to you after ten to twenty years, assuming that you have a "normal" career path.**

This is the best and easiest way of getting a feel for your pension plan and of comparing it to others—but few people bother to do it. Particularly if you are a job hopper, check with the firm's personnel staff to find out how long and how much you are due after specified amounts of service.

▪ **Consider the relative** *safety* **of the pension plan, and how the retirement funds are being invested.**

Are the pension trustees handling their obligations well? In other words, is the money you and the company pay in for your retirement being invested wisely and safely?

Realistically, this is very difficult to assess, and in most cases you won't want to waste your time considering this often technical issue. But if you are concerned, you may want to check the company's annual report or the financial section of the 10K report that is filed with the Securities Exchange Commission for large public corporations; with smaller companies you will have to apply to the pension trustees directly. You want to check the quality of the pension investments—what the money is being invested in and how well the investments have performed relative to the book value of the fund. Better yet, get an outside pension expert to review the management of the pension plan.

One of the most advantageous retirement investment programs today is the Employee Stock Ownership Program (ESOP), by which employee benefits are invested in the corporation's own stock. This gives employees share ownership of their corporation, and certain tax advantages to the employee as well as to the corporation.

▪ **Check to see if the company offers a 401(k) plan: a common company-sponsored savings and retirement plan.**

With a 401(k) plan you make pre-tax contributions from your salary—up to $7,000 per year—and these are matched to a certain percentage by your employer, usually by fifty cents or more on the dollar. The money can be invested in any number of ways including company stock, money market funds, stock or bond funds.

The advantage is obvious: up to $7,000 a year of your money (along with corporate contributions) goes into your retirement investments *before* taxes. When you withdraw this at retirement you must pay tax, but presumably at that point you will be in a lower tax bracket. It is one of the best tax shelters for individual taxpayers.

Some disadvantages: If you withdraw before retirement or age 59½, or the money is withdrawn due to death, disability, or severance, you must pay a 10% penalty on the taxable portion of your 401(k), along with the tax. There are very few exceptions. The same goes for the interest you've earned on your investment; it cannot be withdrawn without paying a penalty in addition to the tax. But on the positive side, many companies now permit *borrowing* against the money in the plan—something you normally can't do with pension plans or IRAs. Find out if the company allows borrowing against the 401(k); currently about half of all companies do.

Check to see how long the vesting period is with the firm's 401(k) as well. For example, if you leave the company before being vested, you may be eligible only for what you put in, or only a certain, smaller percentage of the company's contribution.

According to the U.S. Census Bureau, 6% of all American workers over twenty-five are covered by these plans. Only about 4% of U.S. corporations offer 401(k) plans, but nearly all of the largest companies with over 5,000 employees have them.

Medical Benefits

■ **A normal medical package has a deductible—the amount of medical fees you must pay yourself—of $100 to $200 a year.**

After the deductible is paid, the insurance covers 80% or so of medical expenses up to another limit—usually between $2,000 and $5,000—after which the plan covers 100% of further medical expenses up to a lifetime cap, usually of one million dollars.

Because of rising medical costs, two trends are changing the character of many medical plans. Many companies are raising deductibles, covering less for certain types of medical problems, making you wait over longer periods for reimbursement, and in general getting pickier over what is actually covered and how much you are owed. Particularly when dealing with a small company, find out exactly what is covered and to what amount. Recent estimates are that less than half of all U.S. corporations offer full medical benefits. Another trend is the movement of many companies into Health Maintenance Organizations (HMOs), in which employees are required to use doctors selected by the organization. Some people prefer HMOs because they tend to be easier to use: in many cases you can just walk into a clinic and someone will treat you. There's usually less paperwork as well. Others don't like them; they prefer to choose their own family doctor.

There are several things to check for: Does the plan cover psychiatric expenses? Many don't. Are dental, orthodontic, and vision coverage offered? Vision plans are increasingly common, but many firms still limit their coverage. If the plan includes dental coverage, check also for orthodontic coverage. If you plan on having children, check for pregnancy and dependent coverage. Many plans have *no* pregnancy coverage, while others require you to pay extra for dependent coverage. On the generous side of things, some companies, such as IBM, offer extras such as optional psychiatric coverage for emotionally disturbed children.

Two important items: Particularly when dealing with a smaller company, make sure that *current* medical problems will be covered by your new employer's plan; some plans don't allow this, and you may be left having to pay your own medical expenses. Check also to see if you are covered *between* jobs, either by your old plan or the new.

■ **Many corporations are now offering** *"corporate wellness programs,"* **which are designed to attack potential problems before you have to resort to a doctor's office or a hospital.**

This is a newer aspect of medical benefits that doesn't involve insurance. Some companies maintain exercise rooms and gyms for employees, others offer free membership or will pay for health clubs. Many now offer stress-reduction and addiction programs as well. Don't underestimate the value of these programs: certain large corporations estimate that 10% of their employees use the counseling option annually.

Disability Insurance and Long-Term Care

■ **Disability insurance, which guarantees you a certain income should you become disabled and unable to work, is sometimes deceptively less than you think.**

A basic rule of thumb: be careful. Typically, disability insurance provides you with a certain percentage of your current salary six months after you are injured and unable to work. A normal insurance package may pay 60% of the first $16,000 of your salary, for example, and then 40% of the next $12,500, minus other disability income, including Social Security disability payments.

Disability is one of those things that people assume will never happen to them. But practically speaking, you may want to see if you can increase your benefits in the unfortunate event that it does happen to you. The example above was from a good plan; others may offer far less. Find out where your salary cutoff is and how you can increase it if it's too low. Check to see if the policy has a cost-of-living adjustment, and how it defines disability. Some will pay only if you are completely unable to work, others will pay if you can't work in your regular field. Most coverage falls in between these two extremes.

On a less depressing note, also find out if *short-term* disability insurance is offered. At most large firms, it's part of the standard plan—in California, short-term disability falls under "other insurance," in New York it is mandatory—but elsewhere it can be a valuable optional benefit.

■ **Long-Term Care is still uncommon but, potentially, a very valuable benefit that you should check for.**

Nursing home care and extended home care is not well covered by Medicare, and the costs can be horrendous: upward of $30,000 a year and more. Some insurance companies are now offering people the opportunity to plan *now* for this common post-retirement expense. Costs vary depending on the coverage you want: a low coverage of $50 a day ($18,250 a year) amounts to as little as $150 a year for a young or early-middle-aged person in a group plan. Even if the corporation doesn't pay the premiums, find out if it offers long-term care as an option to which you may contribute personally. If so, you will save on administrative costs, and benefit by group rates.

Vacation, Sick Leave, and Personal Days

■ **The average new employee normally receives one to two weeks of vacation per full year of employment and one to two weeks of sick days and personal days.**

Vacation policy is fairly standard among most corporations; about 75% of all U.S. corporations provide two weeks per year after one full year of employment. Over 50% of U.S. firms now give employees ten or more paid holidays as well. Most firms offer up to four weeks vacation to long-term employees.

Child Care and Parental Leave

■ **Child-care benefits are increasingly common: over 3,000 U.S. firms offer some type of child-care benefit.**

Some firms have centers at their place of work; this, in particular, is becoming more and more common. Other firms offer direct reimbursement for child-care costs (up to a certain limit, of course) that you must arrange. Some companies also offer Adoption Assistance plans, where the firm helps pay for the costs associated with adopting a child, such as agency, legal, and foster-care charges.

■ **Parental leave used to be called maternity leave, but a growing number of companies offer leave to the male parent as well.**

If the company has a parental-leave program, check to see how your benefits are managed if you do take leave, and how the company will view your return to work. Some companies grudgingly allow parental leave, but returning employees may find that the problems outweigh any benefit.

Counseling Services, Legal Plans, and Other Services

■ **Many companies offer to pay or reimburse costs for drug- or alcohol-abuse counseling; others include psychological, financial, retirement, and career-counseling services as well.**

Financial counseling and pre-retirement programs, in particular, are becoming more and more common, but often for a negative reason: many firms expect to pare down their staffs and cut back on middle management employment. Better to let them go with a sound financial base seems to be the reasoning. Some corporations also maintain out-placement services, but you probably won't want to consider this a positive option—unless you plan on being fired.

Legal benefits are useful but minor. Typically, employees receive free legal advice; for more complicated legal problems they're given referrals, for which they'll have to pay regular fees.

Life Insurance

■ **Don't look on life insurance as a major factor in evaluating a benefits package.**

The cost to the company for life insurance is usually low, and the coverage is usually minimal. Normally, the cost of basic life insurance is assumed by your employer and begins the day you start working. It's computed as a percentage of your base annual salary up to a low maximum, usually $100,000. Supplemental insurance is generally available as well—in this case you are asked to pay a low rate, less than 1% of your yearly salary, for up to three times more insurance coverage. For example, someone making $35,000 a year can purchase supplemental coverage of $100,000 for less than $200 per year. Fine, but the same deals are available through many local insurance agents. At any rate, life insurance is a very common benefit; estimates are that over two thirds of all U.S. corporations offer life insurance to regular employees.

Educational Benefits

■ **Many larger corporations—90% of the large Fortune 500 companies—maintain educational programs where the cost of job-related courses or degrees is refunded.**

The scope of educational programs can vary widely, even within the same industry. Some firms offer complete tuition reimbursement, others pay on a sliding scale according to grades: 100% for an A, 90% for a B, and so on. Some companies can be very strict when it comes to defining what constitutes a job-related course, others can be very lax. An extreme example of this came from an employee who somehow managed to be reimbursed for a graduate course in Egyptology . . . which probably had little to do with his job as a financial analyst.

■ **Look also at in-house training programs, and technical or managerial development programs at major universities, where com-**

panies sponsor month-long (or longer) employee-training workshops.

Particularly with large, well-known firms such as IBM or General Electric, the technical or managerial training offered can be very worthwhile, and translate into higher salaries if you leave. As one senior executive put it, "The only thing better on a resume than a Harvard MBA is a General Electric management job. Half of America is run by G.E. grads." Don't underestimate this type of hidden benefit.

Some Final Thoughts About Benefits

■ **A lower salary with substantial benefits can be worth more than a higher salary, in terms of its dollar value as a package.**

Perks and benefits add up. Most large corporations offer a complete and comprehensive benefits package with all or most of the benefits outlined above. Other benefits, which are not standard but may offer you comparable advantages, include: company cars, subsidized cafeterias, company travel packages, and product discounts. All of these may be worth hundreds or even thousands of dollars per year in non-salary benefits. Remember to factor in the tax consequences of these benefits; benefits such as company cars are taxable as income on your tax statements.

> **TIP: When making a job-change decision, consider what you might lose or have to start paying for if you left: extra commuting, lost benefits, the need for a new wardrobe, more or less travel, stricter expense reimbursement, etc. If you're moving, factor in the moving costs beyond the amount the company is willing to assume. Amortize these costs over the expected duration of your stay with the company, and then subtract each year's amount from the salary you've been offered and compare it with your current salary. This is a good way to assess if you've been offered enough.**

■ **Also ask about benefits if you work *part-time*.**

New laws and changing trends have brought benefits to part-timers as well. For example, some major "temp" firms now include vacation time as a standard benefit for people who work with them for at least a year, in addition to other benefits.

NEGOTIATING FOR A BETTER OFFER

After you've looked at the components of a job offer, you'll have some decisions to make. If you absolutely don't like the company and the position, in one sense you're very lucky: it's an easy decision, just don't accept the offer.

In another scenario, you may either like the offer or like it enough to consider it . . . but there's a catch. The salary is too low, or the benefits aren't comprehensive, or certain aspects of the job need alteration. In this instance, you should try to negotiate for a better offer. Easily said, but much harder to do. Negotiating is difficult.

Most negotiations die before they start. The applicant boldly states "I want ten percent more," and the interviewer explains that due to "company policy" he can't pay any more than the first figure. The applicant panics, mumbles "Oh," and that's that. Often he or she then goes home and describes how hard it was to get the interviewer to budge: "I tried and I argued but they didn't give an inch. And you know how tough I can be. . . ." Almost everyone describes his or her negotiating experiences in very graphic and very false terms. Most people fail, and do so meekly. Many successful interviewers and even high-level managers fall completely apart on salary negotiations.

The rest of this chapter is a brief summary designed to *prevent* you from falling apart, to get you past an interviewer's objections, and to help you conclude your negotiations successfully.

For additional information, read:

Perks and Parachutes by John Tarrant. The Stonesong Press, 1985.

You Can Get Anything You Want by Roger Dawson. Simon and Schuster, 1987.

Success! by Michael Korda. Ballantine Books, 1978.

THE BASICS OF NEGOTIATING

Rule #1: Negotiate from Strength

Negotiate when the time is right, when it's easiest for *you* to get what you want.

Your strongest negotiating period is just after you've received an offer (or when it's obvious that the interviewer wants to hire you) but *before* you have accepted the position. This brief period is the best time to negotiate for maximum benefit. The interviewer wants you and you haven't yet committed yourself to anything. Most of the time you'll be negotiating for a better base salary, but make certain that other aspects of the offer are satisfactory as well. If you see any other problems with the quality of your future employment, *now* is the time to push for a better deal.

Rule #2: Know What You Want—Set Your Negotiating Targets

Before you open your mouth, *know* what you want and what compromises you'd be willing to make. As a good poker player would, set your own *internal* strategy and guidelines, and know how far you're willing to risk things.

Set your negotiating limits. Know the approximate salary level you want or feel you deserve, and settle on a reasonable target salary for yourself based on the company's salary ranges and those of the industry. Don't be unrealistic. Generally, at the lower- and middle-management levels, you can reasonably hope to get 10%–20% more than what the interviewer offers you. If the company is offering $25,000 and you're looking for $40,000, realize that your job hunt is probably off-center. You're either setting your career sights too low or your salary sights too high. Unless something is wrong, you can't reasonably hope to negotiate up to that salary.

If you want to negotiate other employment terms, follow the same procedure. Have your limits in mind. Know what you want, what you expect, what you'll settle for.

In all cases, except when you're trying to start over in a new career, aim for a higher salary than your previous job. You want your resume to show upward movement.

Rule #3: Do Your Homework

Good negotiating means preparation. When the interviewer asks "Why?" you must have reasons. When the interviewer says the company "never" pays more, you should be able to mention or suggest exceptions. This means doing some research. Check trade magazines, talk to people at the company or in the same industry. Get the facts before you start negotiating.

Rule #4: Know How Far You're Willing to Go

After setting your salary target, establish how much you need or want this job. If you don't need or want the job, you can obviously go much further than you would if you were desperate to have it. Whatever the case, be prepared to show the interviewer that you are a successful, aggressive applicant in demand by other firms or organizations. Project the image that, although you want this position, you don't *need* it. You're willing to make some compromises, but you expect the same from the interviewer. Naturally, this is much easier if the job doesn't interest you that much.

Rule #5: Study the Interviewer

Make a mental list of the interviewer's motivations for hiring you: What does he or she want or need? What can he or she negotiate on her own, and what must be taken to upper management for approval? Also, what kind of person are you dealing with? Studying the interviewer can give you clues on how best to proceed.

Rule #6: Help the Interviewer

Be prepared to project a helpful attitude, one in which you show that you want to work *with* the interviewer and arrive at a mutually beneficial conclusion. Before the interview, think of ways to convince the interviewer that you should be getting what you want.

Rule #7: Be Prepared to Be Tough

Or firm, if you prefer. Help the interviewer, yes, but be ready for a civilized fight. Beneath the polite words between you and the interviewer is a disagreement. He or she is seeking to get you for less, you are seeking more. This means a fight—usually polite, usually couched in respectful "suggestions" or "ideas," but a fight nonetheless.

Rule #8: Ask Questions

Keep the interviewer on the defensive by asking questions. Many salespeople go a step further and keep on asking questions that require a "yes" answer, figuring that sooner or later the succession of yeses will make it psychologically difficult for the interviewer to refuse. ("Don't you give incremental increases? Isn't my experience above average for the firm?" etc.) Keep the interviewer agreeing with you and he or she will almost be impelled to comply with your request for more money.

WHAT YOU CAN NEGOTIATE FOR

■ **In general, the lower the position, the less negotiating flexibility you have, since the benefits for low-level jobs are usually standardized and salaries and job descriptions are more fixed.**

With lower-level positions, the interviewer doesn't have as much "give" or leeway in what more he can offer you. Also, it's best to face facts: at lower levels you are usually less valuable to the company; if you don't say yes to their offer, they can easily hire someone else. Be careful. Some people get so enthusiastic about tough negotiating techniques that they end up negotiating their way out of a job. Start by being *reasonable.*

You can reasonably ask for:

• an incremental increase in salary

• more vacation time

• a faster career track

> **TIP: If you're young, very often companies that won't part with an extra dime in salary will yield on giving you a faster career track. That translates into more dollars later. One woman wasted hours negotiating for a small $1,000 increase in salary at a rigid Fortune 500 giant. "It was the principle of the thing," she explained. Later she discovered she had won the battle but lost the war. Her experience could have qualified her for a faster career track, which would have gotten her a raise of several thousand dollars in just a few years. She had defeated herself.**

■ **At higher levels, the opportunities for compromise are greater, the methods of agreement are more complex, and the chances of having a successful negotiation are good.**

In addition to a higher salary, those going for higher-level positions may wish to negotiate an employment contract or a termination agreement that will establish a guaranteed duration to your job and continuation of income. Benefits, including stock and bonuses, are also important considerations. In these cases, you should first research the company norms (what most people are paid) and what the "star" employees receive, and then decide what you think you can get if you push for it.

SUCCESSFUL NEGOTIATING

■ **First get the interviewer to state the salary.**

Sometimes you will be pleasantly surprised and the interviewer will name a figure *higher* than you expected. If this happens, keep calm and proceed to argue for a figure 10%–20% higher, secure in the knowledge that, at the very worst, you're getting more than you bargained for. Even if you lose, you win. Normally, though, the figure is less than your target. In that case, it's time to *really* start negotiating.

■ **The best opening ploy was stated before:** *Help the interviewer* **by appearing cooperative and giving reasons for what you want.**

Tell the interviewer what salary you had in mind. Give a higher figure than you expect to get, but not much more than 25% over the figure the interviewer stated. Don't stop there. In the same breath, give the reasons *why* you deserve a higher salary. In this way you'll establish that you're making a reasonable demand, one that will convince the interviewer and the interviewer's *superiors* that indeed you deserve more than "company policy" dictates. *Remember:* Often the interviewer's hands are tied. If he or she offers you more money, it will have to be explained to senior management. Try to make your case before the interviewer reports back with smokescreens such as "company policy," "cost-cutting measures," etc.

> EXAMPLE: **"Hmm. There's a bit of a difference here. My target salary *range* was forty to forty-five thousand, which is in keeping with the unusual breadth of experience I've acquired. It's also in keeping with a normal fifteen percent increase over my current position, which underutilizes all my talents."**

■ *Don't* back yourself into a corner by stating one salary figure, unless you're prepared to give up the job or be embarrassed.

Many inexperienced negotiators commonly do this. They start out tough, and then crumple.

> **EXAMPLE:** *Applicant:* "I need a salary of forty-five thousand dollars. I can't accept anything less."
>
> *Interviewer:* "I'm sorry. Our salary levels aren't that high. I can't offer you more than forty thousand dollars. Maybe you should look elsewhere."
>
> The applicant can hold out, or give up. Most applicants give up.

Avoid this situation by giving the interviewer a salary range. Anticipate the interviewer's objections by giving reasons to prove that you are a special case. Offer the interviewer a *way out.* Give reasons the interviewer can use to justify the higher salary to upper management or to him or herself.

Some good reasons:

- *You're unusually capable.* You're far and above the best candidate for the job, ready and able to hit the ground running and add significantly to the bottom line. This is the "superstar" reason, in which you state the excellent contributions you can make and then show why it's worth it to pay you more.

> **EXAMPLE:** "Thank you for the offer. As you know, I have the background and expertise to take this section of the firm and cut costs significantly without hurting efficiency. But I feel strongly that this unique expertise is worth more. I'm wondering if there's a way to tie in my cost-savings to an incremental bonus system? That way, I'll be getting what I'm worth, and your firm will still be saving dollars."

- *You're more experienced.* You have far more experience than is usual for the position. This experience will enable you to make a more significant contribution to the company than the average employee. Therefore, you're worth more. Give examples.

> **EXAMPLE:** "As we discussed earlier, my background is particularly extensive, more so than the usual candidate for this job.

This means I'm bringing more to the job. Doesn't the company make salary adjustments for MBAs with additional degrees in the field? [If not, why not?]"

TIP: This approach works well with bureaucratic organizations such as the government. Because an entering job level or grade level is usually determined by the extent of formal education or number of years of employment, you should try to convince the interviewer that your background fulfills the bureaucratic requirements for a higher civil service grade.

- *"It's Only Fair."* The salary range for this position throughout the industry is closer to your figure than the interviewer's. In other words, why is the interviewer offering you a below-par salary? Politely put the interviewer on the defensive.

    EXAMPLE: "Let me start by saying that this position really interests me. It offers me the sort of business challenge that I enjoy and one where I know I can contribute significantly to the bottom line. But my research and interviewing experience show that the salary level appears to be a bit below the norm. Is this company policy, or is there a bonus system that we haven't yet discussed?"

- *"I Don't Need This Job Anyway."* You're very interested in the unique challenges of this position, but you're also quite happy in your current position. You had assumed you would be offered the usual 10%–15%–20% increase as an incentive for leaving your job.
    Note: This tactic is best used by people already in a good position.

    EXAMPLE: "As I said in the interview, the scope and challenges of this position make it very appealing. But I view this job as a step up from my current position, and feel that the salary should be set accordingly at a higher range—in keeping with what I can accomplish. Here's the problem: I'm trying to think of a way to accept it, but frankly I'm not certain the financial rewards make it worthwhile. I think you can understand why it would be difficult to leave a successful position without having a reasonable salary increase."

Appendix: Sources

INTRODUCTION

What follows is a foundation for your career "database" that will make your job hunt more effective: a list of useful sources, both general and industry-specific—associations, directories, and publications.

This list isn't designed to take the place of your own research and information-gathering. We strongly recommend you seek out the sources that fit your own, very specific, needs. But in order to make your work a little easier, this list will give you a head start.

A few explanatory notes:

- The following sources are divided into several categories: *general business* (the sources that will fit into most job hunts) and *specific industry* (including accounting, advertising, banking and finance, magazine and book publishing, sales & marketing, manufacturing, and more).

- In most cases, the associations listed are national and have regional offices across the country.

- Associations included in this list have a minimum of 1,000 members. The reasoning: the larger the association, the more likely it will fit into a number of job hunts. Smaller or regional associations, many of which focus on one particular segment of an industry, also exist in every category.

- In choosing sources for this list, we have focused on major associations, directories, and publications in each field. Again, you will find many others that will be helpful in your job hunt—these are intended to give you a research base.

- Sources marked with a star (*) are highly recommended.

GENERAL BUSINESS SOURCES

Associations

American Business Women's Association (ABWA)
P.O. Box 8728
9100 Ward Parkway
Kansas City, MO 64114
816/361-6621
—Almost 120,000 members who are women in business (including executives, business owners, professionals, etc.)
—Of special interest: offers career assessment programs, and scholarships to business women and students

American Management Association (AMA)
135 West 50th Street
New York, NY 10020
212/586-8100
—80,000+ members
—Sponsors educational programs, workshops, and conferences; publishes numerous books; maintains extensive library for research
—Of special interest: publishes membership directory and Executive Employment Guide listing executive search firms, employment agencies, job registers and career counselors

Association of MBA Executives (AMBA)
305 Madison Avenue
New York, NY 10017
212/682-4490
—Over 25,000 members
—Publications include *AMBA Network News, MBA Executive,* and industry reports
—Of special interest: yearly *MBA Employment Guide*

American Society of Professional & Executive Women (ASPEW)
1511 Walnut Street
Philadelphia, PA 19102
215/563-4415
—12,000 members who are careerwomen in a wide variety of fields
—Publishes guides, offers seminars, maintains library and database
—Of special interest: offers executive recruitment

Business Planning Board
P.O. Box 433
Ten Paragon Drive
Montvale, NJ 07645
201/573-6225
—Over 15,000 members: CEOs, CFOs, and other top decision-makers in
their companies
—Of special interest: maintains placement service

*Catalyst
250 Park Avenue South
New York, NY 10003
212/777-8900
—Organization aimed at advancing women in careers
—Of special interest: the National Network of Career Resource Centers,
nationwide network of career counselors, job banks, skills development, referral services, and other career resources
—Publishes Career Development publications, including booklets on career planning, job hunting, and booklets on specific careers

*Forty-Plus Clubs
—Nonprofit cooperative organization in ten cities (no central headquarters); check for listing in major metropolitan phone directories
—Offers extensive aid to job hunters over forty years old including counseling, job hunting techniques, and resume-writing assistance
—Of special interest: brief profiles of members are sent to prospective
employers

*The International Alliance of Professional & Executive Women's Net-
works*
8600 LaSalle Rd.
Towson, MD 21204-3308
301/321-6699
—Association of regional networks for careerwomen
—Offers seminars and workshops; publishes newsletter and annual directory of members

*National Association for Female Executives (NAFE)
127 West 24th Street
New York, NY 10011
212/645-0770

—Over 170,000 members
—Sponsors workshops and seminars; offers management aptitude testing
—Publishes monthly magazine, *Executive Woman*
—Of special interest: the NAFE resume guide and writing service; also sponsors NAFE Network: 1,200 resource groups nationwide for businesswomen

National Management Association (NMA)
2210 Arbor Blvd.
Dayton, OH 45439
513/294-0421
—72,000 members
—Provides seminars and other educational programs

Networks Unlimited
316 Fifth Avenue, Suite 301
New York, NY 10001
212/868-3370
—Designed for people interested in setting up or expanding their network
—Puts out annual membership directory
—Of special interest: maintains placement service

Directories

Career Employment Opportunities Directory
Ready Reference Press
Box 5169
Santa Monica, CA 90405
—Published in four volumes: 1 for Liberal Arts and Social Sciences graduates; 2 Business Administration; 3 Engineering, 4 Sciences
—Listings of companies that are currently hiring; listings include employment opportunities, locations, special programs

Corporate Summaries
National Register Publishing Company
3004 Glenview Road
Wilmette, IL 60091
312/256-6067
—Information on over 10,000 publicly-held companies
—Listings include addresses, financial statistics, etc.

Directory of Career Training & Development Programs
Ready Reference Press
Box 5169
Santa Monica, CA 90405
—Lists management and executive training programs, professional development programs

—Listings include name, program title and purpose, the number of people selected, type of training, qualifications, selection process, name and address of contact
—Good basis for entry-level mailing list

The Directory of Corporate Affiliations
National Register Publishing Company
3004 Glenview Road
Wilmette, IL 60091
312/256-6067
—Profiles of over 4,000 U.S. companies, includes subsidiaries, divisions, and affiliates
—Handy way to trace company back to its parent

Directories in Print
Gale Research Company
Book Tower
Detroit, MI 48226
313/961-2242
—Lists about 8,000 directories, both general and industry-specific
—Listed by industry, also geographically indexed

Directory of Management Consultants
Consultant News
Templeton Road
Fitzwilliam, NH 03447
603/585-2200
—Lists firm, address, phone numbers, contact person, etc.

Dun's Million Dollar Directory
Dun & Bradstreet
1 Pennsylvania Plaza
New York, NY 10013
212/971-6700
—Lists 160,000 U.S. businesses in a variety of industries, including utilities, industrial, transportation, banking, finance; classified alphabetically, by industry, and geographically
—Listings include name, address, phone number, top executives' names and titles, financial statistics, accounting firm, principal bank, and more

Dun's Top 50,000 Companies
Dun & Bradstreet
1 Pennsylvania Plaza
New York, NY 10013
212/971-6700
—The top 50,000 companies of the 160,000 listed in the *Million Dollar Directory*
—As above, listings include address, phone number, executive names and titles, and stats

* Dun & Bradstreet's Reference Book of Corporate Managements
Dun & Bradstreet
99 Church Street
New York, NY 10013
212/312-6500
—Brief biographies of executives—including CEOs, CFOs, directors, presidents and vice-presidents—of top U.S. companies
—Profiles include business address and phone number, title, employment history, education, clubs and memberships, civic and political activities, awards and honors received

* Encyclopedia of Associations
Gale Research Company
Book Tower
Detroit, MI 48226
313/961-2242
—Published in several volumes; the most useful is *Trade & Professional Associations,* which lists over 20,000 associations alphabetically by industry
—Also indexed by name, geographic locations and executive names (special volume for cross-indexing purposes)
—An excellent kick-off point for networking
—Also available online in DIALOG

Guide to American Directories
B. Klein Publications
Coral Springs, FL
305/752-1708
—Similar to the above, but less extensive, this directory lists over 7,000 directories indexed by subject
—Of special interest: under Manufacturers heading, lists industrial directories for each state

Moody's Industrial Manual
Moody's Investor Service, Inc.
99 Church Street
New York, NY 10013
212/553-0300
—Lists 3,000 companies listed on the New York or American Stock Exchanges as well as international companies
—Includes address, phone number and statistics (Moody's also publishes directories for Bank & Finance, Public Utilities, Transportation, Municipals)

* Polk City Directory
R.L. Polk & Company
2001 Elm Hill Pike
Box 1340
Nashville, TN 37202
615/889-3350

—By city, lists names and titles of local executives with brief explanation of their companies

Standard & Poor's Register of Corporations, Directors and Executives
Standard & Poor's Corporation
345 Hudson Street
New York, NY 10014
212/924-6400
—Lists over 45,000 U.S. corporations; includes names and titles of over 400,000 corporate officials, corporation's principal bank and law firm
—Of special interest: Volume 2 contains biographies of 75,000 executives and directors, includes business and home addresses, date and place of birth, and organization/association memberships

* Standard Directory of Advertisers
Standard Rate & Data Service
3004 Glenview Rd.
Wilmette, IL 60091
312/256-6067
—Lists about 17,000 companies that *place* national and/or regional advertising (not a listing of ad agencies)
—Of special interest: each listing includes names and titles of management, financial, advertising, and marketing executives
—An excellent one-stop reference for a resume mailing list

Thomas Register
Thomas Publishing Company
One Pennsylvania Plaza
New York, NY 10013
212/695-0500
—12-volume directory of U.S. manufacturers; Volumes 1–6 contain alphabetical listing of products/services; Volume 7, brandnames only
—Volume 8 is an alphabetical listing of U.S. manufacturers, including name, address, phone number, product lines, executives, branches, representatives, and distributors
—Also available online on DIALOG

Ward's Directory of 51,000 Largest U.S. Corporations
Baldwin H. Ward Publications
929 Petaluma Blvd.
North Petaluma, CA 94952
707/762-0737
—Lists name, address, phone number, president's name, sales and financial data
—Not as easy to read as either *Dun's* or *S&P's* directories; use this as a fallback if the others are unavailable

Ward's Directory of 49,000 Private U.S. Companies
Baldwin H. Ward Publications
929 Petaluma Blvd.
North Petaluma, CA 94952
—Companion directory of the above; lists the same information on top, privately held companies

Who's Who In [State Name]
Gormezano Reference Publications
2921 East Madison Street
Seattle, WA 98112-4237
206/322-1431
—For each state, brief biographies of influential residents

Publications

Barron's National Business and Financial Weekly
Dow Jones & Company, Inc.
22 Cortlandt Street
New York, NY 10007
212/285-5243
—Widely-read business/investments/finance newspaper
—First section contains articles and columns on news, industry trends, and recent developments; second section contains stock tables and statistics

Business Week
McGraw-Hill, Inc.
1221 Avenue of the Americas
New York, NY 10020
212/997-1221
—Special issues include:
　—*Corporate Scoreboard Issue* (March), which lists about 1,200 top companies in business, industrial, and financial categories;
　—*Bank Scoreboard Issue* (April), which ranks the 200 largest U.S. banks

Dun's Business Month
875 Third Avenue
New York, NY 10017
212/605-9400
—Monthly magazine covering business news, trends, developments

Forbes
Forbes, Inc.
60 Fifth Avenue
New York, NY 10011
212/620-2200
—Special issues include:

—*Annual Report on American Industry* (January), which lists about 1,000 top industrial firms; listings include name, sales profit, growth rate, etc.

—*500 Largest Corporations* (mid-May), which ranks corporations by revenue, profits, assets, stock value, etc.

Fortune
Time, Inc.
Time & Life Building
New York, NY 10020
212/556-2581
—Special issues include:
   —*500 Largest U.S. Corporations* (May)
   —*Second 500 Largest U.S. Corporations* (June)
   —*50 Largest Commercial Banks, Life Insurance Companies, Utilities, Financial Services, Retail, Transportation* (July)

* *Inc*
United Marine Publishing
38 Commercial Wharf
Boston, MA 02110
617/227-4700
—Aimed at executives in small to mid-sized companies
—Articles on a variety of business subjects, including financial management, administration, sales & marketing, etc.

International Management
McGraw-Hill, Inc.
1221 Avenue of the Americas
New York, NY 10020
212/997-3608
—Management strategies, trends, developments, and techniques

Computer Databases

Bizdate
Source Telecomputing Corporation
1616 Anderson Road
McLean, VA 22102
703/734-7500
—Current business news updated throughout the day
—Information on a wide range of business subjects
—Available on The Source

D&B—Dun's Financial Records
Dun's Marketing Services
Three Century Drive
Parsippany, NJ 07054
201/455-0900

—Information on over 700,000 companies, including balance sheets, history, comparisons with competitors, and more
—Available on DIALOG

D&B—Dun's Market Identifiers
Dun's Marketing Services
Three Century Drive
Parsippany, NJ 07054
201/455-0900
—Directory of over two million U.S. private and public companies with earnings over $1 million or employing ten or more people
—Profiles include address (headquarters and branches), financial statistics, names and titles of executives
—Available on DIALOG

D&B—Million Dollar Directory
Dun's Marketing Services
Three Century Drive
Parsippany, NJ 07054
201/455-0900
—Lists 160,000 U.S. businesses in a variety of industries, including utilities, industrial, transportation, banking, finance; all with earnings over $500,000
—Listings include name, address, phone number, top executives' names and titles, financial statistics, accounting firm, principal bank, and more
—Available on DIALOG

Disclosure Online
Disclosure, Inc.
5161 River Road
Bethesda, MD 20816
301/951-1300 or 800/638-8076
—Profiles of over 10,000 publicly-held companies that file with the Securities Exchange Commission
—Extensive information includes 10k's, income statements, stockholder's reports, and more
—Available on CompuServe, DIALOG, Dow Jones News/Retrieval, I.P. Sharp, ISYS, Quotron, Warner Computer Systems

Management Contents
Information Access Company
11 David Drive
Belmont, CA 94002
800/227-8431
—Abstracts of articles from over 7,000 business publications, including technical journals, newsletters, reports, and much more
—Available on DIALOG, SDC, BRS, Data-Star, The Source

Moody's Corporate News—U.S.
Moody's Investor Services, Inc.
99 Church Street
New York, NY 10007
212/553-0436
—Up-to-date business news on over 13,000 publicly-held companies, including manufacturers, utilities, savings & loan associations, banks, real estate firms, and more
—Weekly updates with news culled from leading magazines and newspapers, newswire services, stock exchange reports, annual reports, quarterly earning statements, press releases, prospectuses, and other sources
—Available on DIALOG

Moody's Corporate Profiles
Moody's Investor Services, Inc.
99 Church Street
New York, NY 10007
212/553-0436
—Profiles of companies traded on the New York and American Stock Exchanges, as well as most active o-t-c companies—about 3,600 companies total
—As above, weekly updates from a wide variety of sources
—Profiles include extensive financial information
—Available on DIALOG

PTS Annual Reports Abstracts
Predicasts, Inc.
11001 Cedar Avenue
Cleveland, OH 44106
216/795-3000 or 800/321-6388
—Predicasts online, with abstracts dating back to 1982 and information on over 3,000 publicly held companies
—Information from annual reports, 10k statements
—Available on DIALOG, BRS, BRS/BRKTHRU, Data-Star

PTS Promt
Predicasts, Inc.
11001 Cedar Avenue
Cleveland, OH 44106
216/795-3000 or 800/321-6388
—Abstracts from top business publications covering over 120,000 national and international companies
—Available on BRS, Data-Star, DIALOG, VU/TEXT

Standard & Poor's Corporate Descriptions
Standard & Poor's Corporation
25 Broadway
New York, NY 10004
212/208-8622

—Profiles on over 8,000 publicly-held U.S. corporations
—Available on DIALOG

* *Trade & Industry ASAP*
Information Access Company
11 Davis Drive
Belmont, CA 94002
415/591-2333 or 800/227-8431
—Full text from over 100 business and trade magazines (such as *American Banker, Chain Store Age, Advertising Age, Women's Wear Daily* and other top industry publications); also includes top business magazines such as *Forbes, Fortune, Dun's Business Month* and *Money*
—Available on DIALOG

ACCOUNTING

Associations

* *American Institute of Certified Public Accountants (AICPA)*
1211 Avenue of the Americas
New York, NY 10036
212/575-6200
—231,000 members
—Publishes list of accounting firms and practitioners, which lists name and address of individual CPAs and accounting firms by state and city
—Also publishes yearly membership list, handbooks, reports, and a wide range of brochures on a variety of subjects, including *Information for CPA Candidates*
—Annual convention

American Women's Society of Certified Public Accountants (AWSCPA)
500 North Michigan Avenue; Suite 1400
Chicago, IL 60611
312/661-1700
—5,000 members
—In addition to monthly newsletter and quarterly journal, the AWSCPA publishes career information

National Association of Accountants (NAA)
P.O. Box 433
Ten Paragon Drive
Montvale, NJ 07645
201/573-9000
—95,000 members, who are management accountants
—Maintains library
—Of special interest: offers member placement service

National Association of Black Accountants (NABA)
1010 Vermont Ave., N.W.; Suite 901
Washington, DC 20005
202/783-7151
—3,000 members
—Publications include *Guide to Professional Accounting Careers* and *Public Accounting Profession*
—Offers scholarships, career seminars

Directories

AICPA Annual Surveys
American Institute of Certified Public Accountants (AICPA)
1211 Avenue of the Americas
New York, NY 10036
212/575-6200
—Annual directories listing both private practitioners and accounting firms
—National and regional coverage

Publications

Accounting News
Warren, Gorham & Lamont, Inc.
210 South Street
Boston, MA 02111
617/423-2020
—Covers industry news, trends, and developments

Corporate Accounting
Warren, Gorham & Lamont, Inc.
210 South Street
Boston, MA 02111
617/423-2020
—Aimed at corporate accountants
—Articles on corporate accounting trends, developments, and techniques

The CPA Journal
New York State Society of CPAs
600 Third Avenue
New York, NY 10016
212/661-2020
—Explanatory articles on a wide variety of accounting industry areas, including audit, taxation, management services, and more

* *The Journal of Accountancy*
American Institute of Certified Public Accountants
1211 Avenue of the Americas
New York, NY 10036
212/575-6200
—The *AICPA Journal,* an industry must-read
—Articles on both educational and professional subjects

Management Accounting
National Association of Accountants
P.O. Box 433
Ten Paragon Drive
Montvale, NJ 07645
201/573-9000
—Aimed at corporate accountants
—In addition to general industry coverage, includes articles on financial
  and accounting techniques

Computer Database

Accountants
AICPA
1211 Avenue of the Americas
New York, NY 10036
212/575-6200
—Online index of articles on accounting, auditing, taxation, financial
  management, and other fields
—Indexes over 250 periodicals, plus books, pamphlets, and more
—Available on SDC, Orbit

ADVERTISING

Associations

American Association of Advertising Agencies (AAAA)
666 Third Avenue; 13th Floor
New York, NY 10017
212/682-2500
—Association of 640 member *agencies,* not individuals
—Good source of information about the advertising industry in general
  and member agencies; publishes career information
—Publishes yearly roster of members

American Advertising Federation (AAF)
1400 K Street, N.W.; Suite 1000
Washington, DC 20005
202/898-0089

—25,000 members
—Sponsors competition for college students and industry's ADDY awards; holds yearly convention
—Publications include *Communicator* (monthly college newsletter), *American Advertising Magazine* (quarterly)
—Of special interest: publishes career information

Directories

Standard Directory of Advertising Agencies
Standard Rate & Data Service
3004 Glenview Rd.
Wilmette, IL 60091
312/256-6067
—Lists roughly 4,400 agencies
—Listings include address, phone number, billings, clients, and names of executives from top officers to account executives

Creative Black Book
Friendly Publications
80 Irving Place
New York, NY 10003
212/228-9750
—Useful for people on the creative side of advertising (copywriters, art directors, etc.) or those supplying services to agencies (photographers, printers, illustrators, etc.)
—Lists over 12,000 art suppliers, photographers, printers, model agencies, advertising agencies—all services used in advertising
—Split into five geographical sections; listings include company name, address, and phone number

Who's Who in Advertising
Redfield Publishing Co.
P.O. Box 556
Rye, NY 10580
—Lists U.S. and Canadian advertising executives
—Listings include title, affiliation, address, phone number, and area of specialization

Publications

Advertising Age
740 North Rush Street
Chicago, IL 60611
312/649-5200
—Weekly trade journal considered by many to be the industry "bible"
—Comprehensive coverage of advertising/marketing news, issues, people, accounts, trends, and developments

—Especially strong for special issues; among the most useful are: *100 Leading National Advertisers* (September), which contains marketing reports of top advertisers, including statistics and names of marketing personnel and agency account executives for each product/company; *U.S. Agency Income Profiles* issue (March), which profiles top agencies ranked by income; *100 Leading Media Companies* (June); *Research Business Review* (May), which profiles the top market research firms

*Adweek
820 Second Avenue
New York, NY 10017
212/661-8080
—Weekly trade journal *also* considered to be a must-read in the industry
—Smaller than *Ad Age,* less in-depth, easier to read
—Excellent special issue for mailing list: *Adweek Directory of Advertisers* (July), which is split into separate regional editions: East, Southeast, Southwest, Midwest, and West; directory includes agencies, media, and brand names; each listing includes company name, address, and phone number, and names and titles of executives

Business Marketing
220 East 42nd Street
New York, NY 10017
212/210-0100
—Focuses on business-to-business advertising, marketing, and promotion

Madison Avenue
369 Lexington Avenue
New York, NY 10017
212/972-0600
—Monthly magazine covering advertising, with chief emphasis on New York advertising agencies
—Contains industry news, trends, and developments
—Special feature in each issue examines a specific aspect of the industry

Computer Database

PTS MARS
Predicasts, Inc.
11001 Cedar Avenue
Cleveland, OH 44106
216/795-3000 or 800/321-6388
—Information on advertising and marketing from over 110 publications, including *Folio, Ad Age, Adweek*

BANKING/FINANCE

Associations

American Bankers Association
1120 Connecticut Avenue, N.W.
Washington, DC 20036
202/467-4000
—13,000 members
—Sponsors the American Institute of Banking, which offers educational programs (student catalogue of courses is available)
—Publishes *ABA Banking Journal, Banker News,* and other magazines and journals, as well as an annual directory

Bank Administration Institute (BAI)
60 Gould Center
2550 Golf Rd.
Rolling Meadows, IL 60008
312/228-6200
—9,000 members
—Serves as a research facility and information source; sponsors technical conferences
—Of special interest: offers professional development programs
—Publishes the monthly *Magazine of Bank Administration,* as well as other journals

Financial Executives Institute (FEI)
P.O. Box 1938
Ten Madison Ave.
Morristown, NJ 07960
201/898-4600
—12,500 members, who are financial/management executives, including controllers, treasurers, and finance vice-presidents
—Publishes monthly *Financial Executive* and other journals

Financial Managers Society (FMS)
111 East Wacker Drive—Suite 1221
Chicago, IL 60601
312/938-2576
—5,000 members
—Serves as an information exchange for financial/management executives, including chief operating officers and controllers
—Publishes monthly newsletter and yearly directory

Mortgage Bankers Association of America
1125 15th Street, N.W.
Washington, DC 20005
202/861-6500

—Over 1,800 members, including commercial banks, mortgage banking firms, savings and loan associations, and life insurance companies
—Sponsors conferences and seminars; maintains library and School of Mortgage Banking
—Publications include monthly *Mortgage Banker,* which contains industry statistics and other up-to-date data; publishes a yearly directory of members

National Association of Bank Women (NABW)
500 North Michigan Avenue—Suite 1400
Chicago, IL 60601
312/661-1700
—25,000 members, who are women executives in banking and finance
—Publishes *Executive Financial Woman* and newsletter, as well as an annual directory

National Association of Urban Bankers (NAUB)
1101 Connecticut Avenue, N.W.—Suite 700
Washington, DC 20036
202/857-1100
—1,200 members who are minority professionals in banking and finance
—Publishes monthly magazine and quarterly bulletin; awards scholarship to minority student in banking
—Of special interest: sponsors career enhancement and development programs

Directories

American Bank Directory
McFadden Business Publications
6195 Crooked Creek Road
Norcross, GA 30092
404/448-1011
—Covers all U.S. banks
—Lists address, phone number, branches, names and titles of officers and directors, and financial statements

*American Banker Directory of U.S. Banking Executives
American Banker, Inc.
525 West 42nd Street
New York, NY 10036
212/563-1900
—Biographical information on top U.S. bankers
—Indexed by affiliation

* Corporate Finance Blue Book
Macmillan & Co./Professional Books
866 Third Avenue
New York, NY 10022
212/702-2000

—Focuses on executives who make the financial decisions at over 4,200 companies
—Listings include names, titles, and phone numbers of officers in cash management, corporate development, employee benefits, international finance, investor relations, etc.

Directory of American Financial Institutions
McFadden Business Publications
6195 Crooked Creek Road
Norcross, GA 30092
404/448-1011
—Covers all U.S. financial institutions
—Listings include address, phone number, names and titles of officers and directors, and financial statistics

Directory of American Savings & Loan Associations
TK Saunderson Organization
200 East 25th Street
Baltimore, MD 21212
301/235-3383
—Lists over 5,000 S&L associations and their branches
—Listings include name, address, phone number, branch locations, assets, and names of top executives

Moody's Bank & Finance Manual
Moody's Investor Service, Inc.
99 Church Street
New York, NY 10013
212/553-0300
—Lists over 10,000 national, state, and private banks, insurance companies, mutual funds, mortgage and finance companies, real estate investment trusts, savings & loan associations, and other financial firms
—Listings include name, headquarter and branch offices, phone numbers, and names and titles of top executives

Who's Who in Banking
Business Press, Inc.
32 Broadway
New York, NY 10004
—Profiles of top executives in the financial field, including commercial and savings banks, investment banks, saving & loan associations, securities, brokerages, etc.

Who's Who in Finance & Industry
Marquis Who's Who, Inc.
200 East Ohio Street
Chicago, IL 60611
312/787-2008
—Biographical listing of top executives in banking, mutual and pension fund management, real estate, investment services, insurance, financial services, etc.

—Profiles include education, employment history, memberships, awards, political and civic activities, articles and books published, *home* and office addresses

Publications

ABA Banking Journal
American Bankers Association
1120 Connecticut Avenue, N.W.
Washington, DC 20036
202/467-4000
—The official publication of the ABA; publishes monthly articles on banking trends and general industry news

American Banker
American Banker, Inc.
525 West 42nd Street
New York, NY 10036
212/563-1900
—Daily newspaper
—Special issues include *500 Largest Free World Banks; 100 Largest Mutual Savings Banks; 300 Largest Savings & Loan Associations; 100 Largest Finance Companies, Largest US Savings Banks; 300 Largest U.S. Commercial Banks;* and more
—Also available online through NEXIS

Bank Administration
60 East Gould Center
Rolling Meadows, IL 60008
312/228-6200
—Monthly magazine aimed at senior bank management

Bankers Magazine
Warren, Gorham & Lamont
210 South Street
Boston, MA 02111
617/423-2020
—Bi-monthly magazine on banking and money management
—Articles on trends and industry developments

Bankers Monthly
Bankers Monthly, Inc.
601 Skokie Blvd.
Northbrook, IL 60062
312/498-2580
—Monthly; publishes financial statistics for leading banks in each issue
—Annual *Finance Industry Survey Issue*

Business Week: Bank Scoreboard Issue
1221 Avenue of the Americas
New York, NY 10020
212/997-1221
—Published every April
—Ranks the 200 largest U.S. banks by assets; listings include deposits, loans, and other statistics

Institutional Investor
488 Madison Avenue
New York, NY 10022
212/303-3300
—Published monthly
—Useful special issue: *CFO Directory* (July issue), which lists the CFOs and treasurers in over 450 U.S. companies, with their addresses and telephone numbers

Journal of Commercial Bank Lending
Robert Morris Associates
1616 Philadelphia National Bank
Philadelphia, PA 19107
215/665-2850
—Monthly publication aimed at bank credit and loan officers

BROADCASTING (RADIO & TELEVISION)

Associations

*American Women in Radio & Television (AWRT)
1101 Connecticut Avenue, N.W., Suite 700
Washington, DC 20036
202/429-5102
—3,000+ members in a wide range of positions (including administrative, creative, executive) in broadcasting, advertising, public relations, and other fields connected with broadcasting
—Publishes annual membership directory
—Maintains a placement service

Academy of Television Arts & Sciences (ATAS)
4605 Lankershim Blvd., Suite 800
North Hollywood, CA 91602
818/506-7880
—5,200 members
—Most useful as an information source
—Holds workshops and presents speakers; also offers student internships

International Radio & Television Society (IRTS)
420 Lexington Avenue
New York, NY 10170
212/867-6650
—1,800 members
—Sponsors college student summer internship program

National Association of Broadcasters (NAB)
1771 N Street, N.W.
Washington, DC 20036
202/429-5300
—Over 5,000 members
—Maintains a minority placement service

National Cable Television Association (NCTA)
1724 Massachusetts Avenue, N.W.
Washington, DC 20036
202/775-3550
—Over 3,000 members
—In addition to monthly *Tech Line* magazine and periodic reports on industry issues and events, the NCTA puts out *Careers in Cable*—a useful overview of opportunities in the industry

National Radio Broadcasters Association
2033 M Street, N.W., Suite 506
Washington, DC 20036
202/466-2030
—2,000 members
—Publishes various specialized publications and the weekly *Radio Week*

Radio Advertising Bureau
304 Park Avenue South
New York, NY 10010
212/254-4800
—Members include stations, networks, and radio sales reps
—Puts out monthly publications and annual directory of members
—Of special interest: offers training conferences and sales training programs

* Radio-Television News Director Association (RTNDA)
1735 DeSales Street, N.W.
Washington, DC 20036
202/737-8657
—Nearly 3,000 members who are heads of radio and television news departments
—Puts out biweekly and monthly magazines; most important is its annual directory, which lists member names, affiliations and addresses as well as a booklet on career options (primarily aimed at entry-level positions)

Television Bureau of Advertising
477 Madison Avenue
New York, NY 10010
212/759-6800
—Members are networks, television stations, and TV sales reps
—Of special interest: offers sales training courses

Television Information Office
745 Fifth Avenue
New York, NY 10022
212/759-6800
—Useful for research purposes; the TIO maintains an extensive library

Directories

* Broadcasting/Cable Yearbook
Broadcasting Publications, Inc.
1735 DeSales Street, N.W.
Washington, DC 20036
292/638-1022
—Lists all radio, television, and cable TV stations in the United States and Canada
—Listings include address, phone number, format, names and titles of key executives

Television Factbook
Television Digest, Inc.
1836 Jefferson Place, N.W.
Washington, DC 20036
202/872-9200
—Two-volume directory of stations in the U.S. and Canada
—Listings include address, phone number, and names of key executives; also includes names of news department personnel

Publications

* Broadcasting Magazine
Broadcasting Publications, Inc.
1735 DeSales Street, N.W.
Washington, DC 20036
292/638-1022
—This is the industry publication of record; published weekly
—Strong classified ads section

Television Radio Age
Television Editorial Corp.
1270 Avenue of the Americas
New York, NY 10020
212/757-8400
—Aimed at television/radio time buyers and sellers

ENGINEERING

Associations

American Association of Engineering Societies (AAES)
415 Second Street, N.E.
Washington, DC 20002
202/546-2237
—An association of societies representing over one million engineers
—Contact the AAES for information on associations
—Of special interest: publishes the *Directory of Engineering Societies* (every two years); *Engineers Salary Survey* (yearly); *Who's Who in Engineering* (yearly)

American Institute of Aeronautics & Astronautics (AIAA)
1633 Broadway
New York, NY 10019
212/581-4300
—37,000 members who are scientists and engineers
—Maintains library; puts out numerous publications
—Of special interest: publishes career information

American Institute of Chemical Engineers
345 East 47th Street
New York, NY 10017
212/705-7338
—Sponsors continuing education programs; publishes *Chemical Engineering Progress*

Institute of Electrical & Electronics Engineers (IEEE)
345 East 47th Street
New York, NY 10017
212/705-7900
—263,000 members who are scientists and engineers
—Sponsors conferences; offers educational programs, lectures and seminars
—Publishes annual directory of members

Institute of Industrial Engineers (IIEE)
25 Technology Park/Atlanta
Norcross, GA 30092
404/449-0460
—42,000 members
—Maintains research library; sponsors conference, seminars, and workshops
—Puts out several publications including journals

National Society of Professional Engineers (NSPE)
1420 King Street
Alexandria, VA 22314
703/684-2800

—75,000 members
—In addition to reports and other publications, publishes the monthly *Engineering Times*
—Of special interest: sponsors a wide range of educational programs, including career guidance

Society of Women Engineers (SWE)
345 East 47th Street, Room 305
New York, NY 10017
212/705-7855
—13,000 members, both women and men
—Publishes journal as well as career guidance booklets
—Of special interest: career guidance programs, with special attention given to women returning to the work force after extended absence

Publications

Engineering Times
National Society of Professional Engineers
1420 King Street
Alexandria, VA 22314
703/684-2800
—Articles covering a variety of topics including legislation, education, business and more

IEEE Engineering Management Review
IEEE
345 East 47th Street
New York, NY 10017
212/705-7900
—Engineering news, trends and developments

Professional Engineer
National Society of Professional Engineers
1420 King Street
Alexandria, VA 22314
703/684-2800
—Articles on various engineering topics

HIGH TECH

Associations:

Association for Computing Machinery (ACM)
11 West 42nd Street
New York, NY 10036
212/869-7440

—75,000 members who are connected with the computer industry, including engineers, computer scientists, and business systems managers

—Publishes a wide range of publications; sponsors annual conference

—Over thirty special interest groups on specific areas of the computer industry

Association for Systems Management
24587 Bagley Rd.
Cleveland, OH 44138
216/243-6900

—10,000+ members who are executives and specialists in management information systems

—Offers seminars, conferences; maintains library

—Of special interest: offers training in systems management

Society for Information Management (SIM)
One Illinois Center
111 East Wacker Drive, Suite 600
Chicago, IL 60601
312/644-6610

—1,500 members, who are management information systems designers and managers

—Offers educational programs

—Publishes newsletter and journal

Directories

*Directory of Top Computer Executives
Applied Computer Research
P.O. Box 9280
Phoenix, AZ 85068
602/995-5929

—Lists data-processing executives

—Listings include company name, address, phone number

*Directory of Computer Companies, Worldwide
Marquis Who's Who, Inc.
200 East Ohio Street
Chicago, IL 60611
312/787-2008

—Lists about 4,000 computer companies, including hardware manufacturers, software producers, database vendors, consultants, etc.

Directory of Communications Management
Applied Computer Research
P.O. Box 9280
Phoenix, AZ 85068
602/995-5929

—Lists executives at top U.S. companies with data communications responsibilities
—Listings include company name, address, phone number

Information Industry Marketplace
R. R. Bowker
205 East 42nd Street
New York, NY 10017
212/916-1600
—In-depth information on the information industry
—Listings include company name, products offered, and contact people

Publications

Computer Career News
Litton Publishing Group
680 Kinderkamack Road
Oradell, NJ 07649
201/262-3030
—General career information, enhancement, and development, as well as employment opportunities for computer professionals, both scientists and managers

Computer Decisions
Hayden Publishing Company, Inc.
10 Mulholland Drive
Hasbrouck Heights, NJ 07604
201/393-6000
—Monthly magazine focusing on the management and business use of computers

Computer Digest
Gersbeck Publications
200 Park Avenue South
New York, NY 10003
212/777-6400
—Computer industry trends and developments for computer industry professionals

Computer Systems News
CMP Publications
111 East Shore Road
Manhasset, NY 11030
516/365-4600
—General computer industry coverage, including articles on the financial and marketing aspect of the industry

Corporate Times
EML Publications
1214 Oakmead Parkway; Building A
Sunnyvale, CA 94086
408/720-9050
—Aimed at mid- and upper management at high tech companies, including executives, engineers, etc.

Datamation
Dun & Bradstreet Publishing Corp.
875 Third Avenue
New York, NY 10022
212/605-9400
—In-depth coverage of the information field for users, manufacturers, consultants, designers, and other computer professionals

EDN Career News
Cahners Publishing Co.
221 Columbus Ave.
Boston, MA 02116
617/536-7780
—Up-to-date information on careers in design engineering and engineering management

High Technology
Technology Publishing Company
38 Commercial Wharf
Boston, MA 02110
617/227-4700
—Articles revolve around high tech's impact on business and business management

Infosystems
Hitchcock Publications
Hitchcock Building
Wheaton, IL 60188
312/665-1000
—Designed for managers and other people in management-information systems, data-communications, and other areas of computer-based information processing

Journal of Systems Management
24587 Bagley Rd.
Cleveland, OH 44138
216/243-6900
—Monthly trade journal put out by the Association for Systems Management
—Aimed at executives, managers, and systems specialists

Recruiting Databases

Adline
Business People, Incorporated
100 North 7th Street
Minneapolis, MN 55401
612/370-0550
—Listings of want ads from high tech employers; free of charge, you can browse through the ads, then connect with a company's personnel department and transmit your resume

Online Careers
Information Intelligence, Inc.
P.O. Box 31098
Phoenix, AZ 85046
602/996-2283 or 800/228-9982
—Job-hunting database that lists job categories in the information-systems field

---

MAGAZINE PUBLISHING

Associations

American Society of Magazine Editors (ASME)
575 Lexington Avenue
New York, NY 10022
212/752-0050
—Membership consists of senior magazine editors of top U.S. consumer magazines
—Chiefly of interest to the job hunter as a source of industry information

Magazine Publishers Association
575 Lexington Avenue
New York, NY 10022
212/752-0055
—Companion organization of the above; membership consists of the publishers of consumer magazines
—Sponsors seminars and surveys; maintains library and publishes newsletter
—Oversees Publishers Information Bureau, which analyzes industry sales/advertising information and conducts studies and statements on revenues

Directories

Gale Directory of Publications
Gale Research Company
Book Tower
Detroit, MI 48226
313/961-2242
—Directory of U.S. newspapers and magazines listed alphabetically, also indexed geographically
—Listings include name, address, editor, and publisher name

* *Bacon's Publicity Checker: Periodical Volume*
Bacon's Publishing Company
382 South Michigan
Chicago, IL 60604
312/922-2400
—Annual directory
—Includes listings of over 5,500 trade and consumer magazines indexed by subject and industry
—Listings include addresses, phone numbers, names of publishers and editors (including department editors)

Burelle's Consumer & Trade Publications Directory
Burelle's Media Directories
75 East Northfield Avenue
Livingston, NJ 07039
—Covers over 3,500 trade and consumer magazines in eighty different subject categories
—Listings include address, phone number, brief description, and names of top personnel

* *Magazine Industry Market Place (MMP)*
R.R. Bowker Co.
245 West 17th Street
New York, NY 10011
212/645-9700
—Annual directory that covers entire magazine industry, including specific publications, publishers, reference houses, associations, agents, trade events, services, suppliers, etc.
—Listings include address, phone number, and names of department heads and editors
—Of special interest: sections listing associations (national and regional) and employment agencies

Standard Rate & Data Service—Business Publications Rates & Data
Standard Rate & Data Service
5201 Old Orchard Road
Skokie, IL 60076
312/256-6067
—Over 3,000 business, trade, and technical publications
—Lists name, address, phone number, and names of top staff members, and gives brief editorial profiles

Publications

* Folio: The Magazine for Magazine Management
Folio Publishing Co.
125 Elm Street
New Canaan, CT 06840
203/972-0761
—Aimed at managers and executives in every phase of magazine publishing, including general management, editorial, circulation, production, sales/marketing, promotion, art direction

Magazine & Bookseller
North American Publishing Company
401 North Broad Street
Philadelphia, PA 19108
212/371-4100
—Focuses on magazines and mass market paperbacks
—Designed for all aspects of the industry, including publishing, distribution, and sales

Magazine Age
Freed Crown Lee Publishing Company
225 Park Avenue
New York, NY 10169
212/986-7366
—Articles, news, and trends in the advertising side of magazine publishing
—Of special interest: *Top 100 Consumer Magazines* issue (January)

MANUFACTURING

Associations

National Association of Manufacturers
1776 F Street, N.W.
Washington, DC 20006
202/637-3000
—13,000 members in manufacturing and related areas
—Affiliated with 150 state and local manufacturing associations
—Publishes newsletter, journal, and annual *Directory of Officers, Directors and Committees*

Society of Manufacturing Engineers (SME)
P.O. Box 930
One SME Drive
Dearborn, MI 48121
313/271-1500
—80,000 members

—Maintains library; offers variety of courses
—Publishes numerous reports and journals, including the monthly *Manufacturing Engineering*

Directories

Dun & Bradstreet Reference Book of Manufacturers
299 Park Avenue—24th Floor
New York, NY 10171
212/285-7609
—Covers U.S. manufacturers
—Listings include addresses, phone numbers, type of product, number of employees

McRae's Industrial Directory
McRae's Blue Book Inc.
817 Broadway
New York, NY 10003
516/349-1010
—Lists national manufacturers
—Listings include address, phone number, names of top officers, brand names/trademarks, and more

* McRae's State Industrial Directory—[State Name]
McRae's Blue Book Inc.
817 Broadway
New York, NY 10003
516/349-1010
—The regional versions of the above; manufacturing directories for each of the 50 states, and Puerto Rico–Virgin Islands
—Listings include address, phone number, type of product, names of top officers, plant information, etc.
[*Note:* Another place to find state directories is in each state's department of commerce & industry or economic development. For regional directories of a major metropolitan area, contact the major city's chamber of commerce.]

NEWSPAPERS

Associations

International Newspaper Advertising & Marketing Executives (INAME)
P.O. Box 17210
Dulles International Airport
Washington, DC 20041
703/620-0090

—3,500 members in newspaper advertising and marketing
—Publishes news, digest, and membership roster that lists member names, affiliations, addresses, and phone numbers

The Newspaper Fund
P.O. Box 300
Princeton, NJ 08540
—Of special interest to college students: sponsors internship program in editing for students between junior and senior years

Directories

Bacon's Publicity Checker: Newspaper Volume
Bacon's Publishing Company
332 South Michigan
Chicago, IL 60604
312/922-2400
—Annual
—Includes listings of 1,700 daily and 8,000 weekly newspapers, each group indexed geographically
—Listings include address, phone numbers, and names of editors

* *Editor & Publisher International Yearbook*
Editor & Publisher
11 West 19th Street
New York, NY 10011
212/675-4380
—Published annually every March
—Lists U.S. and Canadian daily and Sunday newspapers
—Listings include circulation, advertising rates, names of executives and department editors

* *News Bureaus in the U.S.*
Public Relations Publishing Co., Inc.
888 Seventh Avenue
New York, NY 10106
212/582-7373
—Covers news bureaus of newspapers, magazines, wire services, and syndicates
—Listings include address, phone number, names, and titles of key personnel

Publications

* *Editor & Publisher*
11 West 19th Street
New York, NY 10011
212/675-4380

—Considered to be the industry bible
—Special issues include *Newspaper Advertising Executives* (published in January), which lists top executives on the advertising side of newspaper publishing

---

PUBLIC RELATIONS

Associations

Public Relations Society of America (PRSA)
845 Third Avenue
New York, NY 10022
212/826-1750
—Over 12,000 members in different facets of public relations
—Publishes monthly *Public Relations Journal,* and its annual (July) special issue, the *Register Issue,* which lists members, including name, phone number, and affiliation
—Of special interest: maintains job-referral service

Directories

* *O'Dwyer's Directory of Public Relations Firms*
J. R. O'Dwyer Co., Inc.
271 Madison Avenue
New York, NY 10016
212/679-2471
—Lists almost 1,000 public relations firms
—Listing includes name, address, phone number, names of executives, branch offices, billings, and clients for each agency

O'Dwyer's Directory of Corporate Communications
J. R. O'Dwyer Co., Inc.
271 Madison Avenue
New York, NY 10016
212/679-2471
—Lists information on the public relations and corporate communications departments of over 2,000 top U.S. companies and trade associations
—Listings include name, address, phone number, sales, type of business, names and titles of top public relations staff; also lists the person to whom staff reports, and outside public relations counsel (if any)

Who's Who in Public Relations
PR Publishing Company, Inc.
Meriden, NH 03700
—Brief profiles of top public relations executives, indexed alphabetically and geographically

Publications

Publicity Break
Public Relations Aids, Inc.
330 West 34th Street
New York, NY 10001
212/947-7733
—Articles on different techniques, case histories, industry profiles, and other topics of interest to the public relations professional or publicist

* *Public Relations Journal*
Public Relations Society of America
845 Third Avenue
New York, NY 10022
212/826-1750
—The PRSA monthly journal contains articles on industry trends and developments written by public relations practitioners
—Also contains member updates, ''People in the News''

Public Relations News
127 East 80th Street
New York, NY 10021
212/879-7090
—Articles on public relations trends and techniques
—Includes news on accounts and public relations people

PUBLISHING

Associations

American Booksellers Association
122 East 42nd Street
New York, NY 10168
212/867-9060
—500 members
—Publishes weekly newsletter and monthly magazine, *American Bookseller*
—The annual ABA convention is an industry main event for publishers, agents, authors, and booksellers

Directories

Book Publishers Directory
Gale Research Company
Book Tower
Detroit, MI 48226
313/961-2242

—U.S. book publishers listed alphabetically, also indexed by subject and geographical region

* *Literary Marketplace*
R. R. Bowker Co.
245 West 17th Street
New York, NY 10011
212/645-9700
—Very comprehensive directory covering most aspects of the book publishing industry; lists book publishers, clubs, associations, trade events, conventions, services, and suppliers
—Listings include names of department heads and editors
—Of special interest: listings of associations (national and regional) and employment agencies specializing in publishing

Publications

Publisher's Weekly
205 East 42nd Street
New York, NY 10017
212/916-1600
—Published weekly, covering publishing industry news, trends, and developments
—Brief reviews of new books; special feature articles on different facets of the industry

Special Programs

The New York University Summer Publishing Institute
School of Continuing Education
2 University Place
New York, NY 10003
212/477-9145

The Radcliffe Publishing Procedures Course
6 Ash Street
Cambridge, MA 02138
617/495-8678

Rice University Publishing Program
Office of Continuing Studies
P.O. Box 1892
Houston, TX 77001
713/520-6022

University of Denver Publishing Institute
2199 South University Blvd.
Denver, CO 80208
303/871-2570

PURCHASING

Associations

National Association of Purchasing Management
P.O. Box 418
469 Kinderkamack Road
Oradell, NJ 07649
201/967-8585
—28,000 members in purchasing and materials management for industrial, communications, and utilities companies

Directories

See general business directories, including *Moody's Industrial Manual, Dun's Million Dollar Directory, Dun & Bradstreet's Reference Book of Corporate Managements, Standard Directory of Advertisers, Standard & Poor's Register of Corporations, Directors and Executives,* and the *Thomas Register.*

Publications

Purchasing
270 St. Paul Street
Denver, CO 80206
617/536-7780
—News and developments in industrial purchasing

Purchasing Magazine
Cahners Publishing Co.
221 Columbus Avenue
Boston, MA 02116
617/536-7780
—Articles on industry trends and developments
—Aimed at purchasing professionals

Purchasing World
Huebner Publications Inc.
6521 Davis Industrial Parkway
Solon, OH 44139
216/248-1125
—Aimed at purchasers in manufacturing field

RETAILING

Associations

National Retail Merchants Association (NRMA)
100 West 31st Street
New York, NY 10001
212/244-8780
—Over 55,000 members from department, chain, and specialty stores
—Publishes seven publications, including *Stores Magazine;* sponsors conferences and workshops
—Of special interest: provides advisory service to members

Directories

Department Store and Specialty Store Merchandising and Operations Results of 19——
National Retail Merchants Association
100 West 31 Street
New York, NY 10001
212/244-8780
—Annual directory listing in-depth merchandise and inventory data (gross margin, markdowns, etc.)
—Each listing includes sales and expenses broken down by departments

Fairchild's Financial Manual of Retail Stores
Fairchild Publications
7 East 12th Street
New York, NY 10003
212/741-4280
—Annual directory published every October
—Lists over 500 publicly held companies (general merchandise, discount chains, drug & food stores, mail order, shoe stores, etc.)
—Company listings include address, phone number, names of top officers, number of stores, brief profile, and financial data

Financial and Operational Results of Department and Specialty Stores of 19——
National Retail Merchants Association
100 West 31st Street
New York, NY 10001
212/244-8780
—Annual directory that lists sales, merchandise, and earnings data of U.S. department and specialty stores

Publications

Chain Store Age
Lebhar-Friedman
425 Park Avenue
New York, NY 10022
212/371-9400
—Special issue: *State of the Industry* (June), which includes statistics, a ranked list of the top 100 chains and profiles of the top 25
—Also publishes *Chain Store Age Executive;* special issue: *The $100 Million Club* (August), which gives a ranked list of about 300 stores; and *Chain Store Guide*

Stores
National Retail Merchants Association
100 West 31st Street
New York, NY 10001
212/244-8780
—Monthly magazine put out by the NRMA
—Special issue (July): *Top 100 Stores*

SALES & MARKETING

Associations

* *American Marketing Association*
250 South Wacker Drive, Suite 200
Chicago, IL 60606
312/648-0536
—42,000 members who are marketing and market research executives, sales and promotions managers, etc.
—Puts out annual roster with member names; includes index by member affiliation; directory also lists firms that provide marketing services (market research companies, advertising agencies, consultants, etc.) and includes names of top officers and type of service
—New York chapter of AMA puts out an annual guide: the *International Directory of Marketing Research Houses and Services,* that contains listings of firms, names of top officers, and type of services offered

International Marketing Institute (IMI)
29 Garden Street
Cambridge, MA 02138
617/547-9873
—4,000 members
—Provides seminars and other educational programs, including an in-depth skills improvement workshop offered every summer
—Of special interest: maintains a placement service

National Network of Women in Sales (NNWS)
P.O. Box 95269
Schaumburg, IL 60195
312/577-1944
—Members are women in sales or those seeking jobs in sales
—Of special interest: NNWS maintains a placement service, job bank, and resume file

Sales & Marketing Executives International (SMEI)
6151 Wilson Mills Road, Suite 200
Cleveland, OH 44143
216/473-2100
—Over 25,000 sales and marketing executive members
—Sponsors studies, workshops, etc.; works with Junior Achievement and Distributive Education clubs
—Puts out yearly membership directory
—Of special interest: maintains placement service

Publications

Business Marketing
Crain Communications
740 Rush Street
Chicago, IL 60601
—Monthly magazine that focuses on business-to-business advertising and marketing

Journal of Marketing
American Marketing Association
250 South Wacker Drive, Suite 200
Chicago, IL 60606
312/648-0536
—Monthly journal considered a must-read in the industry

Marketing Times
Sales and Marketing Executives International
330 West 42nd Street
New York, NY 10017
212/239-1919
—Covers a wide range of marketing industry subjects, including market research and advertising

The Marketing News
American Marketing Association
250 South Wacker Drive, Suite 200
Chicago, IL 60606
312/993-9504
—Covers industry news, marketing trends, and developments

Sales and Marketing Management
Bill Publications
633 Third Avenue
New York, NY 10017
212/986-4800
—Monthly trade journal covering management techniques, industry trends, etc.

CO-OP PROGRAMS FOR COLLEGE STUDENTS

Co-op programs, which arrange for college students in their junior and senior years to work at a company in their field of study, are growing more common and gaining in popularity. For good reason: roughly 40% of co-op students continue working for their co-op employer after graduation. It is a beneficial arrangement for both the student and the employer. The student gets invaluable experience and a headstart at the beginning of his or her career; the employer trains the student and winds up with an employee who is already well-versed in the job, company procedure, and the corporate culture.

For free booklets about co-op programs, write:

Co-op Education and Co-op Education Undergraduate Program Directory
National Commission for Co-op Education
P.O. Box 775
Boston, MA 02117

Index